I0754247

Poetical Works of

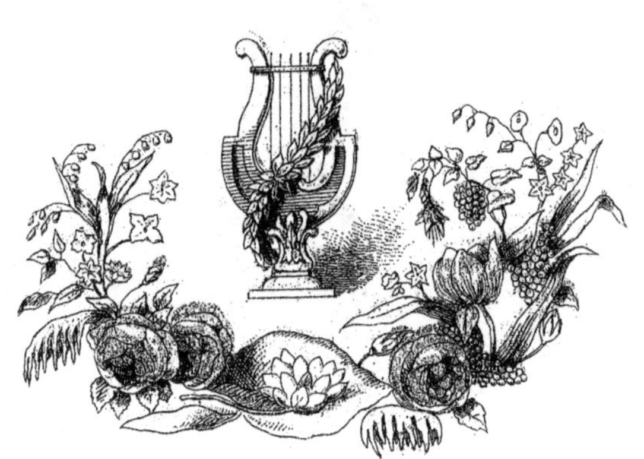

BOSTON:

18[illegible]

THE

POETICAL WORKS

OF

THOMAS HOOD.

BOSTON:
CROSBY, NICHOLS, LEE & COMPANY.
1861.

CONTENTS.

POEMS.

HUMOROUS POEMS.

THE PLEA

OF

THE MIDSUMMER FAIRIES.

TO CHARLES LAMB.

My dear Friend: I thank my literary fortune that I am not reduced, like many better wits, to barter dedications, for the hope or promise of patronage, with some nominally great man; but that where true affection points, and honest respect, I am free to gratify my head and heart by a sincere inscription. An intimacy and dearness, worthy of a much earlier date than our acquaintance can refer to, direct me at once to your name; and with this acknowledgment of your ever kind feeling towards me, I desire to record a respect and admiration for you as a writer, which no one acquainted with our literature, save Elia himself, will think disproportionate or misplaced. If I had not these better reasons to govern me, I should be guided to the same selection by your intense yet critical relish for the works of our great Dramatist, and for that favorite play in particular which has furnished the subject of my verses.

It is my design, in the following Poem, to celebrate by an allegory that immortality which Shakspeare has conferred on the Fairy mythology by his Midsummer Night's Dream. But for him, those pretty children of our childhood would leave barely their names to our maturer years; they belong, as the mites upon the plum, to the bloom of fancy, a thing generally too frail and beautiful to withstand the rude handling of Time: but the Poet has made this most perishable part of the mind's creation equal to the most enduring; he has so intertwined the Elfins with human sympathies, and linked them by so many delightful associations with the productions of nature, that they are as real to the mind's eye as their green magical circles to the outer sense.

It would have been a pity for such a race to go extinct, even though they were but as the butterflies that hover about the leaves and blossoms of the visible world.

I am, my dear friend,

Yours, most truly,

T. Hood.

THE PLEA OF

THE MIDSUMMER FAIRIES.

'TWAS in that mellow season of the year
When the hot Sun singes the yellow leaves
Till they be gold, and with a broader sphere
The Moon looks down on Ceres and her sheaves;
When more abundantly the spider weaves,
And the cold wind breathes from a chillier clime;
That forth I fared, on one of those still eves,
Touched with the dewy sadness of the time,
To think how the bright months had spent their prime.

So that, wherever I addressed my way,
I seemed to track the melancholy feet
Of him that is the Father of Decay,
And spoils at once the sour weed and the sweet; —
Wherefore regretfully I made retreat
To some unwasted regions of my brain,
Charmed with the light of summer and the heat,
And bade that bounteous season bloom again,
And sprout fresh flowers in mine own domain.

It was a shady and sequestered scene,
Like those famed gardens of Boccaccio,
Planted with his own laurels ever green,

And roses that for endless summer blow;
And there were fountain springs to overflow
Their marble basins; and cool green arcades
Of tall o'erarching sycamores, to throw
Athwart the dappled path their dancing shades;
With timid conies cropping the green blades.

And there were crystal pools, peopled with fish,
Argent and gold; and some of Tyrian skin,
Some crimson-barred; — and ever at a wish
They rose obsequious till the wave grew thin
As glass upon their backs, and then dived in,
Quenching their ardent scales in watery gloom;
Whilst others with fresh hues rowed forth to win
My changeable regard, — for so we doom
Things born of thought to vanish or to bloom.

And there were many birds of many dyes,
From tree to tree still faring to and fro,
And stately peacocks with their splendid eyes,
And gorgeous pheasants with their golden glow,
Like Iris just bedabbled in her bow,
Besides some vocalists, without a name,
That oft on fairy errands come and go,
With accents magical; — and all were tame,
And peckéd at my hand where'er I came.

And for my sylvan company, in lieu
Of Pampinea with her lively peers,
Sate Queen Titania with her pretty crew,
All in their liveries quaint, with elfin gears;
For she was gracious to my childish years,
And made me free of her enchanted round;
Wherefore this dreamy scene she still endears,

And plants her court upon a verdant mound,
Fenced with umbrageous woods and groves profound.

"Ah, me," she cries, "was ever moonlight seen
So clear and tender for our midnight trips?
Go some one forth, and with a trump convene
My lieges all!" — Away the goblin skips
A pace or two apart, and deftly strips
The ruddy skin from a sweet rose's cheek,
Then blows the shuddering leaf between his lips,
Making it utter forth a shrill small shriek,
Like a frayed bird in the gray owlet's beak.

And, lo! upon my fixed delighted ken
Appeared the loyal Fays. Some by degrees
Crept from the primrose buds that opened then,
And some from bell-shaped blossoms like the bees,
Some from the dewy meads, and rushy leas,
Flew up like chafers when the rustics pass;
Some from the rivers, others from tall trees
Dropped, like shed blossoms, silent to the grass,
Spirits and elfins small, of every class.

Peri and Pixy, and quaint Puck the Antic,
Brought Robin Goodfellow, that merry swain;
And stealthy Mab, queen of old realms romantic,
Came too, from distance, in her tiny wain,
Fresh dripping from a cloud — some bloomy rain,
Then circling the bright Moon, had washed her car,
And still bedewed it with a various stain:
Lastly came Ariel, shooting from a star,
Who bears all fairy embassies afar.

But Oberon, that night elsewhere exiled,
Was absent, whether some distempered spleen

Kept him and his fair mate unreconciled,
Or warfare with the Gnome (whose race had been
Sometimes obnoxious) kept him from his queen,
And made her now peruse the starry skies
Prophetical with such an absent mien;
Howbeit, the tears stole often to her eyes,
And oft the Moon was incensed with her sighs —

Which made the elves sport drearily, and soon
Their hushing dances languished to a stand,
Like midnight leaves when, as the Zephyrs swoon,
All on their drooping stems they sink unfanned, —
So into silence drooped the fairy band,
To see their empress dear so pale and still,
Crowding her softly round on either hand,
As pale as frosty snowdrops, and as chill,
To whom the sceptred dame reveals her ill.

"Alas!" quoth she, "ye know our fairy lives
Are leased upon the fickle faith of men;
Not measured out against fate's mortal knives
Like human gossamers, we perish when
We fade, and are forgot in worldly ken, —
Though poesy has thus prolonged our date,
Thanks be to the sweet Bard's auspicious pen
That rescued us so long! — howbeit of late
I feel some dark misgivings of our fate.

"And this dull day my melancholy sleep
Hath been so thronged with images of woe,
That even now I cannot choose but weep
To think this was some sad prophetic show
Of future horror to befall us so, —
Of mortal wreck and uttermost distress, —

Yea, our poor empire's fall and overthrow,—
For this was my long vision's dreadful stress,
And when I waked my trouble was not less.

"Whenever to the clouds I tried to seek,
Such leaden weight dragged these Icarian wings,
My faithless wand was wavering and weak,
And slimy toads had trespassed in our rings—
The birds refused to sing for me—all things
Disowned their old allegiance to our spells;
The rude bees pricked me with their rebel stings;
And, when I passed, the valley-lily's bells
Rang out, methought, most melancholy knells.

"And ever on the faint and flagging air
A doleful spirit with a dreary note
Cried in my fearful ear, 'Prepare! prepare!'
Which soon I knew came from a raven's throat,
Perched on a cypress bough not far remote,—
A cursèd bird, too crafty to be shot,
That alway cometh with his soot-black coat
To make hearts dreary: for he is a blot
Upon the book of life, as well ye wot!—

"Wherefore some while I bribed him to be mute,
With bitter acorns stuffing his foul maw,
Which barely I appeased, when some fresh bruit
Startled me all aheap!—and soon I saw
The horridest shape that ever raised my awe,—
A monstrous giant, very huge and tall,
Such as in elder times, devoid of law,
With wicked might grieved the primeval ball,
And this was sure the deadliest of them all!

"Gaunt was he as a wolf of Languedoc,
With bloody jaws, and frost upon his crown;
So from his barren poll one hoary lock
Over his wrinkled front fell far adown,
Well nigh to where his frosty brows did frown
Like jagged icicles at cottage eaves;
And for his coronal he wore some brown
And bristled ears gathered from Ceres' sheaves,
Entwined with certain sere and russet leaves.

"And, lo! upon a mast reared far aloft,
He bore a very bright and crescent blade,
The which he waved so dreadfully, and oft,
In meditative spite, that, sore dismayed,
I crept into an acorn cup for shade;
Meanwhile the horrid effigy went by:
I trow his look was dreadful, for it made
The trembling birds betake them to the sky,
For every leaf was lifted by his sigh.

"And ever, as he sighed, his foggy breath
Blurred out the landscape like a flight of smoke:
Thence knew I this was either dreary Death
Or Time, who leads all creatures to his stroke.
Ah, wretched me!" — Here, even as she spoke,
The melancholy Shape came gliding in,
And leaned his back against an antique oak,
Folding his wings, that were so fine and thin,
They scarce were seen against the Dryad's skin.

Then what a fear seized all the little rout!
Look how a flock of panicked sheep will stare —
And huddle close — and start — and wheel about,
Watching the roaming mongrel here and there, —

So did that sudden Apparition scare
All close aheap those small affrighted things;
Nor sought they now the safety of the air,
As if some leaden spell withheld their wings;
But who can fly that ancientest of Kings?

Whom now the Queen, with a forestalling tear
And previous sigh, beginneth to entreat,
Bidding him spare, for love, her lieges dear:
"Alas!" quoth she, "is there no nodding wheat
Ripe for thy crooked weapon, and more meet,
Or withered leaves to ravish from the tree, —
Or crumbling battlements for thy defeat?
Think but what vaunting monuments there be
Builded in spite and mockery of thee.

"O, fret away the fabric walls of Fame,
And grind down marble Cæsars with the dust:
Make tombs inscriptionless — raze each high name,
And waste old armors of renown with rust:
Do all of this, and thy revenge is just:
Make such decays the trophies of thy prime,
And check Ambition's overweening lust,
That dares exterminating war with Time, —
But we are guiltless of that lofty crime.

"Frail, feeble sprites! — the children of a dream!
Leased on the sufferance of fickle men,
Like motes dependent on the sunny beam,
Living but in the sun's indulgent ken,
And when that light withdraws, withdrawing then;
So do we flutter in the glance of youth
And fervid fancy, — and so perish when
The eye of faith grows aged; — in sad truth,
Feeling thy sway, O Time! though not thy tooth!

"Where be those old divinities forlorn
That dwelt in trees, or haunted in a stream?
Alas! their memories are dimmed and torn,
Like the remainder tatters of a dream;
So will it fare with our poor thrones. I deem;—
For us the same dark trench Oblivion delves,
That holds the wastes of every human scheme.
O, spare us then,—and these, our pretty elves.
We soon, alas! shall perish of ourselves!"

Now as she ended, with a sigh, to name
Those old Olympians, scattered by the whirl
Of fortune's giddy wheel, and brought to shame,
Methought a scornful and malignant curl
Showed on the lips of that malicious churl,
To think what noble havocs he had made:
So that I feared he all at once would hurl
The harmless fairies into endless shade,—
Howbeit he stopped a while to whet his blade.

Pity it was to hear the elfins' wail
Rise up in concert from their mingled dread;
Pity it was to see them, all so pale,
Gaze on the grass, as for a dying bed;—
But Puck was seated on a spider's thread,
That hung between two branches of a brier,
And 'gan to swing and gambol heels o'er head,
Like any Southwark tumbler on a wire,
For him no present grief could long inspire.

Meanwhile the Queen, with many piteous drops,
Falling like tiny sparks full fast and free,
Bedews a pathway from her throne;—and stops
Before the foot of her arch enemy,
And with her little arms enfolds his knee,

That shows more gristly from that fair embrace;
But she will ne'er depart. "Alas!" quoth she,
"My painful fingers I will here enlace,
Till I have gained your pity for our race.

"What have we ever done to earn this grudge
And hate — (if not too humble for thy hating?) —
Look o'er our labors and our lives, and judge
If there be any ills of our creating;
For we are very kindly creatures, dating
With nature's charities still sweet and bland: —
O, think this murder worthy of debating!" —
Herewith she makes a signal with her hand,
To beckon some one from the Fairy band.

Anon I saw one of those elfin things,
Clad all in white, like any chorister,
Come fluttering forth on his melodious wings,
That made soft music at each little stir,
But something louder than a bee's demur
Before he lights upon a bunch of broom,
And thus 'gan he with Saturn to confer, —
And, O, his voice was sweet, touched with the gloom
Of that sad theme that argued of his doom!

Quoth he, "We make all melodies our care,
That no false discords may offend the Sun,
Music's great master — tuning every where
All pastoral sounds and melodies, each one
Duly to place and season, so that none
May harshly interfere. We rouse at morn
The shrill, sweet lark; and when the day is done,
Hush silent pauses for the bird forlorn,
That singeth with her breast against a thorn.

"We gather in loud choirs the twittering race,
That make a chorus with their single note;
And tend on new-fledged birds in every place,
That duly they may get their tunes by rote;
And oft, like echoes, answering remote,
We hide in thickets from the feathered throng,
And strain in rivalship each throbbing throat,
Singing in shrill responses all day long,
Whilst the glad truant listens to our song.

"Wherefore, great King of Years, as thou dost love
The raining music from a morning cloud,
When vanished larks are carolling above,
To wake Apollo with their pipings loud; —
If ever thou hast heard in leafy shroud
The sweet and plaintive Sappho of the dell,
Show thy sweet mercy on this little crowd,
And we will muffle up the sheepfold bell
Whene'er thou listenest to Philomel."

Then Saturn thus: "Sweet is the merry lark,
That carols in man's ear so clear and strong;
And youth must love to listen in the dark
That tuneful elegy of Tereus' wrong;
But I have heard that ancient strain too long,
For sweet is sweet but when a little strange,
And I grow weary for some newer song;
For wherefore had I wings, unless to range
Through all things mutable from change to change?

"But wouldst thou hear the melodies of Time,
Listen when sleep and drowsy darkness roll
Over hushed cities, and the midnight chime
Sounds from their hundred clocks, and deep bells toll
Like a last knell over the dead world's soul,

Saying, Time shall be final of all things,
Whose late, last voice must elegize the whole, —
O, then I clap aloft my brave, broad wings,
And make the wide air tremble while it rings!"

Then next a fair Eve-Fay made meek address,
Saying, "We be the handmaids of the Spring,
In sign whereof, May, the quaint broideress,
Hath wrought her samplers on our gauzy wing.
We tend upon buds' birth and blossoming,
And count the leafy tributes that they owe —
As, so much to the earth — so much to fling
In showers to the brook — so much to go
In whirlwinds to the clouds that made them grow.

"The pastoral cowslips are our little pets,
And daisy stars, whose firmament is green;
Pansies, and those veiled nuns, meek violets,
Sighing to that warm world from which they screen;
And golden daffodils, plucked for May's Queen;
And lonely harebells, quaking on the heath;
And Hyacinth, long since a fair youth seen,
Whose tuneful voice, turned fragrance in his breath,
Kissed by sad Zephyr, guilty of his death.

"The widowed primrose weeping to the moon,
And saffron crocus, in whose chalice bright
A cool libation hoarded for the noon
Is kept — and she that purifies the light,
The virgin lily, faithful to her white,
Whereon Eve wept in Eden for her shame;
And the most dainty rose, Aurora's spright,
Our every godchild, by whatever name —
Spare us our lives, for we did nurse the same!"

Then that old Mower stamped his heel, and struck
His hurtful scythe against the harmless ground,
Saying, "Ye foolish imps, when am I stuck
With gaudy buds, or like a wooer crowned
With flowery chaplets, save when they are found
Withered? — Whenever have I plucked a rose,
Except to scatter its vain leaves around?
For so all gloss of beauty I oppose,
And bring decay on every flower that blows.

"Or when am I so wroth as when I view
The wanton pride of Summer; — how she decks
The birthday world with blossoms ever new,
As if Time had not lived, and heaped great wrecks
Of years on years? — O, then I bravely vex
And catch the gay Months in their gaudy plight,
And slay them with the wreaths about their necks,
Like foolish heifers in the holy rite,
And raise great trophies to my ancient might!"

Then saith another, "We are kindly things,
And like her offspring nestle with the dove, —
Witness these hearts embroidered on our wings,
To show our constant patronage of love: —
We sit at even, in sweet bowers above
Lovers, and shake rich odors on the air,
To mingle with their sighs; and still remove
The startling owl, and bid the bat forbear
Their privacy, and haunt some other where.

"And we are near the mother when she sits
Beside her infant in its wicker bed;
And we are in the fairy scene that flits
Across its tender brain: sweet dreams we shed,
And whilst the tender little soul is fled

Away, to sport with our young elves, the while
We touch the dimpled cheek with roses red,
And tickle the soft lips until they smile,
So that their careful parents they beguile.

"O, then, if ever thou hast breathed a vow
At Love's dear portal, or at pale moon-rise
Crushed the dear curl on a regardful brow
That did not frown thee from thy honey prize —
If ever thy sweet son sat on thy thighs,
And wooed thee from thy careful thoughts within
To watch the harmless beauty of his eyes,
Or glad thy fingers on his smooth, soft skin,
For love's dear sake, let us thy pity win!"

Then Saturn fiercely thus: "What joy have I
In tender babes, that have devoured mine own,
Whenever to the light I heard them cry,
Till foolish Rhea cheated me with stone?
Whereon, till now, is my great hunger shown,
In monstrous dints of my enormous tooth;
And, — but the peopled world is too full grown
For hunger's edge, — I would consume all youth
At one great meal, without delay or ruth!

"For I am well-nigh crazed and wild to hear
How boastful fathers taunt me with their breed,
Saying, 'We shall not die nor disappear,
But in these other selves ourselves succeed,
Even as ripe flowers pass into their seed
Only to be renewed from prime to prime,'
All of which boastings I am forced to read,
Besides a thousand challenges to Time
Which bragging lovers have compiled in rhyme.

"Wherefore, when they are sweetly met o' nights,
There will I steal, and with my hurried hand
Startle them suddenly from their delights
Before their next encounter hath been planned,
Ravishing hours in little minutes spanned;
But when they say farewell, and grieve apart,
Then like a leaden statue I will stand,
Meanwhile their many tears incrust my dart,
And with a ragged edge cut heart from heart."

Then next a merry Woodsman, clad in green,
Stept vanward from his mates, that idly stood
Each at his proper ease, as they had been
Nursed in the liberty of old Shérwood,
And wore the livery of Robin Hood,
Who wont in forest shades to dine and sup, —
So came this chief right frankly, and made good
His haunch against his axe, and thus spoke up,
Doffing his cap, which was an acorn's cup:

"We be small foresters and gay, who tend
On trees and all their furniture of green,
Training the young boughs airily to bend,
And show blue snatches of the sky between;
Or knit more close intricacies, to screen
Birds' crafty dwellings, as may hide them best,
But most the timid blackbird's — she, that seen,
Will bear black poisonous berries to her nest,
Lest man should cage the darlings of her breast.

"We bend each tree in proper attitude,
And founting willows train in silvery falls;
We frame all shady roofs and arches rude,
And verdant aisles leading to Dryads' halls,
Or deep recesses where the Echo calls; —

We shape all plumy trees against the sky,
And carve tall elms' Corinthian capitals,—
When sometimes, as our tiny hatchets ply,
Men say, the tapping woodpecker is nigh.

"Sometimes we scoop the squirrel's hollow cell,
And sometimes carve quaint letters on trees' rind,
That haply some lone musing wight may spell
Dainty Aminta,—gentle Rosalind,—
Or chastest Laura,—sweetly called to mind
In sylvan solitudes, ere he lies down;—
And sometimes we enrich gray stems, with twined
And vagrant ivy,—or rich moss, whose brown
Burns into gold as the warm sun goes down.

"And, lastly, for mirth's sake and Christmas cheer,
We bear the seedling berries, for increase,
To graft the Druid oaks, from year to year,
Careful that mistletoe may never cease;—
Wherefore, if thou dost prize the shady peace
Of sombre forests, or to see light break
Through sylvan cloisters, and in spring release
Thy spirit amongst leaves from careful ake,
Spare us our lives for the Green Dryad's sake."

Then Saturn, with a frown: "Go forth, and fell
Oak for your coffins, and thenceforth lay by
Your axes for the rust, and bid farewell
To all sweet birds, and the blue peeps of sky
Through tangled branches, for ye shall not spy
The next green generation of the tree;
But hence with the dead leaves, whene'er they fly,
Which in the bleak air I would rather see,
Than flights of the most tuneful birds that be.

"For I dislike all prime, and verdant pets,
Ivy except, that on the aged wall
Preys with its worm-like roots, and daily frets
The crumbled tower it seems to league withal,
King-like, worn down by its own coronal:—
Neither in forest haunts love I to won,
Before the golden plumage 'gins to fall,
And leaves the brown bleak limbs with few leaves on,
Or bare — like Nature in her skeleton.

"For then sit I amongst the crooked boughs,
Wooing dull Memory with kindred sighs;
And there in rustling nuptials we espouse,
Smit by the sadness in each other's eyes;—
But Hope must have green bowers and blue skies,
And must be courted with the gauds of spring;
Whilst Youth leans godlike on her lap, and cries,
What shall we always do, but love and sing?—
And Time is reckoned a discarded thing."

Here in my dream it made me fret to see
How Puck, the antic, all this dreary while
Had blithely jested with calamity,
With mistimed mirth mocking the doleful style
Of his sad comrades, till it raised my bile
To see him so reflect their grief aside,
Turning their solemn looks to half a smile—
Like a straight stick shown crooked in the tide;—
But soon a novel advocate I spied.

Quoth he, "We teach all natures to fulfil
Their fore-appointed crafts, and instincts meet,—
The bee's sweet alchemy,—the spider's skill,—
The pismire's care to garner up his wheat,—
And rustic masonry to swallows fleet,—

The lapwing's cunning to preserve her nest,—
But most that lesser pelican, the sweet
And shrilly ruddock, with its bleeding breast,
Its tender pity of poor babes distrest.

" Sometimes we cast our shapes, and in sleek skins
Delve with the timid mole, that aptly delves
From our example; so the spider spins,
And eke the silk-worm, patterned by ourselves:
Sometimes we travail on the summer shelves
Of early bees, and busy toils commence,
Watched of wise men, that know not we are elves,
But gaze and marvel at our stretch of sense,
And praise our human-like intelligence.

" Wherefore, by thy delight in that old tale,
And plaintive dirges the late robins sing,
What time the leaves are scattered by the gale,
Mindful of that old forest burying;—
As thou dost love to watch each tiny thing,
For whom our craft most curiously contrives,
If thou hast caught a bee upon the wing,
To take his honey-bag,—spare us our lives,
And we will pay the ransom in full hives."

"Now by my glass," quoth Time, "ye do offend
In teaching the brown bees that careful lore,
And frugal ants, whose millions would have end,
But they lay up for need a timely store,
And travail with the seasons evermore;
Whereas Great Mammoth long hath passed away,
And none but I can tell what hide he wore;
Whilst purblind men, the creatures of a day,
In riddling wonder his great bones survey."

Then came an elf, right beauteous to behold,
Whose coat was like a brooklet that the sun
Hath all embroidered with its crooked gold,
It was so quaintly wrought and overrun
With spangled traceries, — most meet for one
That was a warden of the pearly streams; —
And as he stept out of the shadows dun,
His jewels sparkled in the pale moon's gleams,
And shot into the air their pointed beams.

Quoth he, "We bear the gold and silver keys
Of bubbling springs and fountains, that below
Course through the veiny earth,—which, when they freeze
Into hard chrysolites, we bid to flow,
Creeping like subtle snakes, when, as they go,
We guide their windings to melodious falls,
At whose soft murmurings so sweet and low
Poets have turned their smoothest madrigals,
To sing to ladies in their banquet-halls.

"And when the hot sun with his steadfast heat
Parches the river god, — whose dusty urn
Drips miserly, till soon his crystal feet
Against his pebbly floor wax faint and burn,
And languid fish, unpoised, grow sick and yearn, —
Then scoop we hollows in some sandy nook,
And little channels dig, wherein we turn
The thread-worn rivulet, that all forsook
The Naiad-lily, pining for her brook.

"Wherefore, by thy delight in cool green meads,
With living sapphires daintily inlaid, —
In all soft songs of waters and their reeds, —
And all reflections in a streamlet made,
Haply of thy own love, that, disarrayed,

Kills the fair lily with a livelier white,—
By silver trouts upspringing from green shade,
And winking stars reduplicate at night,
Spare us, poor ministers, to such delight."

Howbeit his pleading and his gentle looks
Moved not the spiteful Shade:—Quoth he, "Your taste
Shoots wide of mine, for I despise the brooks
And slavish rivulets that run to waste
In noontide sweats, or, like poor vassals, haste
To swell the vast dominion of the sea,
In whose great presence I am held disgraced,
And neighbored with a king that rivals me
In ancient might and hoary majesty.

"Whereas I ruled in chaos, and still keep
The awful secrets of that ancient dearth,
Before the briny fountains of the deep
Brimmed up the hollow cavities of earth;—
I saw each trickling Sea-God at his birth,
Each pearly Naiad with her oozy locks,
And infant Titans of enormous girth,
Whose huge young feet yet stumbled on the rocks,
Stunning the early world with frequent shocks.

"Where now is Titan, with his cumbrous brood,
That scared the world?—By this sharp scythe they fell,
And half the sky was curdled with their blood:
So have all primal giants sighed farewell.
No Wardens now by sedgy fountains dwell,
Nor pearly Naiads. All their days are done
That strove with Time, untimely, to excel;
Wherefore I razed their progenies, and none
But my great shadow intercepts the sun!"

Then saith the timid Fay, "O, mighty Time!
Well hast thou wrought the cruel Titans' fall,
For they were stained with many a bloody crime:
Great giants work great wrongs, — but we are small,
For Love goes lowly; — but Oppression's tall,
And with surpassing strides goes foremost still
Where Love indeed can hardly reach at all;
Like a poor dwarf o'erburthened with good will,
That labors to efface the tracks of ill.

"Man even strives with Man, but we eschew
The guilty feud, and all fierce strifes abhor;
Nay, we are gentle as sweet heaven's dew,
Beside the red and horrid drops of war,
Weeping the cruel hates men battle for,
Which worldly bosoms nourish in our spite:
For in the gentle breast we ne'er withdraw,
But only when all love hath taken flight,
And youth's warm gracious heart is hardened quite.

"So are our gentle natures intertwined
With sweet humanities, and closely knit
In kindly sympathy with human kind.
Witness how we befriend, with elfin-wit,
All hopeless maids and lovers, — nor omit
Magical succors unto hearts forlorn: —
We charm man's life, and do not perish it; —
So judge us by the helps we showed this morn
To one who held his wretched days in scorn.

"'Twas nigh sweet Amwell; — for the Queen had tasked
Our skill to-day amidst the silver Lea,
Whereon the noontide sun had not yet basked;
Wherefore some patient man we thought to see,
Planted in moss-grown rushes to the knee,

Beside the cloudy margin cold and dim ;—
Howbeit no patient fishermen was he
That cast his sudden shadow from the brim,
Making us leave our toils to gaze on him.

"His face was ashy pale, and leaden care
Had sunk the levelled arches of his brow,
Once bridges for his joyous thoughts to fare
Over those melancholy springs and slow,
That from his piteous eyes began to flow,
And fell anon into the chilly stream ;
Which, as his mimicked image showed below,
Wrinkled his face with many a needless seam,
Making grief sadder in its own esteem.

"And, lo! upon the air we saw him stretch
His passionate arms ; and, in a wayward strain,
He 'gan to elegize that fellow-wretch
That with mute gestures answered him again,
Saying, 'Poor slave, how long wilt thou remain
Life's sad weak captive in a prison strong,
Hoping with tears to rust away thy chain,
In bitter servitude to worldly wrong ?—
Thou wear'st that mortal livery too long!'

"This, with mere spleenful speeches and some tears,
When he had spent upon the imaged wave,
Speedily I convened my elfin peers
Under the lily-cups, that we might save
This woful mortal from a wilful grave
By shrewd diversions of his mind's regret,
Seeing he was mere Melancholy's slave,
That sank wherever a dark cloud he met,
And straight was tangled in her secret net.

"Therefore, as still he watched the water's flow,
Daintily we transformed, and with bright fins
Came glancing through the gloom; some from below
Rose like dim fancies when a dream begins,
Snatching the light upon their purple skins;
Then under the broad leaves made slow retire;
One like a golden galley bravely wins
Its radiant course, — another glows like fire, —
Making that wayward man our pranks admire.

"And so he banished thought, and quite forgot
All contemplation of that wretched face;
And so we wiled him from that lonely spot
Along the river's brink; till, by Heaven's grace,
He met a gentle haunter of the place,
Full of sweet wisdom gathered from the brooks,
Who there discussed his melancholy case
With wholesome texts learned from kind Nature's books,
Meanwhile he newly trimmed his lines and hooks."

Herewith the Fairy ceased. Quoth Ariel now —
"Let me remember how I saved a man,
Whose fatal noose was fastened on a bough,
Intended to abridge his sad life's span;
For haply I was by when he began
His stern soliloquy in life's dispraise,
And overheard his melancholy plan,
How he had made a vow to end his days,
And therefore followed him in all his ways,

"Through brake and tangled copse, for much he loathed
All populous haunts, and roamed in forests rude,
To hide himself from man. But I had clothed
My delicate limbs with plumes, and still pursued
Where only foxes and wild cats intrude,

Till we were come beside an ancient tree
Late blasted by a storm. Here he renewed
His loud complaints, — choosing that spot to be
The scene of his last horrid tragedy.

"It was a wild and melancholy glen,
Made gloomy by tall firs and cypress dark,
Whose roots, like any bones of buried men,
Pushed through the rotten sod for fear's remark;
A hundred horrid stems, jagged and stark,
Wrestled with crooked arms in hideous fray,
Besides sleek ashes, with their dappled bark,
Like crafty serpents climbing for a prey,
With many blasted oaks, moss-grown and gray.

"But here upon this final desperate clause
Suddenly I pronounced so sweet a strain,
Like a panged nightingale it made him pause,
Till half the frenzy of his grief was slain,
The sad remainder oozing from his brain
In timely ecstasies of healing tears,
Which through his ardent eyes began to drain; —
Meanwhile the deadly fates unclosed their shears: —
So pity me and all my fated peers!"

Thus Ariel ended, and was some time hushed:
When with the hoary shape a fresh tongue pleads,
And red as rose the gentle Fairy blushed
To read the record of her own good deeds: —
"It chanced," quoth she, "in seeking through the meads
For honeyed cowslips, sweetest in the morn,
Whilst yet the buds were hung with dewy beads,
And Echo answered to the huntsman's horn,
We found a babe left in the swaths forlorn.

"A little, sorrowful, deserted thing,
Begot of love, and yet no love begetting;
Guiltless of shame, and yet for shame to wring;
And too soon banished from a mother's petting,
To churlish nurture and the wide world's fretting,
For alien pity and unnatural care; —
Alas! to see how the cold dew kept wetting
His childish coats, and dabbled all his hair,
Like gossamers across his forehead fair.

"His pretty, pouting mouth, witless of speech,
Lay half-way open, like a rose-lipped shell;
And his young cheek was softer than a peach,
Whereon his tears, for roundness, could not dwell,
But quickly rolled themselves to pearls, and fell,
Some on the grass, and some against his hand,
Or haply wandered to the dimpled well,
Which love beside his mouth had sweetly planned,
Yet not for tears, but mirth and smilings bland.

"Pity it was to see those frequent tears
Falling regardless from his friendless eyes;
There was such beauty in those twin blue spheres,
As any mother's heart might leap to prize;
Blue were they, like the zenith of the skies
Softened betwixt two clouds, both clear and mild; —
Just touched with thought, and yet not over wise,
They showed the gentle spirit of a child,
Not yet by care or any craft defiled.

"Pity it was to see the ardent sun
Scorching his helpless limbs — it shone so warm;
For kindly shade or shelter he had none,
Nor mother's gentle breast, come fair or storm.
Meanwhile I bade my pitying mates transform

Like grasshoppers, and then, with shrilly cries,
All round the infant noisily we swarm,
Haply some passing rustic to advise —
Whilst providential Heaven our care espies,

"And sends full soon a tender-hearted hind,
Who, wondering at our loud, unusual note,
Strays curiously aside, and so doth find
The orphan child laid in the grass remote,
And laps the foundling in his russet coat,
Who thence was nurtured in his kindly cot: —
But how he prospered let proud London quote,
How wise, how rich, and how renowned he got,
And chief of all her citizens, I wot.

"Witness his goodly vessels on the Thames,
Whose holds were fraught with costly merchandise, —
Jewels from Ind, and pearls for courtly dames,
And gorgeous silks that Samarcand supplies:
Witness that Royal Bourse he bade arise,
The mart of merchants from the East and West;
Whose slender summit, pointing to the skies,
Still bears, in token of his grateful breast,
The tender grasshopper, his chosen crest —

"The tender grasshopper, his chosen crest,
That all the summer, with a tuneful wing,
Makes merry chirpings in its grassy nest,
Inspirited with dew to leap and sing: —
So let us also live, eternal King!
Partakers of the green and pleasant earth: —
Pity it is to slay the meanest thing
That, like a mote, shines in the smile of mirth: —
Enough there is of joy's decrease and dearth!

"Enough of pleasure, and delight, and beauty,
Perished and gone, and hasting to decay; —
Enough to sadden even thee, whose duty
Or spite it is to havoc and to slay:
Too many a lovely race, razed quite away,
Hath left large gaps in life and human loving: —
Here then begin thy cruel war to stay,
And spare fresh sighs, and tears, and groans, reproving
Thy desolating hand for our removing."

Now here I heard a shrill and sudden cry,
And looking up, I saw the antic Puck
Grappling with Time, who clutched him like a fly,
Victim of his own sport, — the jester's luck!
He, whilst his fellows grieved, poor wight, had stuck
His freakish gauds upon the Ancient's brow,
And now his ear, and now his beard, would pluck;
Whereas the angry churl had snatched him now,
Crying, "Thou impish mischief, who art thou?"

"Alas!" quoth Puck, "a little random elf,
Born in the sport of nature, like a weed,
For simple, sweet enjoyment of myself,
But for no other purpose, worth, or need;
And yet withal of a most happy breed;
And there is Robin Goodfellow besides,
My partner dear in many a prankish deed
To make dame Laughter hold her jolly sides,
Like merry mummers twain on holy tides.

"'Tis we that bob the angler's idle cork,
Till even the patient man breathes half a curse;
We steal the morsel from the gossip's fork,
And curdling looks with secret straws disperse,
Or stop the sneezing chanter at mid verse:

And when an infant's beauty prospers ill,
We change, some mothers say, the child at nurse;
But any graver purpose to fulfil,
We have not wit enough, and scarce the will.

"We never let the canker melancholy
To gather on our faces like a rust,
But gloss our features with some change of folly,
Taking life's fabled miseries on trust,
But only sorrowing when sorrow must:
We ruminate no sage's solemn cud,
But own ourselves a pinch of lively dust
To frisk upon a wind, — whereas the flood
Of tears would turn us into heavy mud.

"Beshrew those sad interpreters of nature,
Who gloze her lively, universal law,
As if she had not formed our cheerful feature
To be so tickled with the slightest straw!
So let them vex their mumping mouths, and draw
The corners downward, like a watery moon,
And deal in gusty sighs and rainy flaw —
We will not woo foul weather all too soon,
Or nurse November on the lap of June.

"For ours are winging sprites, like any bird,
That shun all stagnant settlements of grief;
And even in our rest our hearts are stirred,
Like insects settled on a dancing leaf: —
This is our small philosophy in brief,
Which thus to teach hath set me all agape:
But dost thou relish it? O, hoary chief!
Unclasp thy crooked fingers from my nape,
And I will show thee many a pleasant scrape."

Then Saturn thus: — shaking his crooked blade
O'erhead, which made aloft a lightning flash
In all the fairies' eyes, dismally frayed!
His ensuing voice came like the thunder crash —
Meanwhile the bolt shatters some pine or ash —
"Thou feeble, wanton, foolish, fickle thing!
Whom nought can frighten, sadden, or abash, —
To hope my solemn countenance to wring
To idiot smiles! — but I will prune thy wing!

"Lo! this most awful handle of my scythe
Stood once a May-pole, with a flowery crown,
Which rustics danced around, and maidens blithe,
To wanton pipings; — but I plucked it down,
And robed the May Queen in a church-yard gown,
Turning her buds to rosemary and rue;
And all their merry minstrelsy did drown,
And laid each lusty leaper in the dew; —
So thou shalt fare — and every jovial crew!"

Here he lets go the struggling imp, to clutch
His mortal engine with each grisly hand,
Which frights the elfin progeny so much,
They huddle in a heap, and trembling stand
All round Titania, like the queen bee's band,
With sighs and tears and very shrieks of woe! —
Meanwhile, some moving argument I planned,
To make the stern Shade merciful, — when, lo!
He drops his fatal scythe without a blow!

For, just at need, a timely Apparition
Steps in between, to bear the awful brunt;
Making him change his horrible position,
To marvel at this comer, brave and blunt,
That dares Time's irresistible affront,

Whose strokes have scarred even the gods of old; —
Whereas this seemed a mortal, at mere hunt
For conies, lighted by the moonshine cold,
Or stalker of stray deer, stealthy and bold.

Who, turning to the small assembled fays,
Doffs to the lily queen his courteous cap,
And holds her beauty for a while in gaze,
With bright eyes kindling at this pleasant hap;
And thence upon the fair moon's silver map,
As if in question of this magic chance,
Laid like a dream upon the green earth's lap;
And then upon old Saturn turns askance,
Exclaiming, with a glad and kindly glance: —

"O, these be Fancy's revellers by night!
Stealthy companions of the downy moth —
Diana's motes, that flit in her pale light,
Shunners of Sunbeams in diurnal sloth; —
These be the feasters on night's silver cloth, —
The gnat with shrilly trump is their convener,
Forth from their flowery chambers, nothing loth,
With lulling tunes to charm the air serener,
Or dance upon the grass to make it greener.

"These be the pretty genii of the flowers,
Daintily fed with honey and pure dew —
Midsummer's phantoms in her dreaming hours,
King Oberon and all his merry crew,
The darling puppets of romance's view;
Fairies, and sprites, and goblin elves, we call them,
Famous for patronage of lovers true; —
No harm they act, neither shall harm befall them,
So do not thus with crabbed frowns appall them."

O, what a cry was Saturn's then!—it made
The fairies quake. "What care I for their pranks,
However they may lovers choose to aid,
Or dance their roundelays on flowery banks?—
Long must they dance before they earn my thanks,—
So step aside, to some far safer spot,
Whilst with my hungry scythe I mow their ranks,
And leave them in the sun, like weeds, to rot,
And with the next day's sun to be forgot."

Anon, he raised afresh his weapon keen;
But still the gracious Shade disarmed his aim,
Stepping with brave alacrity between,
And made his sere arm powerless and tame.
His be perpetual glory, for the shame
Of hoary Saturn in that grand defeat!—
But I must tell how here Titania came
With all her kneeling lieges, to entreat
His kindly succor, in sad tones, but sweet.

Saying, "Thou seest a wretched queen before thee,
The fading power of a failing land,
Who for her kingdom kneeleth to implore thee,
Now menaced by this tyrant's spoiling hand;
No one but thee can hopefully withstand
That crooked blade, he longeth so to lift.
I pray thee blind him with his own vile sand,
Which only times all ruins by its drift,
Or prune his eagle wings that are so swift.

"Or take him by that sole and grizzled tuft
That hangs upon his bald and barren crown;
And we will sing to see him so rebuffed,
And lend our little mights to pull him down,
And make brave sport of his malicious frown,

For all his boastful mockery o'er men.
For thou wast born, I know, for this renown,
By my most magical and inward ken,
That readeth even at Fate's forestalling pen.

"Nay, by the golden lustre of thine eye,
And by thy brow's most fair and ample span,
Thought's glorious palace, framed for fancies high,
And by thy cheek thus passionately wan,
I know the signs of an immortal man,—
Nature's chief darling, an illustrious mate,
Destined to foil old Death's oblivious plan,
And shine untarnished by the fogs of Fate,
Time's famous rival till the final date!

"O, shield us, then, from this usurping Time,
And we will visit thee in moonlight dreams;
And teach thee tunes, to wed unto thy rhyme,
And dance about thee in all midnight gleams,
Giving thee glimpses of our magic schemes,
Such as no mortal's eye hath ever seen;
And, for thy love to us in our extremes,
Will ever keep thy chaplet fresh and green,
Such as no poet's wreath hath ever been!

"And we'll distil thee aromatic dews,
To charm thy sense, when there shall be no flowers:
And flavored sirups in thy drinks infuse,
And teach the nightingale to haunt thy bowers,
And with our games divert thy weariest hours,
With all that elfin wits can e'er devise.
And, this churl dead, there'll be no hasting hours
To rob thee of thy joys, as now joy flies:"—
Here she was stopped by Saturn's furious cries.

Whom, therefore, the kind Shade rebukes anew,
Saying, "Thou haggard Sin, go forth, and scoop
Thy hollow coffin in some church-yard yew,
Or make the autumnal flowers turn pale, and droop
Or fell the bearded corn, till gleaners stoop
Under fat sheaves, — or blast the piny grove : —
But here thou shalt not harm this pretty group,
Whose lives are not so frail and feebly wove,
But leased on Nature's loveliness and love.

"'Tis these that free the small entangled fly,
Caught in the venomed spider's crafty snare ; —
These be the petty surgeons that apply
The healing balsams to the wounded hare,
Bedded in bloody fern, no creature's care ! —
These be providers for the orphan brood,
Whose tender mother hath been slain in air,
Quitting with gaping bill her darlings' food,
Hard by the verge of her domestic wood.

"'Tis these befriend the timid trembling stag,
When, with a bursting heart beset with fears,
He feels his saving speed begin to flag ;
For then they quench the fatal taint with tears,
And prompt fresh shifts in his alarumed ears,
So piteously they view all bloody morts ;
Or if the gunner, with his arm, appears,
Like noisy pyes and jays, with harsh reports,
They warn the wild fowl of his deadly sports.

"For these are kindly ministers of nature,
To soothe all covert hurts and dumb distress ;
Pretty they be, and very small of stature, —
For mercy still consorts with littleness ;

Wherefore the sum of good is still the less,
And mischief grossest in this world of wrong;—
So do these charitable dwarfs redress
The ten-fold ravages of giants strong,
To whom great malice and great might belong.

"Likewise to them are Poets much beholden
For secret favors in the midnight glooms;
Brave Spenser quaffed out of their goblets golden,
And saw their tables spread of prompt mushrooms,
And heard their horns of honeysuckle blooms
Sounding upon the air most soothing soft,
Like humming bees busy about the brooms,—
And glanced this fair queen's witchery full oft,
And in her magic wain soared far aloft.

"Nay, I myself, though mortal, once was nursed
By fairy gossips, friendly at my birth,
And in my childish ear glib Mab rehearsed
Her breezy travels round our planet's girth,
Telling me wonders of the moon and earth;
My gramarye at her grave lap I conned,
Where Puck hath been convened to make me mirth;
I have had from Queen Titania tokens fond,
And toyed with Oberon's permitted wand.

"With figs and plums and Persian dates they fed me,
And delicate cates after my sunset meal,
And took me by my childish hand, and led me
By craggy rocks crested with keeps of steel,
Whose awful bases deep dark woods conceal,
Staining some dead lake with their verdant dyes:
And when the West sparkled at Phœbus' wheel,
With fairy euphrasy they purged mine eyes,
To let me see their cities in the skies.

" 'Twas they first schooled my young imagination
To take its flights like any new-fledged bird,
And showed the span of wingéd meditation
Stretched wider than things grossly seen or heard.
With sweet swift Ariel how I soared and stirred
The fragrant blooms of spiritual bowers!
'Twas they endeared what I have still preferred,
Nature's blest attributes and balmy powers,
Her hills and vales and brooks, sweet birds and flowers

" Wherefore with all true loyalty and duty
Will I regard them in my honoring rhyme,
With love for love, and homages to beauty,
And magic thoughts gathered in night's cool clime,
With studious verse trancing the dragon Time,
Strong as old Merlin's necromantic spells;
So these dear monarchs of the summer's prime
Shall live unstartled by his dreadful yells,
Till shrill larks warn them to their flowery cells."

Look how a poisoned man turns livid black,
Drugged with a cup of deadly hellebore,
That sets his horrid features all at rack, —
So seemed these words into the ear to pour
Of ghastly Saturn, answering with a roar
Of mortal pain and spite and utmost rage,
Wherewith his grisly arm he raised once more,
And bade the clustered sinews all engage,
As if at one fell stroke to wreck an age.

Whereas the blade flashed on the dinted ground,
Down through his steadfast foe, yet made no scar
On that immortal Shade, or death-like wound;
But Time was long benumbed, and stood ajar,
And then with baffled rage took flight afar,

To weep his hurt in some Cimmerian gloom,
Or meaner fames (like mine) to mock and mar,
Or sharp his scythe for royal strokes of doom,
Whetting its edge on some old Cæsar's tomb.

Howbeit he vanished in the forest shade,
Distantly heard, as if some grumbling pard,
And, like Narcissus, to a sound decayed; —
Meanwhile the fays clustered the gracious Bard,
The darling centre of their dear regard:
Besides of sundry dances on the green,
Never was mortal man so brightly starred,
Or won such pretty homages, I ween.
"Nod to him, Elves!" cries the melodious queen.

"Nod to him, Elves, and flutter round about him,
And quite enclose him with your pretty crowd,
And touch him lovingly, for that, without him,
The silk-worm now had spun our dreary shroud; —
But he hath all dispersed death's tearful cloud,
And Time's dread effigy scared quite away:
Bow to him, then, as though to me ye bowed,
And his dear wishes prosper and obey
Wherever love and wit can find a way!

"'Noint him with fairy dews of magic savors,
Shaken from orient buds still pearly wet,
Roses and spicy pinks, — and, of all favors,
Plant in his walks the purple violet,
And meadow-sweet under the hedges set,
To mingle breaths with dainty eglantine
And honeysuckles sweet, — nor yet forget
Some pastoral flowery chaplets to entwine,
To vie the thoughts about his brow benign.

"Let no wild things astonish him or fear him,
But tell them all how mild he is of heart,
Till e'en the timid hares go frankly near him,
And eke the dappled does, yet never start;
Nor shall their fawns into the thickets dart,
Nor wrens forsake their nests among the leaves,
Nor speckled thrushes flutter far apart; —
But bid the sacred swallow haunt his eaves,
To guard his roof from lightning and from thieves.

"Or when he goes the nimble squirrel's visitor,
Let the brown hermit bring his hoarded nuts,
For, tell him, this is Nature's kind Inquisitor, —
Though man keeps cautious doors that conscience shuts,
For conscious wrong all curious quest rebuts, —
Nor yet shall bees uncase their jealous stings,
However he may watch their straw-built huts; —
So let him learn the crafts of all small things,
Which he will hint most aptly when he sings."

Here she leaves off, and with a graceful hand
Waves thrice three splendid circles round his head;
Which, though deserted by the radiant wand,
Wears still the glory which her waving shed,
Such as erst crowned the old Apostle's head;
To show the thoughts there harbored were divine,
And on immortal contemplations fed: —
Goodly it was to see that glory shine
Around a brow so lofty and benign! —

Goodly it was to see the elfin brood
Contend for kisses of his gentle hand,
That had their mortal enemy withstood,
And stayed their lives, fast ebbing with the sand.
Long while this strife engaged the pretty band;

But now bold Chanticleer, from farm to farm,
Challenged the dawn creeping o'er eastern land,
And well the fairies knew that shrill alarm,
Which sounds the knell of every elfish charm.

And soon the rolling mist, that 'gan arise
From plashy mead and undiscovered stream,
Earth's morning incense to the early skies,
Crept o'er the failing landscape of my dream.
Soon faded then the Phantom of my theme —
A shapeless shade, that fancy disavowed,
And shrank to nothing in the mist extreme.
Then flew Titania, — and her little crowd,
Like flocking linnets, vanished in a cloud.

HERO AND LEANDER.

TO S. T. COLERIDGE.

It is not with a hope my feeble praise
Can add one moment's honor to thy own,
That with thy mighty name I grace these lays;
I seek to glorify myself alone;
For that some precious favor thou hast shown
To my endeavor in a bygone time,
And by this token I would have it known
Thou art my friend, and friendly to my rhyme!
It is my dear ambition now to climb
Still higher in thy thought, — if my bold pen
May thrust on contemplations more sublime. —
But I am thirsty for thy praise, for when
We gain applauses from the great in name,
We seem to be partakers of *their* fame.

HERO AND LEANDER.

O Bards of old! what sorrows have ye sung,
And tragic stories, chronicled in stone,—
Sad Philomel restored her ravished tongue,
And transformed Niobe in dumbness shown;
Sweet Sappho on her love forever calls,
And Hero on the drowned Leander falls.

Was it that spectacles of sadder plights
Should make our blisses relish the more high?
Then all fair dames, and maidens, and true knights,
Whose flourished fortunes prosper in Love's eye,
Weep here, unto a tale of ancient grief,
Traced from the course of an old bas-relief.

There stands Abydos!—here is Sestos' steep,
Hard by the gusty margin of the sea,
Where sprinkling waves continually do leap;
And that is where those famous lovers be,
A builded gloom shot up into the gray,
As if the first tall watch-tower of the day.

Lo! how the lark soars upward and is gone!
Turning a spirit as he nears the sky,
His voice is heard, though body there is none,
And rain-like music scatters from on high;
But Love would follow with a falcon spite,
To pluck the minstrel from his dewy height.

For Love hath framed a ditty of regrets,
Tuned to the hollow sobbings on the shore,
A vexing sense, that with like music frets,
And chimes this dismal burthen o'er and o'er,
Saying, Leander's joys are past and spent,
Like stars extinguished in the firmament.

For ere the golden crevices of morn
Let in those regal luxuries of light,
Which all the variable east adorn,
And hang rich fringes on the skirts of night,
Leander, weaning from sweet Hero's side,
Must leave a widow where he found a bride.

Hark! how the billows beat upon the sand!
Like pawing steeds, impatient of delay;
Meanwhile their rider, lingering on the land,
Dallies with Love, and holds farewell at bay
A too short span. — How tedious slow is grief!
But parting renders time both sad and brief.

"Alas! (he sighed) that this first glimpsing light,
Which makes the wide world tenderly appear,
Should be the burning signal for my flight,
From all the world's best image, which is here;
Whose very shadow, in my fond compare,
Shines far more bright than Beauty's self elsewhere.'

Their cheeks are white as blossoms of the dark,
Whose leaves close up, and show the outward pale,
And those fair mirrors where their joys did spark,
All dim and tarnished with a dreary veil,
No more to kindle till the night's return,
Like stars replenished at Joy's golden urn.

Even thus they creep into the spectral gray,
That cramps the landscape in its narrow brim,
As when two shadows by old Lethe stray,
He clasping her, and she entwining him;
Like trees wind-parted that embrace anon,
True love so often goes before 'tis gone.

For what rich merchant but will pause in fear,
To trust his wealth to the unsafe abyss?
So Hero dotes upon her treasure here,
And sums the loss with many an anxious kiss,
Whilst her fond eyes grow dizzy in her head,
Fear aggravating fear with shows of dread.

She thinks how many have been sunk and drowned,
And spies their snow-white bones below the deep,
Then calls huge congregated monsters round,
And plants a rock wherever he would leap;
Anon she dwells on a fantastic dream,
Which she interprets of that fatal stream

Saying, "That honeyed fly I saw was thee,
Which lighted on a water-lily's cup,
When, lo! the flower, enamoured of my bee,
Closed on him suddenly, and locked him up,
And he was smothered in her drenching dew;
Therefore this day thy drowning I shall rue."

But next, remembering her virgin fame,
She clips him in her arms, and bids him go,
But seeing him break loose repents her shame,
And plucks him back upon her bosom's snow;
And tears unfix her iced resolve again,
As steadfast frosts are thawed by showers of rain.

O for a type of parting! — Love to love
Is like the fond attraction of two spheres,
Which needs a godlike effort to remove,
And then sink down their sunny atmospheres
In rain and darkness on each ruined heart,
Nor yet their melodies will sound apart.

So brave Leander sunders from his bride;
The wrenching pang disparts his soul in twain;
Half stays with her, half goes towards the tide,
And life must ache until they join again.
Now wouldst thou know the wideness of the wound,
Mete every step he takes upon the ground.

And for the agony and bosom-throe,
Let it be measured by the wide vast air,
For that is infinite, and so is woe,
Since parted lovers breathe it every where.
Look how it heaves Leander's laboring chest,
Panting, at poise, upon a rocky crest!

From which he leaps into the scooping brine,
That shocks his bosom with a double chill;
Because, all hours, till the slow sun's decline,
That cold divorcer will betwixt them still;
Wherefore he likens it to Styx' foul tide,
Where life grows death upon the other side.

Then sadly he confronts his two-fold toil
Against rude waves and an unwilling mind,
Wishing, alas! with the stout rower's toil,
That like a rower he might gaze behind,
And watch that lonely statue he hath left
On her bleak summit, weeping and bereft!

Yet turning oft, he sees her troubled locks
Pursue him still the furthest that they may;
Her marble arms that overstretch the rocks,
And her pale passioned hands that seem to pray
In dumb petition to the gods above:
Love prays devoutly when it prays for love!

Then with deep sighs he blows away the wave,
That hangs superfluous tears upon his cheek,
And bans his labor like a hopeless slave,
That, chained in hostile galley, faint and weak,
Plies on despairing through the restless foam,
Thoughtful of his lost love, and far-off home.

The drowsy mist before him chill and dank,
Like a dull lethargy o'erleans the sea,
When he rows on against the utter blank
Steering as if to dim eternity,—
Like Love's frail ghost departing with the dawn;
A failing shadow in the twilight drawn.

And soon is gone,—or nothing but a faint
And failing image in the eye of thought;
That mocks his model with an after-paint,
And stains an atom like the shape she sought;
Then with her earnest vows she hopes to fee
The old and hoary majesty of sea.

"O King of waves, and brother of high Jove,
Preserve my sumless venture there afloat;
A woman's heart, and its whole wealth of love,
Are all embarked upon that little boat;
Nay, but two loves, two lives, a double fate
A perilous voyage for so dear a freight.

"If impious mariners be stained with crime,
Shake not in awful rage thy hoary locks;
Lay by thy storms until another time,
Lest my frail bark be dashed against the rocks:
Or rather smooth thy deeps that he may fly
Like Love himself, upon a seeming sky!

"Let all thy herded monsters sleep beneath,
Nor gore him with crooked tusks, or wreathéd horns;
Let no fierce sharks destroy him with their teeth,
Nor spine-fish wound him with their venomed thorns:
But if he faint, and timely succor lack,
Let ruthful dolphins rest him on their back.

"Let no false dimpling whirlpools suck him in,
Nor slimy quicksands smother his sweet breath;
Let no jagged corals tear his tender skin,
Nor mountain billows bury him in death;"—
And with that thought forestalling her own fears,
She drowned his painted image in her tears.

By this, the climbing sun, with rest repaired,
Looked through the gold embrasures of the sky,
And asked the drowsy world how she had fared;—
The drowsy world shone brightened in reply;
And smiling off her fogs, his slanting beam
Spied young Leander in the middle stream.

His face was pallid, but the hectic morn
Had hung a lying crimson on his cheeks,
And slanderous sparkles in his eyes forlorn;
So death lies ambushed in consumptive streaks;
But inward grief was writhing o'er its task,
As heart-sick jesters weep behind the mask.

He thought of Hero and the lost delight,
Her last embracings, and the space between;
He thought of Hero and the future night,
Her speechless rapture and enamoured mien,
When, lo! before him, scarce two galleys' space,
His thoughts confronted with another face!

Her aspect's like a moon divinely fair,
But makes the midnight darker that it lies on;
'Tis so beclouded with her coal-black hair
That densely skirts her luminous horizon,
Making her doubly fair, thus darkly set,
As marble lies advantaged upon jet.

She's all too bright, too argent, and too pale,
To be a woman; — but a woman's double,
Reflected on the wave so faint and frail,
She tops the billows like an air-blown bubble;
Or dim creation of a morning dream,
Fair as the wave-bleached lily of the stream.

The very rumor strikes his seeing dead:
Great beauty like great fear first stuns the sense:
He knows not if her lips be blue or red,
Nor of her eyes can give true evidence:
Like murder's witness swooning in the court,
His sight falls senseless by its own report.

Anon resuming, it declares her eyes
Are tinct with azure, like two crystal wells
That drink the blue complexion of the skies,
Or pearls out-peeping from their silvery shells:
Her polished brow, it is an ample plain,
To lodge vast contemplations of the main.

6

Her lips might corals seem, but corals near,
Stray through her hair like blossoms on a bower;
And o'er the weaker red still domineer,
And make it pale by tribute to more power;
Her rounded cheeks are of still paler hue,
Touched by the bloom of water, tender blue.

Thus he beholds her rocking on the water,
Under the glossy umbrage of her hair,
Like pearly Amphitrite's fairest daughter,
Naiad, or Nereid, or Siren fair,
Mislodging music in her pitiless breast,
A nightingale within a falcon's nest.

They say there be such maidens in the deep,
Charming poor mariners, that all too near
By mortal lullabies fall dead asleep,
As drowsy men are poisoned through the ear;
Therefore Leander's fears begin to urge,
This snowy swan is come to sing his dirge.

At which he falls into a deadly chill,
And strains his eyes upon her lips apart;
Fearing each breath to feel that prelude shrill,
Pierce through his marrow, like a breath-blown dart
Shot sudden from an Indian's hollow cane,
With mortal venom fraught, and fiery pain.

Here, then, poor wretch, how he begins to crowd
A thousand thoughts within a pulse's space;
There seemed so brief a pause of life allowed,
His mind stretched universal, to embrace
The whole wide world, in an extreme farewell, —
A moment's musing — but an age to tell.

For there stood Hero, widowed at a glance,
The foreseen sum of many a tedious fact,
Pale cheeks, dim eyes, and withered countenance,
A wasted ruin that no wasting lacked;
Time's tragic consequents ere time began,
A world of sorrow in a tear-drop's span.

A moment's thinking is an hour in words,—
An hour of words is little for some woes;
Too little breathing a long life affords,
For love to paint itself by perfect shows;
Then let his love and grief unwronged lie dumb,
Whilst Fear, and that it fears, together come.

As when the crew, hard by some jutty cape,
Struck pale and panicked by the billows' roar,
Lay by all timely measures of escape,
And let their bark go driving on the shore;
So frayed Leander, drifting to his wreck,
Gazing on Scylla, falls upon her neck.

For he hath all forgot the swimmer's art,
The rower's cunning, and the pilot's skill,
Letting his arms fall down in languid part,
Swayed by the waves, and nothing by his will,
Till soon he jars against that glossy skin,
Solid like glass, though seemingly as thin.

Lo! how she startles at the warning shock,
And straightway girds him to her radiant breast,
More like his safe smooth harbor than his rock;
Poor wretch, he is so faint and toil-opprest,
He cannot loose him from his grappling foe,
Whether for love or hate, she lets not go.

His eyes are blinded with the sleety brine,
His ears are deafened with the wildering noise;
He asks the purpose of her fell design,
But foamy waves choke up his struggling voice;
Under the ponderous sea his body dips,
And Hero's name dies bubbling on his lips.

Look how a man is lowered to his grave;
A yearning hollow in the green earth's lap;
So he is sunk into the yawning wave,
The plunging sea fills up the watery gap;
Anon he is all gone, and nothing seen,
But likeness of green turf and hillocks green.

And where he swam the constant sun lies sleeping,
Over the verdant plain that makes his bed;
And all the noisy waves go freshly leaping,
Like gamesome boys over the church-yard dead;
The light in vain keeps looking for his face,
Now screaming sea fowl settle in his place.

Yet weep and watch for him, though all in vain!
Ye moaning billows, seek him as ye wander!
Ye gazing sunbeams, look for him again!
Ye winds, grow hoarse with asking for Leander!
Ye did but spare him for more cruel rape,
Sea storm and ruin in a female shape!

She says 'tis love hath bribed her to this deed,
The glancing of his eyes did so bewitch her.
O bootless theft! unprofitable meed!
Love's treasury is sacked, but she no richer;
The sparkles of his eyes are cold and dead,
And all his golden looks are turned to lead!

She holds the casket, but her simple hand
Hath spilled its dearest jewel by the way;
She hath life's empty garment at command,
But her own death lies covert in the prey;
As if a thief should steal a tainted vest,
Some dead man's spoil, and sicken of his pest.

Now she compels him to her deeps below,
Hiding his face beneath her plenteous hair,
Which jealously she shakes all round her brow,
For dread of envy, though no eyes are there
But seals', and all brute tenants of the deep,
Which heedless through the wave their journeys keep.

Down and still downward through the dusky green
She bore him, murmuring with joyous haste
In too rash ignorance, as he had been
Born to the texture of that watery waste;
That which she breathed and sighed, the emerald wave,
How could her pleasant home become his grave!

Down and still downward through the dusky green
She bore her treasure, with a face too nigh
To mark how life was altered in its mien,
Or how the light grew torpid in his eye,
Or how his pearly breath, unprisoned there,
Flew up to join the universal air.

She could not miss the throbbings of his heart,
Whilst her own pulse so wantoned in its joy;
She could not guess he struggled to depart,
And when he strove no more, the hapless boy!
She read his mortal stillness for content,
Feeling no fear where only love was meant.

Soon she alights upon her ocean-floor,
And straight unyokes her arms from her fair prize;
Then on his lovely face begins to pore,
As if to glut her soul; — her hungry eyes
Have grown so jealous of her arms' delight;
It seems, she hath no other sense but sight.

But, O, sad marvel! O, most bitter strange!
What dismal magic makes his cheek so pale?
Why will he not embrace, — why not exchange
Her kindly kisses; — wherefore not exhale
Some odorous message from life's ruby gates,
Where she his first sweet embassy awaits?

Her eyes, poor watchers, fixed upon his looks,
Are grappled with a wonder near to grief,
As one who pores on undeciphered books,
Strains vain surmise, and dodges with belief;
So she keeps gazing with a mazy thought,
Framing a thousand doubts that end in nought.

Too stern inscription for a page so young,
The dark translation of his look was death!
But death was written in an alien tongue,
And learning was not by to give it breath;
So one deep woe sleeps buried in its seal,
Which Time, untimely, hasteth to reveal.

Meanwhile she sits unconscious of her hap,
Nursing Death's marble effigy, which there
With heavy head lies pillowed in her lap,
And elbows all unhinged; — his sleeking hair
Creeps o'er her knees, and settles where his hand
Leans with lax fingers crooked against the sand;

And there lies spread in many an oozy trail,
Like glossy weeds hung from a chalky base,
That shows no whiter than his brow is pale;
So soon the wintry death had bleached his face
Into cold marble, — with blue chilly shades,
Showing wherein the freezy blood pervades.

And o'er his steadfast cheek a furrowed pain
Hath set, and stiffened like a storm in ice,
Showing by drooping lines the deadly strain
Of mortal anguish; — yet you might gaze twice
Ere Death it seemed, and not his cousin, Sleep,
That through those creviced lids did underpeep.

But all that tender bloom about his eyes,
Is Death's own violets, which his utmost rite
It is to scatter when the red rose dies;
For blue is chilly, and akin to white:
Also he leaves some tinges on his lips,
Which he hath kissed with such cold frosty nips.

"Surely," quoth she, "he sleeps, the senseless thing,
Oppressed and faint with toiling in the stream!"
Therefore she will not mar his rest, but sing
So low, her tune shall mingle with his dream;
Meanwhile, her lily fingers tasks to twine
His uncrispt locks uncurling in the brine.

"O lovely boy!" — thus she attuned her voice, —
"Welcome, thrice welcome, to a sea-maid's home;
My love-mate thou shalt be, and true heart's choice;
How have I longed such a twin-self should come, —
A lonely thing, till this sweet chance befell,
My heart kept sighing like a hollow shell.

"Here thou shalt live beneath this secret dome,
An ocean-bower; defended by the shade
Of quiet waters, a cool emerald gloom
To lap thee all about. Nay, be not frayed.
Those are but shady fishes that sail by
Like antic clouds across my liquid sky!

"Look how the sunbeam burns upon their scales,
And shows rich glimpses of their Tyrian skins;
They flash small lightnings from their vigorous tails,
And winking stars are kindled at their fins;
These shall divert thee in thy weariest mood,
And seek thy hand for gamesomeness and food.

"Lo! those green pretty leaves with tassel bells,
My flowerets those, that never pine for drowth;
Myself did plant them in the dappled shells,
That drink the wave with such a rosy mouth,—
Pearls wouldst thou have beside? crystals to shine?
I had such treasures once,—now they are thine.

"Now, lay thine ear against this golden sand,
And thou shalt hear the music of the sea,
Those hollow tunes it plays against the land,—
Is't not a rich and wondrous melody?
I have lain hours, and fancied in its tone
I heard the languages of ages gone!

"I too can sing when it shall please thy choice,
And breathe soft tunes through a melodious shell,
Though heretofore I have but set my voice
To some long sighs, grief harmonized, to tell
How desolate I fared;—but this sweet change
Will add new notes of gladness to my range!

"Or bid me speak, and I will tell thee tales,
Which I have framed out of the noise of waves;
Ere now, I have communed with senseless gales,
And held vain colloquies with barren caves;
But I could talk to thee whole days and days,
Only to word my love a thousand ways.

"But if thy lips will bless me with their speech,
Then ope, sweet oracles! and I'll be mute;
I was born ignorant for thee to teach,
Nay, all love's lore to thy dear looks impute;
Then ope thine eyes, fair teachers, by whose light
I saw to give away my heart aright!"

But cold and deaf the sullen creature lies,
Over her knees, and with concealing clay
Like hoarding Avarice locks up his eyes,
And leaves her world impoverished of day;
Then at his cruel lips she bends to plead,
But there the door is closed against her need.

Surely he sleeps, — so her false wits infer!
Alas! poor sluggard, ne'er to wake again!
Surely he sleeps, yet without any stir
That might denote a vision in his brain;
Or if he does not sleep, he feigns too long,
Twice she hath reached the ending of her song.

Therefore, 'tis time she tells him to uncover
Those radiant jesters, and disperse her fears,
Whereby her April face is shaded over,
Like rainy clouds just ripe for showering tears;
Nay, if he will not wake, so poor she gets,
Herself must rob those locked up cabinets.

With that she stoops above his brow, and bids
Her busy hands forsake his tangled hair,
And tenderly lift up those coffer-lids,
That she may gaze upon the jewels there,
Like babes that pluck an early bud apart,
To know the dainty color of its heart.

Now, picture one, soft creeping to a bed,
Who slowly parts the fringe-hung canopies,
And then starts back to find the sleeper dead;
So she looks in on his uncovered eyes,
And seeing all within so drear and dark,
Her own bright soul dies in her like a spark.

Backward she falls, like a pale prophetess,
Under the swoon of holy divination:
And what had all surpassed her simple guess,
She now resolves in this dark revelation;
Death's very mystery, — oblivious death; —
Long sleep, — deep night, and an entrancéd breath.

Yet life, though wounded sore, not wholly slain,
Merely obscured, and not extinguished, lies;
Her breath, that stood at ebb, soon flows again,
Heaving her hollow breast with heavy sighs,
And light comes in and kindles up the gloom,
To light her spirit from its transient tomb.

Then like the sun, awakened at new dawn,
With pale bewildered face she peers about,
And spies blurred images obscurely drawn,
Uncertain shadows in a haze of doubt;
But her true grief grows shapely by degrees,
A perished creature lying on her knees.

And now she knows how that old Murther preys,
Whose quarry on her lap lies newly slain:
How he roams all abroad and grimly slays,
Like a lean tiger in Love's own domain;
Parting fond mates, — and oft in flowery lawns
Bereaves mild mothers of their milky fawns.

O, too dear knowledge! O, pernicious earning!
Foul curse engraven upon beauty's page!
Even now the sorrow of that deadly learning
Ploughs up her brow, like an untimely age,
And on her cheek stamps verdict of death's truth
By canker blights upon the bud of youth!

For as unwholesome winds decay the leaf,
So her cheeks' rose is perished by her sighs,
And withers in the sickly breath of grief;
Whilst unacquainted rheum bedims her eyes,
Tears, virgin tears, the first that ever leapt
From those young lids, now plentifully wept.

Whence being shed, the liquid crystalline
Drops straightway down, refusing to partake
In gross admixture with the baser brine,
But shrinks and hardens into pearls opaque,
Hereafter to be worn on arms and ears;
So one maid's trophy is another's tears!

"O, foul Arch-Shadow, thou old cloud of Night,"
(Thus in her frenzy she began to wail,)
"Thou blank oblivion — blotter out of light,
Life's ruthless murderer, and dear Love's bale!
Why hast thou left thy havoc incomplete,
Leaving me here, and slaying the more sweet?

"Lo! what a lovely ruin thou hast made!
Alas! alas! thou hast no eyes to see,
And blindly slew'st him in misguided shade.
Would I had lent my doting sense to thee!
But now I turn to thee, a willing mark,
Thine arrows miss me in the aimless dark!

"O, doubly cruel!—twice misdoing spite,
But I will guide thee with my helping eyes,
Or walk the wide world through, devoid of sight,
Yet thou shalt know me by my many sighs.
Nay, then thou shouldst have spared my rose, false Death,
And known Love's flower by smelling his sweet breath;

"Or, when thy furious rage was round him dealing,
Love should have grown from touching of his skin;
But like cold marble thou art all unfeeling,
And hast no ruddy springs of warmth within,
And being but a shape of freezing bone,
Thy touching only turned my love to stone!

"And here, alas! he lies across my knees,
With cheeks still colder than the stilly wave,
The light beneath his eyelids seems to freeze;
Here then, since Love is dead and lacks a grave,
O, come and dig it in my sad heart's core—
That wound will bring a balsam for its sore!

"For art thou not a sleep where sense of ill
Lies stingless, like a sense benumbed with cold,
Healing all hurts only with sleep's good will?
So shall I slumber, and perchance behold
My living love in dreams,—O, happy night,
That lets me company his banished spright!

"O, poppy death! — sweet poisoner of sleep;
Where shall I seek for thee, oblivious drug,
That I may steep thee in my drink, and creep
Out of life's coil? Look, Idol! how I hug
Thy dainty image in this strict embrace,
And kiss this clay-cold model of thy face!

"Put out, put out these sun-consuming lamps!
I do but read my sorrows by their shine;
O, come and quench them with thy oozy damps,
And let my darkness intermix with thine;
Since love is blinded, wherefore should I see?
Now love is death, — death will be love to me!

"Away, away, this vain complaining breath,
It does but stir the troubles that I weep;
Let it be hushed and quieted, sweet Death;
The wind must settle ere the wave can sleep, —
Since love is silent I would fain be mute;
O, Death, be gracious to my dying suit!"

Thus far she pleads, but pleading nought avails her,
For Death, her sullen burthen, deigns no heed;
Then with dumb craving arms, since darkness fails her,
She prays to heaven's fair light, as if her need
Inspired her there were gods to pity pain,
Or end it, — but she lifts her arms in vain!

Poor gilded Grief! the subtle light by this
With mazy gold creeps through her watery mine,
And, diving downward through the green abyss,
Lights up her palace with an amber shine;
There, falling on her arms, — the crystal skin
Reveals the ruby tide that fares within.

Look how the fulsome beam would hang a glory
On her dark hair, but the dark hairs repel it;
Look how the perjured glow suborns a story
On her pale lips, but lips refuse to tell it;
Grief will not swerve from grief, however told
On coral lips, or charactered in gold;

Or else, thou maid! safe anchored on Love's neck,
Listing the hapless doom of young Leander,
Thou wouldst not shed a tear for that old wreck,
Sitting secure where no wild surges wander;
Whereas the woe moves on with tragic pace,
And shows its sad reflection in thy face.

Thus having travelled on, and tracked the tale
Like the due course of an old bas-relief,
Where Tragedy pursues her progress pale,
Brood here a while upon that sea-maid's grief,
And take a deeper imprint from the frieze
Of that young Fate, with Death upon her knees.

Then whilst the melancholy Muse withal
Resumes her music in a sadder tone,
Meanwhile the sunbeam strikes upon the wall,
Conceive that lovely siren to live on,
Even as Hope whispered, the Promethean light
Would kindle up the dead Leander's spright.

"'Tis light," she says, "that feeds the glittering stars,
And those were stars set in his heavenly brow;
But this salt cloud, this cold sea vapor, mars
Their radiant breathing, and obscures them now;
Therefore I'll lay him in the clear blue air,
And see how these dull orbs will kindle there."

Swiftly as dolphins glide, or swifter yet,
With dead Leander in her fond arms' fold,
She cleaves the meshes of that radiant net
The sun hath twined above of liquid gold,
Nor slacks till on the margin of the land
She lays his body on the glowing sand.

There, like a pearly waif, just past the reach
Of foamy billows he lies cast. Just then,
Some listless fishers, straying down the beach,
Spy out this wonder. Thence the curious men,
Low crouching, creep into a thicket brake,
And watch her doings till their rude hearts ache.

First she begins to chafe him till she faints,
Then falls upon his mouth with kisses many,
And sometimes pauses in her own complaints
To list his breathing, but there is not any, —
Then looks into his eyes where no light dwells;
Light makes no pictures in such muddy wells.

The hot sun parches his discovered eyes,
The hot sun beats on his discolored limbs,
The sand is oozy whereupon he lies,
Soiling his fairness; — then away she swims,
Meaning to gather him a daintier bed,
Plucking the cool fresh weeds, brown, green, and red.

But, simple-witted thief, while she dives under,
Another robs her of her amorous theft;
The ambushed fishermen creep forth to plunder,
And steal the unwatched treasure she has left;
Only his void impression dints the sands:
Leander is purloined by stealthy hands!

Lo! how she shudders off the beaded wave!
Like Grief all over tears, and senseless falls,
His void imprint seems hollowed for her grave;
Then, rising on her knees, looks round and calls
On Hero! Hero!—having learned this name
Of his last breath, she calls him by the same.

Then with her frantic hands she rends her hairs,
And casts them forth, sad keepsakes, to the wind,
As if in plucking those she plucked her cares;
But grief lies deeper, and remains behind
Like a barbed arrow, rankling in her brain,
Turning her very thoughts to throbs of pain.

Anon her tangled locks are left alone,
And down upon the sand she meekly sits,
Hard by the foam, as humble as a stone,
Like an enchanted maid beside her wits,
That ponders with a look serene and tragic,
Stunned by the mighty mystery of magic.

Or think of Ariadne's utter trance,
Crazed by the flight of that disloyal traitor,
Who left her gazing on the green expanse
That swallowed up his track,—yet this would mate l
Even in the cloudy summit of her woe,
When o'er the far sea-brim she saw him go.

For even so she bows, and bends her gaze
O'er the eternal waste, as if to sum
Its waves by weary thousands all her days,
Dismally doomed! meanwhile the billows come,
And coldly dabble with her quiet feet,
Like any bleaching stones they wont to greet.

And thence into her lap have boldly sprung,
Washing her weedy tresses to and fro,
That round her crouching knees have darkly hung;
But she sits careless of waves' ebb and flow,
Like a lone beacon on a desert coast,
Showing where all her hope was wrecked and lost.

Yet whether in the sea or vaulted sky,
She knoweth not her love's abrupt resort,
So like a shape of dreams he left her eye,
Winking with doubt. Meanwhile, the churls' report
Has thronged the beach with many a curious face,
That peeps upon her from its hiding-place.

And here a head, and there a brow half seen,
Dodges behind a rock. Here on his hands
A mariner his crumpled cheeks doth lean
Over a rugged crest. Another stands,
Holding his harmful arrow at the head,
Still checked by human caution and strange dread.

One stops his ears, — another close beholder
Whispers unto the next his grave surmise;
This crouches down, — and just above his shoulder,
A woman's pity saddens in her eyes,
And prompts her to befriend that lonely grief,
With all sweet helps of sisterly relief.

And down the sunny beach she paces slowly,
With many doubtful pauses by the way;
Grief hath an influence so hushed and holy, —
Making her twice attempt, ere she can lay
Her hand upon that sea-maid's shoulder white,
Which makes her startle up in wild affright.

And, like a seal, she leaps into the wave,
That drowns the shrill remainder of her scream;
Anon the sea fills up the watery cave,
And seals her exit with a foamy seam, —
Leaving those baffled gazers on the beach,
Turning in uncouth wonder each to each.

Some watch, some call, some see her head emerge,
Wherever a brown weed falls through the foam;
Some point to white eruptions of the surge: —
But she is vanished to her shady home,
Under the deep, inscrutable, — and there
Weeps in a midnight made of her own hair.

Now here the sighing winds, before uuheard,
Forth from their cloudy caves begin to blow,
Till all the surface of the deep is stirred,
Like to the panting grief it hides below;
And heaven is covered with a stormy rack
Soiling the waters with its inky black.

The screaming fowl resigns her finny prey,
And labors shoreward with a bending wing,
Rowing against the wind her toilsome way;
Meanwhile, the curling billows chafe, and fling
Their dewy frost still further on the stones,
That answer to the wind with hollow groans.

And here and there a fisher's far-off bark
Flies with the sun's last glimpse upon its sail,
Like a bright flame amid the waters dark,
Watched with the hope and fear of maidens pale,
And anxious mothers that upturn their brows,
Freighting the gusty wind with frequent vows,

For that the horrid deep has no sure track
To guide love safe into his homely haven.
And, lo! the storm grows blacker in its wrath,
O'er the dark billow brooding like a raven,
That bodes of death and widow's sorrowing,
Under the dusty covert of his wing.

And so day ended. But no vesper spark
Hung forth its heavenly sign; but sheets of flame
Played round the savage features of the dark,
Making night horrible. That night, there came
A weeping maiden to high Sestos' steep,
And tore her hair and gazed upon the deep,

And waved aloft her bright and ruddy torch,
Whose flame the boastful wind so rudely fanned,
That oft it would recoil, and basely scorch
The tender covert of her sheltering hand;
Which yet, for love's dear sake, disdained retire,
And, like a glorying martyr, braved the fire.

For that was love's own sign and beacon guide
Across the Hellespont's wide weary space,
Wherein he nightly struggled with the tide;
Look what a red it forges on her face,
As if she blushed at holding such a light,
Even in the unseen presence of the night!

Whereas her tragic cheek is truly pale,
And colder than the rude and ruffian air
That howls into her ear a horrid tale
Of storm, and wreck, and uttermost despair,
Saying, "Leander floats amid the surge,
And those are dismal waves that sing his dirge."

And, hark! — a grieving voice, trembling and faint,
Blends with the hollow sobbings of the sea;
Like the sad music of a siren's plaint,
But shriller than Leander's voice should be,
Unless the wintry death had changed its tone, —
Wherefore she thinks she hears his spirit moan.

For now, upon each brief and breathless pause
Made by the raging winds, it plainly calls
On Hero! Hero! — whereupon she draws
Close to the dizzy brink, that ne'er appalls
Her brave and constant spirit to recoil,
However the wild billows toss and toil.

"O! dost thou live under the deep, deep sea?
I thought such love as thine could never die;
If thou hast gained an immortality
From the kind pitying sea-god, so will I;
And this false cruel tide, that used to sever
Our hearts, shall be our common home forever!

"There we will sit and sport upon one billow,
And sing our ocean-ditties all the day,
And lie together on the same green pillow,
That curls above us with its dewy spray;
And ever in one presence live and dwell,
Like two twin pearls within the self-same shell."

One moment, then, upon the dizzy verge
She stands; — with face upturned against the sky;
A moment more, upon the foamy surge
She gazes, with a calm despairing eye;
Feeling that awful pause of blood and breath
Which life endures when it confronts with death; —

Then from the giddy deep she madly springs,
Grasping her maiden robes, that vainly kept
Panting abroad, like unavailing wings,
To save her from her death. — The sea-maid wept,
And in a crystal cave her corse enshrined;
No meaner sepulchre should Hero find!

THE ELM TREE:

A DREAM IN THE WOODS.

"And this our life, exempt from public haunt,
Finds tongues in trees." AS YOU LIKE IT.

'TWAS in a shady avenue,
Where lofty elms abound—
And from a tree
There came to me
A sad and solemn sound,
That sometimes murmured overhead,
And sometimes underground.

Amongst the leaves it seemed to sigh,
Amid the boughs to moan;
It muttered in the stem, and then
The roots took up the tone;
As if beneath the dewy grass
The dead began to groan.

No breeze there was to stir the leaves;
No bolts that tempests launch,
To rend the trunk or rugged bark;
No gale to bend the branch;
No quake of earth to heave the roots,
That stood so stiff and stanch.

No bird was preening up aloft,
  To rustle with its wing;
No squirrel, in its sport or fear,
  From bough to bough to spring;
    The solid bole
    Had ne'er a hole
  To hide a living thing!

No scooping hollow cell to lodge
  A furtive beast or fowl,
    The martin, bat,
    Or forest cat
  That nightly loves to prowl,
Nor ivy nook so apt to shroud
  The moping, snoring owl.

But still the sound was in my ear,
  A sad and solemn sound,
That sometimes murmured overhead,
  And sometimes underground —
'Twas in a shady avenue
  Where lofty elms abound.

O, hath the Dryad still a tongue
  In this ungenial clime?
Have sylvan spirits still a voice
  As in the classic prime —
To make the forest voluble,
  As in the olden time?

The olden time is dead and gone;
  Its years have filled their sum —
And even in Greece — her native Greece —
  The sylvan nymph is dumb —
From ash, and beech, and aged oak,
  No classic whispers come.

From poplar, pine, and drooping birch,
  And fragrant linden trees,
    No living sound
    E'er hovers round,
  Unless the vagrant breeze,
The music of the merry bird,
  Or hum of busy bees.

But busy bees forsake the elm
  That bears no bloom aloft —
The finch was in the hawthorn-bush,
  The blackbird in the croft;
And among the firs the brooding dove,
  That else might murmur soft.

Yet still I heard that solemn sound,
  And sad it was to boot,
From every overhanging bough,
  And each minuter shoot;
From rugged trunk and mossy rind,
  And from the twisted root.

From these, — a melancholy moan;
  From those, — a dreary sigh;
As if the boughs were wintry bare,
  And wild winds sweeping by —
Whereas the smallest fleecy cloud
  Was steadfast in the sky.

No sign or touch of stirring air
  Could either sense observe —
The zephyr had not breath enough
  The thistle-down to swerve,
Or force the filmy gossamers
  To take another curve.

In still and silent slumber hushed
  All Nature seemed to be:
From heaven above, or earth beneath,
  No whisper came to me—
Except the solemn sound and sad
  From that MYSTERIOUS TREE!

A hollow, hollow, hollow sound,
  As is that dreamy roar
When distant billows boil and bound
  Along a shingly shore—
But the ocean brim was far aloof,
  A hundred miles or more.

No murmur of the gusty sea,
  No tumult of the beach,
However they may foam and fret,
  The bounded sense could reach—
Methought the trees in mystic tongue
  Were talking each to each!—

Mayhap, rehearsing ancient tales
  Of greenwood love or guilt,
    Of whispered vows
    Beneath their boughs;
  Or blood obscurely spilt;
Or of that near-hand mansion-house
  A royal Tudor built.

Perchance, of booty won or shared
  Beneath the starry cope—
Or where the suicidal wretch
  Hung up the fatal rope;
Or Beauty kept an evil tryste,
  Ensnared by Love and Hope.

Of graves, perchance, untimely scooped
At midnight dark and dank —
And what is underneath the sod
Whereon the grass is rank —
Of old intrigues,
And privy leagues,
Tradition leaves in blank.

Of traitor lips that muttered plots —
Of kin who fought and fell —
God knows the undiscovered schemes,
The arts and acts of hell,
Performed long generations since,
If trees had tongues to tell!

With wary eyes, and ears alert,
As one who walks afraid,
I wandered down the dappled path
Of mingled light and shade —
How sweetly gleamed that arch of blue
Beyond the green arcade!

How cheerly shone the glimpse of heaven
Beyond that verdant aisle!
All overarched with lofty elms,
That quenched the light, the while,
As dim and chill
As serves to fill
Some old cathedral pile!

And many a gnarlèd trunk was there,
That ages long had stood,
Till Time had wrought them into shapes
Like Pan's fantastic brood;
Or still more foul and hideous forms
That pagans carve in wood!

A crouching Satyr lurking here —
   And there a Goblin grim —
As staring full of demon life
   As Gothic sculptor's whim —
A marvel it had scarcely been
   To hear a voice from him!

Some whisper from that horrid mouth
   Of strange, unearthly tone;
Or wild infernal laugh, to chill
   One's marrow in the bone.
But no — it grins like rigid Death,
   And silent as a stone!

As silent as its fellows be,
   For all is mute with them —
The branch that climbs the leafy roof —
   The rough and mossy stem —
      The crooked root,
      And tender shoot,
   Where hangs the dewy gem.

One mystic tree alone there is,
   Of sad and solemn sound —
That sometimes murmurs overhead,
   And sometimes underground —
In all that shady avenue,
   Where lofty elms abound.

PART II.

The scene is changed! No green arcade,
   No trees all ranged a-row —

But scattered like a beaten host,
  Dispersing to and fro;
With here and there a sylvan corse,
  That fell before the foe.

The foe that down in yonder dell
  Pursues his daily toil;
As witness many a prostrate trunk,
  Bereft of leafy spoil,
Hard by its wooden stump, whereon
  The adder loves to coil.

Alone he works — his ringing blows
  Have banished bird and beast;
The hind and fawn have cantered off
  A hundred yards at least;
And on the maple's lofty top
  The linnet's song has ceased.

No eye his labor overlooks,
  Or when he takes his rest;
Except the timid thrush that peeps
  Above her secret nest,
Forbid by love to leave the young
  Beneath her speckled breast.

The woodman's heart is in his work,
  His axe is sharp and good;
With sturdy arm and steady aim
  He smites the gaping wood;
    From distant rocks
    His lusty knocks
  Reëcho many a rood.

His axe is keen, his arm is strong;
  The muscles serve him well;
His years have reached an extra span,
  The number none can tell;
But still his life-long task has been
  The timber tree to fell.

Through summer's parching sultriness
  And winter's freezing cold,
      From sapling youth
      To virile growth,
  And age's rigid mould,
His energetic axe hath rung
  Within that forest old.

Aloft, upon his poising steel
  The vivid sunbeams glance—
About his head and round his feet
  The forest shadows dance;
And bounding from his russet coat
  The acorn drops askance.

His face is like a Druid's face,
  With wrinkles furrowed deep,
And tanned by scorching suns as brown
  As corn that's ripe to reap;
But the hair on brow, and cheek, and chin,
  Is white as wool of sheep.

His frame is like a giant's frame;
  His legs are long and stark;
His arms like limbs of knotted yew;
  His hands like rugged bark;
      So he felleth still,
      With right good will,
  As if to build an ark!

O! well within *his* fatal path
The fearful tree might quake
Through every fibre, twig, and leaf,
With aspen tremor shake;
Through trunk and root,
And branch and shoot,
A low complaining make!

O! well to *him* the tree might breathe
A sad and solemn sound,
A sigh that murmured overhead,
And groans from underground;
As in that shady avenue
Where lofty elms abound!

But calm and mute the maple stands,
The plane, the ash, the fir,
The elm, the beech, the drooping birch,
Without the least demur;
And e'en the aspen's hoary leaf
Makes no unusual stir.

The pines — those old gigantic pines,
That writhe — recalling soon
The famous human group that writhes
With snakes in wild festoon —
In ramous wrestlings interlaced
A forest Laocoon —

Like Titans of primeval girth
By tortures overcome,
Their brown enormous limbs they twine,
Bedewed with tears of gum —
Fierce agonies that ought to yell,
But, like the marble, dumb.

Nay, yonder blasted elm that stands
  So like a man of sin,
Who, frantic, flings his arms abroad
  To feel the worm within —
For all that gesture, so intense,
  It makes no sort of din!

An universal silence reigns
  In rugged bark or peel,
Except that very trunk which rings
  Beneath the biting steel —
Meanwhile the woodman plies his axe
  With unrelenting zeal!

No rustic song is on his tongue,
  No whistle on his lips;
But, with a quiet thoughtfulness
  His trusty tool he grips,
And, stroke on stroke, keeps hacking out
  The bright and flying chips.

Stroke after stroke, with frequent dint
  He spreads the fatal gash;
Till, lo! the remnant fibres rend,
  With harsh and sudden crash,
And on the dull-resounding turf
  The jarring branches lash!

O! now the forest trees may sigh,
  The ash, the poplar tall,
The elm, the birch, the drooping beech,
  The aspens — one and all,
    With solemn groan
    And hollow moan
  Lament a comrade's fall!

A goodly elm, of noble girth,
  That, thrice the human span —
While on their variegated course
  The constant seasons ran —
Through gale, and hail, and fiery bolt,
  Had stood erect as man.

But now, like mortal man himself,
  Struck down by hand of God,
Or heathen idol tumbled prone
  Beneath the Eternal's nod,
In all its giant bulk and length
  It lies along the sod!

Ay, now the forest trees may grieve
  And make a common moan
Around that patriarchal trunk
  So newly overthrown;
And with a murmur recognize
  A doom to be their own!

The echo sleeps: the idle axe,
  A disregarded tool,
Lies crushing with its passive weight
  The toad's reputed stool —
The woodman wipes his dewy brow
  Within the shadows cool.

No zephyr stirs: the ear may catch
  The smallest insect hum;
But on the disappointed sense
  No mystic whispers come;
No tone of sylvan sympathy,
  The forest trees are dumb.

No leafy noise, nor inward voice,
  No sad and solemn sound,
That sometimes murmurs overhead,
  And sometimes underground;
As in that shady avenue,
  Where lofty elms abound!

PART III.

The deed is done: the tree is low
  That stood so long and firm;
The woodman and his axe are gone,
  His toil has found its term;
And where he wrought the speckled thrush
  Securely hunts the worm.

The cony from the sandy bank
  Has run a rapid race,
Through thistle, bent, and tangled fern,
  To seek the open space;
And on its haunches sits erect
  To clean its furry face.

The dappled fawn is close at hand,
  The hind is browsing near,—
And on the larch's lowest bough
  The ousel whistles clear;
    But checks the note
    Within its throat,
  As choked with sudden fear!

With sudden fear her wormy quest
  The thrush abruptly quits —
Through thistle, bent, and tangled fern
  The startled cony flits;
And on the larch's lowest bough
  No more the ousel sits.

With sudden fear
The dappled deer
  Effect a swift escape;
But well might bolder creatures start
  And fly, or stand agape,
With rising hair and curdled blood,
  To see so grim a Shape!

The very sky turns pale above;
  The earth grows dark beneath;
The human terror thrills with cold,
  And draws a shorter breath —
An universal panic owns
  The dread approach of DEATH!

With silent pace, as shadows come,
  And dark as shadows be,
The grisly phantom takes his stand
  Beside the fallen tree,
And scans it with his gloomy eyes,
  And laughs with horrid glee —

A dreary laugh and desolate,
  Where mirth is void and null,
As hollow as its echo sounds
  Within the hollow skull —
"Whoever laid this tree along,
  His hatchet was not dull!

"The human arm and human tool
Have done their duty well!
But after sound of ringing axe
Must sound the ringing knell;
When elm or oak
Have felt the stroke
My turn it is to fell.

"No passive unregarded tree,
A senseless thing of wood,
Wherein the sluggish sap ascends
To swell the vernal bud —
But conscious, moving, breathing trunks,
That throb with living blood!

"No forest monarch yearly clad
In mantle green or brown;
That unrecorded lives, and falls
By hand of rustic clown —
But kings who don the purple robe,
And wear the jewelled crown.

"Ah! little recks the royal mind,
Within his banquet hall,
While tapers shine, and music breathes,
And beauty leads the ball, —
He little recks the oaken plank
Shall be his palace wall!

"Ah, little dreams the haughty peer,
The while his falcon flies —
Or on the blood-bedabbled turf
The antlered quarry dies —
That in his own ancestral park
The narrow dwelling lies.

"But haughty peer and mighty king
  One doom shall overwhelm!
    The oaken cell
    Shall lodge him well
  Whose sceptre ruled a realm —
While he who never knew a home
  Shall find it in the elm!

"The tattered, lean, dejected wretch,
  Who begs from door to door,
And dies within the cressy ditch,
  Or on the barren moor,
The friendly elm shall lodge and clothe
  That houseless man and poor!

"Yea, this recumbent, ragged trunk,
  That lies so long and prone,
With many a fallen acorn-cup,
  And mast and firry cone —
This rugged trunk shall hold its share
  Of mortal flesh and bone!

"A miser hoarding heaps of gold,
  But pale with ague-fears —
A wife lamenting love's decay,
  With secret, cruel tears,
Distilling bitter, bitter drops
  From sweets of former years —

"A man within whose gloomy mind
  Offence had darkly sunk,
Who out of fierce Revenge's cup
  Hath madly, darkly drunk —
Grief, Avarice, and Hate shall sleep
  Within this very trunk!

"This massy trunk that lies along,
And many more must fall —
For the very knave
Who digs the grave,
The man who spreads the pall,
And he who tolls the funeral bell,
The elm shall have them all!

"The tall abounding elm that grows
In hedge-rows up and down:
In field and forest, copse and park,
And in the peopled town,
With colonies of noisy rooks
That nestle on its crown.

"And well the abounding elm may grow
In field and hedge so rife,
In forest, copse, and wooded park,
And 'mid the city's strife,
For every hour that passes by
Shall end a human life!"

The phantom ends: the shade is gone;
The sky is clear and bright;
On turf, and moss, and fallen tree,
There glows a ruddy light;
And bounding through the golden fern
The rabbit comes to bite.

The thrush's mate beside her sits
And pipes a merry lay;
The dove is in the evergreens;
And on the larch's spray
The fly-bird flutters up and down,
To catch its tiny prey.

9

The gentle hind and dappled fawn
  Are coming up the glade;
Each harmless furred and feathered thing
  Is glad, and not afraid —
But on my saddened spirit still
  The shadow leaves a shade.

A secret, vague, prophetic gloom,
  As though by certain mark
I knew the fore-appointed tree
  Within whose rugged bark
This warm and living frame shall find
  Its narrow house and dark.

That mystic tree which breathed to me
  A sad and solemn sound,
That sometimes murmured overhead,
  And sometimes underground;
Within that shady avenue
  Where lofty elms abound.

THE DREAM OF EUGENE ARAM.

'Twas in the prime of summer time,
    An evening calm and cool,
And four and twenty happy boys
    Came bounding out of school:
There were some that ran, and some that leapt
    Like troutlets in a pool.

Away they sped with gamesome minds
    And souls untouched by sin;

To a level mead they came, and there
They drave the wickets in:
Pleasantly shone the setting sun
Over the town of Lynn.

Like sportive deer they coursed about,
And shouted as they ran, —
Turning to mirth all things of earth,
As only boyhood can;
But the Usher sat remote from all,
A melancholy man!

His hat was off, his vest apart,
To catch heaven's blessèd breeze;
For a burning thought was in his brow,
And his bosom ill at ease:
So he leaned his head on his hands, and read
The book between his knees!

Leaf after leaf he turned it o'er,
Nor ever glanced aside,
For the peace of his soul he read that book
In the golden eventide:
Much study had made him very lean,
And pale, and leaden-eyed.

At last he shut the ponderous tome;
With a fast and fervent grasp
He strained the dusky covers close,
And fixed the brazen hasp:
"O, God! could I so close my mind,
And clasp it with a clasp!"

Then leaping on his feet upright,
Some moody turns he took —

Now up the mead, then down the mead,
 And past a shady nook,—
And, lo! he saw a little boy
 That pored upon a book!

"My gentle lad, what is't you read—
 Romance or fairy fable?
Or is it some historic page,
 Of kings and crowns unstable?"
The young boy gave an upward glance,—
 "It is 'The Death of Abel.'"

The Usher took six hasty strides,
 As smit with sudden pain,—
Six hasty strides beyond the place,
 Then slowly back again;
And down he sat beside the lad,
 And talked with him of Cain;

And, long since then, of bloody men,
 Whose deeds tradition saves;
Of lonely folk cut off unseen,
 And hid in sudden graves;
Of horrid stabs in groves forlorn,
 And murders done in caves;

And how the sprites of injured men
 Shriek upward from the sod,—
Ay, how the ghostly hand will point
 To show the burial clod;
And unknown facts of guilty acts
 Are seen in dreams from God!

He told how murderers walk the earth
 Beneath the curse of Cain,—

With crimson clouds before their eyes,
And flames about their brain;
For blood has left upon their souls
Its everlasting stain!

"And well," quoth he, "I know, for truth,
Their pangs must be extreme, —
Woe, woe, unutterable woe, —
Who spill life's sacred stream!
For why? Methought, last night, I wrought
A murder, in a dream!

"One that had never done me wrong —
A feeble man and old;
I led him to a lonely field, —
The moon shone clear and cold:
Now here, said I, this man shall die,
And I will have his gold!

"Two sudden blows with a ragged stick,
And one with a heavy stone,
One hurried gash with a hasty knife, —
And then the deed was done:
There was nothing lying at my foot
But lifeless flesh and bone!

"Nothing but lifeless flesh and bone,
That could not do me ill;
And yet I feared him all the more,
For, lying there so still:
There was a manhood in his look,
That murder could not kill!

"And, lo, the universal air
Seemed lit with ghastly flame; —

Ten thousand thousand dreadful eyes
    Were looking down in blame:
I took the dead man by his hand,
    And called upon his name!

"O, God! it made me quake to see
    Such sense within the slain!
But when I touched the lifeless clay,
    The blood gushed out amain!
For every clot, a burning spot
    Was scorching in my brain!

"My head was like an ardent coal,
    My heart as solid ice;
My wretched, wretched soul, I knew,
    Was at the devil's price:
A dozen times I groaned; the dead
    Had never groaned but twice!

"And now, from forth the frowning sky,
    From the heaven's topmost height,
I heard a voice — the awful voice
    Of the blood-avenging sprite: —
'Thou guilty man! take up thy dead
    And hide it from my sight!'

"I took the dreary body up,
    And cast it in a stream, —
A sluggish water, black as ink,
    The depth was so extreme: —
My gentle Boy, remember this
    Is nothing but a dream!

"Down went the corse with a hollow plunge,
    And vanished in the pool;

Anon I cleansed my bloody hands,
And washed my forehead cool,
And sat among the urchins young,
That evening, in the school.

"O, Heaven! to think of their white souls,
And mine so black and grim!
I could not share in childish prayer,
Nor join in evening hymn:
Like a devil of the pit I seemed,
'Mid holy cherubim!

"And peace went with them, one and all,
And each calm pillow spread;
But Guilt was my grim chamberlain
That lighted me to bed;
And drew my midnight curtains round,
With fingers bloody red!

"All night I lay in agony,
In anguish dark and deep;
My fevered eyes I dared not close,
But stared aghast at Sleep:
For Sin had rendered unto her
The keys of hell to keep!

"All night I lay in agony,
From weary chime to chime,
With one besetting horrid hint,
That racked me all the time;
A mighty yearning, like the first
Fierce impulse unto crime!

"One stern tyrannic thought, that made
All other thoughts its slave;

Stronger and stronger every pulse
    Did that temptation crave, —
Still urging me to go and see
    The Dead Man in his grave!

"Heavily I rose up, as soon
    As light was in the sky,
And sought the black accurséd pool
    With a wild misgiving eye;
And I saw the Dead in the river bed,
    For the faithless stream was dry.

"Merrily rose the lark, and shook
    The dew-drop from its wing;
But I never marked its morning flight,
    I never heard it sing:
For I was stooping once again
    Under the horrid thing.

"With breathless speed, like a soul in chase,
    I took him up and ran; —
There was no time to dig a grave
    Before the day began:
In a lonesome wood, with heaps of leaves,
    I hid the murdered man!

"And all that day I read in school,
    But my thought was other where;
As soon as the mid-day task was done,
    In secret I was there:
And a mighty wind had swept the leaves,
    And still the corse was bare!

"Then down I cast me on my face,
    And first began to weep,

For I knew my secret then was one
That earth refused to keep:
Or land or sea, though he should be
Ten thousand fathoms deep.

"So wills the fierce avenging Sprite,
Till blood for blood atones!
Ay, though he's buried in a cave,
And trodden down with stones,
And years have rotted off his flesh, —
The world shall see his bones!

"O, God! that horrid, horrid dream
Besets me now awake!
Again — again, with dizzy brain,
The human life I take;
And my red right hand grows raging hot,
Like Cranmer's at the stake.

"And still no peace for the restless clay
Will wave or mould allow;
The horrid thing pursues my soul, —
It stands before me now!"
The fearful Boy looked up, and saw
Huge drops upon his brow.

That very night, while gentle sleep
The urchin eyelids kissed,
Two stern-faced men set out from Lynn,
Through the cold and heavy mist:
And Eugene Aram walked between,
With gyves upon his wrist.

THE HAUNTED HOUSE.

A ROMANCE.

"A jolly place," said he, "in times of old,
But something ails it now; the place is curst."
HART-LEAP WELL, BY WORDSWORTH.

PART I.

SOME dreams we have are nothing else but dreams,
Unnatural and full of contradictions;
Yet others of our most romantic schemes
Are something more than fictions.

It might be only on enchanted gound;
It might be merely by a thought's expansion;
But in the spirit, or the flesh, I found
An old deserted mansion.

A residence for woman, child, and man,
A dwelling-place, — and yet no habitation;
A house, — but under some prodigious ban
Of excommunication.

Unhinged the iron gates half open hung,
Jarred by the gusty gales of many winters,
That from its crumbled pedestal had flung
One marble globe in splinters.

No dog was at the threshold, great or small;
No pigeon on the roof — no household creature —
No cat demurely dozing on the wall —
Not one domestic feature.

No human figure stirred, to go or come;
No face looked forth from shut or open casement:
No chimney smoked — there was no sign of home
From parapet to basement.

With shattered panes the grassy court was starred;
The time-worn coping-stone had tumbled after;
And through the ragged roof the sky shone, barred
With naked beam and rafter.

O'er all there hung a shadow and a fear;
A sense of mystery the spirit daunted,
And said, as plain as whisper in the ear,
The place is haunted!

The flower grew wild and rankly as the weed,
Roses with thistles struggled for espial,
And vagrant plants of parasitic breed
Had overgrown the dial.

But, gay or gloomy, steadfast or infirm,
No heart was there to heed the hour's duration;
All times and tides were lost in one long term
Of stagnant desolation.

The wren had built within the porch, she found
Its quiet loneliness so sure and thorough;
And on the lawn, — within its turfy mound, —
The rabbit made his burrow.

The rabbit wild and gray, that flitted through
The shrubby clumps, and frisked, and sat, and vanished,
But leisurely and bold, as if he knew
His enemy was banished.

The wary crow, — the pheasant from the woods, —
Lulled by the still and everlasting sameness,
Close to the mansion, like domestic broods,
Fed with a "shocking tameness."

The coot was swimming in the reedy pond,
Beside the water-hen, so soon affrighted;
And in the weedy moat the heron, fond
Of solitude, alighted.

The moping heron, motionless and stiff,
That on a stone, as silently and stilly,
Stood, an apparent sentinel, as if
To guard the water lily.

No sound was heard, except, from far away,
The ringing of the whitwall's shrilly laughter,
Or, now and then, the chatter of the jay,
That Echo murmured after.

But Echo never mocked the human tongue;
Some weighty crime, that Heaven could not pardon,
A secret curse on that old building hung,
And its deserted garden.

The beds were all untouched by hand or tool;
No footstep marked the damp and mossy gravel,
Each walk as green as is the mantled pool
For want of human travel.

The vine unpruned, and the neglected peach,
Drooped from the wall with which they used to grapple;
And on the cankered tree, in easy reach,
Rotted the golden apple.

But awfully the truant shunned the ground,
The vagrant kept aloof, and daring poacher:
In spite of gaps that through the fences round
Invited the encroacher.

For over all there hung a cloud of fear;
A sense of mystery the spirit daunted,
And said, as plain as whisper in the ear,
The place is haunted!

The pear and quince lay squandered on the grass;
The mould was purple with unheeded showers
Of bloomy plums — a wilderness it was
Of fruits, and weeds, and flowers!

The marigold amidst the nettles blew,
The gourd embraced the rose-bush in its ramble,
The thistle and the stock together grew,
The hollyhock and bramble.

The bear-bine with the lilac interlaced;
The sturdy burdock choked its slender neighbor,
The spicy pink. All tokens were effaced
Of human care and labor.

The very yew formality had trained
To such a rigid pyramidal stature,
For want of trimming had almost regained
The raggedness of nature.

The fountain was a-dry — neglect and time
Had marred the work of artisan and mason,
And efts and croaking frogs, begot of slime,
Sprawled in the ruined basin.

The statue, fallen from its marble base,
Amidst the refuse leaves, and herbage rotten,
Lay like the idol of some bygone race,
Its name and rites forgotten.

On every side the aspect was the same,
All ruined, desolate, forlorn and savage:
No hand or foot within the precinct came
To rectify or ravage.

For over all there hung a cloud of fear;
A sense of mystery the spirit daunted,
And said, as plain as whisper in the ear,
The place is haunted!

PART II.

O, very gloomy is the house of woe,
Where tears are falling while the bell is knelling,
With all the dark solemnities which show
That Death is in the dwelling!

O, very, very dreary is the room
Where love, domestic love, no longer nestles,
But, smitten by the common stroke of doom,
The corpse lies on the trestles!

But house of woe, and hearse, and sable pall,
The narrow home of the departed mortal,
Ne'er looked so gloomy as that ghostly hall,
With its deserted portal!

The centipede along the threshold crept,
The cobweb hung across in mazy tangle,
And in its winding-sheet the maggot slept,
At every nook and angle.

The keyhole lodged the earwig and her brood;
The emmets of the steps had old possession,
And marched in search of their diurnal food
In undisturbed procession.

As undisturbed as the prehensile cell
Of moth or maggot, or the spider's tissue;
For never foot upon that threshold fell,
To enter or to issue.

O'er all there hung the shadow of a fear;
A sense of mystery the spirit daunted,
And said, as plain as whisper in the ear,
The place is haunted!

Howbeit, the door I pushed — or so I dreamed —
Which slowly, slowly gaped, — the hinges creaking
With such a rusty eloquence, it seemed
That Time himself was speaking.

But Time was dumb within that mansion old,
Or left his tale to the heraldic banners
That hung from the corroded walls, and told
Of former men and manners.

Those tattered flags, that with the opened door
Seemed the old wave of battle to remember,
While fallen fragments danced upon the floor
Like dead leaves in December.

The startled bats flew out — bird after bird —
The screech-owl overhead began to flutter,
And seemed to mock the cry that she had heard
Some dying victim utter!

A shriek that echoed from the joisted roof,
And up the stair, and further still and further,
Till in some ringing chamber far aloof
It ceased its tale of murther!

Meanwhile the rusty armor rattled round,
The banner shuddered, and the ragged streamer;
All things the horrid tenor of the sound
Acknowledged with a tremor.

The antlers, where the helmet hung and belt,
Stirred as the tempest stirs the forest branches,
Or as the stag had trembled when he felt
The bloodhound at his haunches.

The window jingled in its crumbled frame,
And through its many gaps of destitution
Dolorous moans and hollow sighings came,
Like those of dissolution.

The wood-louse dropped, and rolled into a ball,
Touched by some impulse occult or mechanic;
And nameless beetles ran along the wall
In universal panic.

The subtle spider, that from overhead
Hung like a spy on human guilt and error,
Suddenly turned, and up its slender thread
Ran with a nimble terror.

The very stains and fractures on the wall,
Assuming features solemn and terrific,
Hinted some tragedy of that old hall,
Locked up in hieroglyphic.

Some tale that might, perchance, have solved the doubt,
Wherefore amongst those flags so dull and livid
The banner of the Bloody Hand shone out,
So ominously vivid.

Some key to that inscrutable appeal,
Which made the very frame of Nature quiver,
And every thrilling nerve and fibre feel
So ague-like a shiver.

For over all there hung a cloud of fear;
A sense of mystery the spirit daunted,
And said, as plain as whisper in the ear,
The place is haunted!

If but a rat had lingered in the house,
To lure the thought into a social channel!
But not a rat remained, or tiny mouse,
To squeak behind the panel.

Huge drops rolled down the walls, as if they wept;
And where the cricket used to chirp so shrilly
The toad was squatting, and the lizard crept
On that damp hearth and chilly.

For years no cheerful blaze had sparkled there,
Or glanced on coat of buff or knightly metal;
The slug was crawling on the vacant chair,—
The snail upon the settle.

The floor was redolent of mould and must,
The fungus in the rotten seams had quickened;
While on the oaken table coats of dust
Perennially had thickened.

No mark of leathern jack or metal can,
No cup, no horn, no hospitable token, —
All social ties between that board and man
Had long ago been broken.

There was so foul a rumor in the air,
The shadow of a presence so atrocious,
No human creature could have feasted there,
Even the most ferocious.

For over all there hung a cloud of fear;
A sense of mystery the spirit daunted,
And said, as plain as whisper in the ear,
The place is haunted!

PART III.

'Tis hard for human actions to account,
Whether from reason or from impulse only —
But some internal prompting bade me mount
The gloomy stairs and lonely.

Those gloomy stairs, so dark, and damp, and cold,
With odors as from bones and relics carnal,
Deprived of rite and consecrated mould,
The chapel vault or charnel.

Those dreary stairs, where with the sounding stress
Of every step so many echoes blended,
The mind, with dark misgivings, feared to guess
How many feet ascended.

The tempest with its spoils had drifted in,
Till each unwholesome stone was darkly spotted,
As thickly as the leopard's dappled skin,
With leaves that rankly rotted.

The air was thick, and in the upper gloom
The bat — or something in its shape — was winging;
And on the wall, as chilly as a tomb,
The death's-head moth was clinging.

That mystic moth, which, with a sense profound
Of all unholy presence, augurs truly;
And with a grim significance flits round
The taper burning bluely.

Such omens in the place there seemed to be,
At every crooked turn, or on the landing,
The straining eyeball was prepared to see
Some apparition standing.

For over all there hung a cloud of fear;
A sense of mystery the spirit daunted,
And said, as plain as whisper in the ear,
The place is haunted!

Yet no portentous shape the sight amazed;
Each object plain, and tangible, and valid;
But from their tarnished frames dark figures gazed,
And faces spectre-pallid.

Not merely with the mimic life that lies
Within the compass of art's simulation;
Their souls were looking through their painted eyes
With awful speculation.

On every lip a speechless horror dwelt;
On every brow the burthen of affliction;
The old ancestral spirits knew and felt
The house's malediction.

Such earnest woe their features overcast,
They might have stirred, or sighed, or wept, or spoken;
But, save the hollow moaning of the blast,
The stillness was unbroken.

No other sound or stir of life was there,
Except my steps in solitary clamber,
From flight to flight, from humid stair to stair,
From chamber into chamber.

Deserted rooms of luxury and state,
That old magnificence had richly furnished
With pictures, cabinets of ancient date,
And carvings gilt and burnished.

Rich hangings, storied by the needle's art,
With Scripture history or classic fable;
But all had faded, save one ragged part,
Where Cain was slaying Abel.

The silent waste of mildew and the moth
Had marred the tissue with a partial ravage;
But undecaying frowned upon the cloth
Each feature stern and savage.

The sky was pale; the cloud a thing of doubt;
Some hues were fresh, and some decayed and duller;
But still the BLOODY HAND shone strangely out
With vehemence of color!

The BLOODY HAND that with a lurid stain
Shone on the dusty floor, a dismal token,
Projected from the casement's painted pane,
Where all beside was broken.

The BLOODY HAND significant of crime,
That, glaring on the old heraldic banner,
Had kept its crimson unimpaired by time,
In such a wondrous manner!

O'er all there hung the shadow of a fear;
A sense of mystery the spirit daunted,
And said, as plain as whisper in the ear,
The place is haunted!

The death-watch ticked behind the panelled oak,
Inexplicable tremors shook the arras,
And echoes strange and mystical awoke,
The fancy to embarrass.

Prophetic hints that filled the soul with dread,
But through one gloomy entrance pointing mostly,
The while some secret inspiration said,
That chamber is the ghostly!

Across the door no gossamer festoon
Swung pendulous — no web — no dusty fringes,
No silky chrysalis or white cocoon
About its nooks and hinges.

The spider shunned the interdicted room,
The moth, the beetle, and the fly were banished,
And where the sunbeam fell athwart the gloom
The very midge had vanished.

One lonely ray that glanced upon a bed,
As if with awful aim direct and certain,
To show the BLOODY HAND in burning red
Embroidered on the curtain.

And yet no gory stain was on the quilt —
The pillow in its place had slowly rotted;
The floor alone retained the trace of guilt,
Those boards obscurely spotted.

Obscurely spotted to the door, and thence
With mazy doubles to the grated casement —
O, what a tale they told of fear intense,
Of horror and amazement!

What human creature in the dead of night
Had coursed like hunted hare that cruel distance?
Had sought the door, the window, in his flight,
Striving for dear existence?

What shrieking spirit in that bloody room
Its mortal frame had violently quitted? —
Across the sunbeam, with a sudden gloom,
A ghostly shadow flitted.

Across the sunbeam, and along the wall,
But painted on the air so very dimly,
It hardly veiled the tapestry at all,
Or portrait frowning grimly.

O'er all there hung the shadow of a fear;
A sense of mystery the spirit daunted,
And said, as plain as whisper in the ear,
The place is haunted!

THE BRIDGE OF SIGHS.

"Drowned! drowned!"—HAMLET.

ONE more unfortunate,
Weary of breath,
Rashly importunate,
Gone to her death!

Take her up tenderly,
Lift her with care;
Fashioned so slenderly,
Young, and so fair!

Look at her garments
Clinging like cerements;
Whilst the wave constantly
Drips from her clothing;
Take her up instantly,
Loving, not loathing.—

Touch her not scornfully;
Think of her mournfully,
Gently and humanly;
Not of the stains of her,
All that remains of her
Now is pure womanly.

Make no deep scrutiny
Into her mutiny
Rash and undutiful:
Past all dishonor,
Death has left on her
Only the beautiful.

Still, for all slips of hers,
One of Eve's family —
Wipe those poor lips of hers
Oozing so clammily.

Loop up her tresses
Escaped from the comb,
Her fair auburn tresses;
Whilst wonderment guesses
Where was her home?

Who was her father?
Who was her mother?
Had she a sister?
Had she a brother?
Or was there a dearer one
Still, and a nearer one
Yet, than all other?

Alas for the rarity
Of Christian charity
Under the sun!
O, it was pitiful!
Near a whole city full,
Home she had none.

Sisterly, brotherly,
Fatherly, motherly

Feelings had changed:
Love, by harsh evidence,
Thrown from its eminence;
Even God's providence
Seeming estranged.

Where the lamps quiver
So far in the river,
With many a light
From window and casement,
From garret to basement,
She stood with amazement,
Houseless by night.

The bleak wind of March
Made her tremble and shiver;
But not the dark arch,
Or the black flowing river:
Mad from life's history,
Glad to death's mystery
Swift to be hurled —
Any where, any where
Out of the world!

In she plunged boldly,
No matter how coldly
The rough river ran, —
Over the brink of it,
Picture it — think of it,
Dissolute man!
Lave in it, drink of it,
Then, if you can!

Take her up tenderly,
Lift her with care;

Fashioned so slenderly,
Young, and so fair!

Ere her limbs frigidly
Stiffen too rigidly,
Decently, — kindly, —
Smooth, and compose them;
And her eyes, close them,
Staring so blindly!

Dreadfully staring
Through muddy impurity,
As when with the daring
Last look of despairing
Fixed on futurity.

Perishing gloomily,
Spurred by contumely,
Cold inhumanity,
Burning insanity,
Into her rest. —
Cross her hands humbly,
As if praying dumbly,
Over her breast!

Owning her weakness,
Her evil behavior,
And leaving, with meekness,
Her sins to her Saviour!

THE SONG OF THE SHIRT.

WITH fingers weary and worn,
With eyelids heavy and red,
A woman sat in unwomanly rags,
Plying her needle and thread —
Stitch! stitch! stitch!
In poverty, hunger, and dirt,
And still with a voice of dolorous pitch
She sang the "Song of the Shirt!"

"Work! work! work!
While the cock is crowing aloof!
And work — work — work,
Till the stars shine through the roof!
It's O! to be a slave
Along with the barbarous Turk,
Where woman has never a soul to save,
If this is Christian work!

"Work — work — work
Till the brain begins to swim!
Work — work — work
Till the eyes are heavy and dim!
Seam, and gusset, and band,
Band, and gusset, and seam,
Till over the buttons I fall asleep,
And sew them on in a dream!

"O, men, with sisters dear!
O, men, with mothers and wives!
It is not linen you're wearing out,
But human creatures' lives!

Stitch — stitch — stitch,
In poverty, hunger, and dirt,
Sewing at once, with a double thread,
A shroud as well as a shirt.

"But why do I talk of death?
That phantom of grisly bone,
I hardly fear his terrible shape,
It seems so like my own —
It seems so like my own,
Because of the fasts I keep;
O, God! that bread should be so dear,
And flesh and blood so cheap!

"Work — work — work!
My labor never flags;
And what are its wages? A bed of straw,
A crust of bread — and rags.
That shattered roof — and this naked floor —
A table — a broken chair —
And a wall so blank, my shadow I thank
For sometimes falling there!

"Work — work — work!
From weary chime to chime,
Work — work — work,
As prisoners work for crime!
Band, and gusset, and seam,
Seam, and gusset, and band,
Till the heart is sick, and the brain benumbed,
As well as the weary hand.

"Work — work — work,
In the dull December light,

And work — work — work,
When the weather is warm and bright —
While underneath the eaves
The brooding swallows cling,
As if to show me their sunny backs,
And twit me with the spring.

"O! but to breathe the breath
Of the cowslip and primrose sweet —
With the sky above my head,
And the grass beneath my feet,
For only one short hour
To feel as I used to feel,
Before I knew the woes of want,
And the walk that costs a meal!

"O! but for one short hour!
A respite however brief!
No blessed leisure for love or hope,
But only time for grief!
A little weeping would ease my heart,
But in their briny bed
My tears must stop, for every drop
Hinders needle and thread!"

With fingers weary and worn,
With eyelids heavy and red,
A woman sat in unwomanly rags,
Plying her needle and thread —
Stitch! stitch! stitch!
In poverty, hunger, and dirt,
And still with a voice of dolorous pitch, —
Would that its tone could reach the rich! —
She sang this "Song of the Shirt!"

THE LADY'S DREAM.

THE lady lay in her bed,
 Her couch so warm and soft,
But her sleep was restless and broken still;
 For, turning often and oft
From side to side, she muttered and moaned,
 And tossed her arms aloft.

At last she startled up,
 And gazed on the vacant air,
With a look of awe, as if she saw
 Some dreadful phantom there —
And then in the pillow she buried her face
 From visions ill to bear.

The very curtain shook,
 Her terror was so extreme;
And the light that fell on the broidered quilt
 Kept a tremulous gleam;
And her voice was hollow, and shook as she cried:
 "O, me! that awful dream!

"That weary, weary walk,
 In the church-yard's dismal ground!
And those horrible things, with shady wings,
 That came and flitted round, —
Death, death, and nothing but death,
 In every sight and sound!

"And, O! those maidens young,
 Who wrought in that dreary room,

With figures drooping and spectres thin,
  And cheeks without a bloom ; —
And the voice that cried, 'For the pomp of pride,
  We haste to an early tomb!

"'For the pomp and pleasure of pride,
  We toil like Afric slaves,
And only to earn a home at last,
  Where yonder cypress waves ;'
And then they pointed — I never saw
  A ground so full of graves!

"And still the coffins came,
  With their sorrowful trains and slow;
Coffin after coffin still,
  A sad and sickening show;
From grief exempt, I never had dreamt
  Of such a world of woe!

"Of the hearts that daily break,
  Of the tears that hourly fall,
Of the many, many troubles of life,
  That grieve this earthly ball —
Disease, and Hunger, and Pain, and Want,
  But now I dreamt of them all!

"For the blind and the cripple were there,
  And the babe that pined for bread,
And the houseless man, and the widow poor
  Who begged — to bury the dead;
The naked, alas! that I might have clad,
  The famished I might have fed!

"The sorrow I might have soothed,
  And the unregarded tears;

For many a thronging shape was there,
  From long-forgotten years, —
Ay, even the poor rejected Moor,
  Who raised my childish fears!

"Each pleading look, that long ago
  I scanned with a heedless eye,
Each face was gazing as plainly there
  As when I passed it by:
Woe, woe for me if the past should be
  Thus present when I die!

"No need of sulphureous lake,
  No need of fiery coal,
But only that crowd of human kind
  Who wanted pity and dole —
In everlasting retrospect —
  Will wring my sinful soul!

"Alas! I have walked through life
  Too heedless where I trod;
Nay, helping to trample my fellow-worm,
  And fill the burial sod —
Forgetting that even the sparrow falls
  Not unmarked of God!

"I drank the richest draughts;
  And ate whatever is good —
Fish, and flesh, and fowl, and fruit,
  Supplied my hungry mood;
But I never remembered the wretched ones
  That starve for want of food!

"I dressed as the noble dress,
  In cloth of silver and gold,

With silk, and satin, and costly furs,
  In many an ample fold;
But I never remembered the naked limbs
  That froze with winter's cold.

"The wounds I might have healed!
  The human sorrow and smart!
And yet it never was in my soul
  To play so ill a part;
But evil is wrought by want of thought,
  As well as want of heart!"

She clasped her fervent hands,
  And the tears began to stream;
Large, and bitter, and fast they fell,
  Remorse was so extreme;
And yet, O, yet, that many a dame
  Would dream the Lady's Dream!

THE WORKHOUSE CLOCK.

AN ALLEGORY.

There's a murmur in the air,
A noise in every street —
The murmur of many tongues,
The noise of numerous feet —
While round the workhouse door
The laboring classes flock,
For why? — the overseer of the poor
Is setting the workhouse clock.

Who does not hear the tramp
Of thousands speeding along
Of either sex and various stamp,
Sickly, crippled, or strong,
Walking, limping, creeping
From court, and alley, and lane,
But all in one direction sweeping,
Like rivers that seek the main?
Who does not see them sally
From mill, and garret, and room,
In lane, and court, and alley,
From homes in poverty's lowest valley,
Furnished with shuttle and loom —
Poor slaves of Civilization's galley —
And in the road and footways rally,
As if for the day of doom?

Some, of hardly human form,
Stunted, crooked, and crippled by toil;
Dingy with smoke and dust and oil,
And smirched besides with vicious soil,
Clustering, mustering, all in a swarm.
Father, mother, and careful child,
Looking as if it had never smiled —
The seamstress, lean, and weary, and wan,
With only the ghosts of garments on —
The weaver, her sallow neighbor,
The grim and sooty artisan;
Every soul — child, woman, or man,
Who lives — or dies — by labor.

Stirred by an overwhelming zeal,
And sociál impulse, a terrible throng!
Leaving shuttle, and needle, and wheel,

Furnace, and grindstone, spindle, and reel,
Thread, and yarn, and iron, and steel —
Yea, rest and the yet untasted meal —
Gushing, rushing, crushing along,
A very torrent of Man!
Urged by the sighs of sorrow and wrong,
Grown at last to a hurricane strong,
Stop its course who can!
Stop who can its onward course
And irresistible moral force;
O! vain and idle dream!
For surely as men are all akin,
Whether of fair or sable skin,
According to Nature's scheme,
That human movement contains within
A blood-power stronger than steam.

Onward, onward, with hasty feet,
They swarm — and westward still —
Masses born to drink and eat,
But starving amidst Whitechapel's meat,
And famishing down Cornhill!
Through the Poultry — but still unfed —
Christian charity, hang your head!
Hungry — passing the Street of Bread;
Thirsty — the Street of Milk;
Ragged — beside the Ludgate mart,
So gorgeous, through mechanic art,
With cotton, and wool, and silk!

At last, before that door
That bears so many a knock
Ere ever it opens to sick or poor,
Like sheep they huddle and flock —

And would that all the good and wise
Could see the million of hollow eyes,
With a gleam derived from hope and the skies,
Upturned to the workhouse clock!

O! that the parish powers,
Who regulate labor's hours,
The daily amount of human trial,
Weariness, pain, and self-denial,
Would turn from the artificial dial
That striketh ten or eleven,
And go, for once, by that older one
That stands in the light of Nature's sun,
And takes its time from Heaven!

THE LAY OF THE LABORER.

A SPADE! a rake! a hoe!
  A pickaxe, or a bill!
A hook to reap, or a scythe to mow,
  A flail, or what ye will —
And here's a ready hand
  To ply the needful tool,
And skilled enough, by lessons rough,
  In Labor's rugged school.

To hedge, or dig the ditch,
  To lop or fell the tree,
To lay the swarth on the sultry field,
  Or plough the stubborn lea;

The harvest stack to bind,
  The wheaten rick to thatch,
And never fear in my pouch to find
  The tinder or the match.

To a flaming barn or farm
  My fancies never roam;
The fire I yearn to kindle and burn
  Is on the hearth of home;
Where children huddle and crouch
  Through dark long winter days,
Where starving children huddle and crouch,
  To see the cheerful rays,
A-glowing on the haggard cheek,
  And not in the haggard's blaze!

To Him who sends a drought
  To parch the fields forlorn,
The rain to flood the meadows with mud,
  The blight to blast the corn,
To Him I leave to guide
  The bolt in its crooked path,
To strike the miser's rick, and show
  The skies blood-red with wrath.

A spade! a rake! a hoe!
  A pickaxe, or a bill!
A hook to reap, or a scythe to mow,
  A flail, or what ye will —
The corn to thrash, or the hedge to plash,
  The market-team to drive,
Or mend the fence by the cover side,
  And leave the game alive.

Ay, only give me work,
And then you need not fear
That I shall snare his worship's hare,
Or kill his grace's deer;
Break into his lordship's house,
To steal the plate so rich;
Or leave the yeoman that had a purse
To welter in the ditch.

Wherever Nature needs,
Wherever Labor calls,
No job I'll shirk of the hardest work,
To shun the workhouse walls;
Where savage laws begrudge
The pauper babe its breath,
And doom a wife to a widow's life,
Before her partner's death.

My only claim is this,
With labor stiff and stark
By lawful turn my living to earn,
Between the light and dark;
My daily bread and nightly bed,
My bacon, and drop of beer —
But all from the hand that holds the land,
And none from the overseer!

No parish money, or loaf,
No pauper badges for me, —
A son of the soil by right of toil
Entitled to my fee.
No alms I ask, give me my task;
Here are the arm, the leg,
The strength, the sinews of a man,
To work, and not to beg.

Still one of Adam's heirs,
  Though doomed by chance of birth
To dress so mean, and to eat the lean
  Instead of the fat of the earth;
To make such humble meals
  As honest labor can,
A bone and a crust, with a grace to God,
  And little thanks to man!

A spade! a rake! a hoe!
  A pickaxe, or a bill!
A hook to reap, or a scythe to mow,
  A flail, or what ye will—
Whatever the tool to ply,
  Here is a willing drudge,
With muscle and limb, and woe to him
  Who does their pay begrudge!

Who every weekly score
  Docks labor's little mite,
Bestows on the poor at the temple door,
  But robbed them over night.
The very shilling he hoped to save,
  As health and morals fail,
Shall visit me in the New Bastile
  The Spital, or the Gaol!

FAIR INES.

O SAW ye not fair Ines?
She's gone into the west,
To dazzle when the sun is down,
And rob the world of rest:

She took our daylight with her,
The smiles that we love best,
With morning blushes on her cheek,
And pearls upon her breast.

O turn again, fair Ines,
Before the fall of night,
For fear the moon should shine alone,
And stars unrivalled bright;
And blessèd will the lover be
That walks beneath their light,
And breathes the love against thy cheek
I dare not even write!

Would I had been, fair Ines,
That gallant cavalier,
Who rode so gayly by thy side,
And whispered thee so near!—
Were there no bonny dames at home,
Or no true lovers here,
That he should cross the seas to win
The dearest of the dear?

I saw thee, lovely Ines,
Descend along the shore,
With bands of noble gentlemen,
And banners waved before:
And gentle youth and maidens gay,
And snowy plumes they wore;—
It would have been a beauteous dream,
—If it had been no more!

Alas, alas! fair Ines,
She went away with song,

With music waiting on her steps,
And shoutings of the throng;
But some were sad, and felt no mirth,
But only music's wrong,
In sounds that sang farewell, farewell,
To her you've loved so long.

Farewell, farewell, fair Ines!
That vessel never bore
So fair a lady on its deck,
Nor danced so light before, —
Alas for pleasure on the sea,
And sorrow on the shore!
The smile that blest one lover's heart
Has broken many more!

THE DEPARTURE OF SUMMER.

SUMMER is gone on swallows' wings,
And earth has buried all her flowers:
No more the lark, the linnet sings,
But silence sits in faded bowers.
There is a shadow on the plain
Of Winter ere he comes again, —
There is in woods a solemn sound
Of hollow warnings whispered round,
As Echo in her deep recess
For once had turned a prophetess.
Shuddering Autumn stops to list,
And breathes his fear in sudden sighs,
With clouded face, and hazel eyes
That quench themselves, and hide in mist.

Yes, Summer's gone like pageant bright;
Its glorious days of golden light
Are gone — the mimic suns that quiver,
Then melt in Time's dark-flowing river.
Gone the sweetly-scented breeze
That spoke in music to the trees;
Gone for damp and chilly breath,
As if fresh blown o'er marble seas,
Or newly from the lungs of Death.
Gone its virgin roses' blushes,
Warm as when Aurora rushes
Freshly from the god's embrace,
With all her shame upon her face.
Old Time hath laid them in the mould;
Sure he is blind as well as old,
Whose hand relentless never spares
Young cheeks so beauty-bright as theirs!
Gone are the flame-eyed lovers now
From where so blushing-blest they tarried
Under the hawthorn's blossom-bough,
Gone; for Day and Night are married.
All the light of love is fled: —
Alas! that negro breasts should hide
The lips that were so rosy red,
At morning and at even-tide!

Delightful Summer! then adieu
Till thou shalt visit us anew:
But who without regretful sigh
Can say adieu, and see thee fly?
Not he that e'er hath felt thy power,
His joy expanding like a flower
That cometh after rain and snow,
Looks up at heaven, and learns to glow: —

Not he that fled from Babel-strife
To the green Sabbath-land of life,
To dodge dull Care 'mid clustered trees,
And cool his forehead in the breeze, —
Whose spirit, weary-worn perchance,
Shook from its wings a weight of grief,
And perched upon an aspen-leaf,
For every breath to make it dance.

Farewell! — on wings of sombre stain,
That blacken in the last blue skies,
Thou fly'st; but thou wilt come again
On the gay wings of butterflies.
Spring at thy approach will sprout
Her new Corinthian beauties out,
Leaf-woven homes, where twitter-words
Will grow to songs, and eggs to birds;
Ambitious buds shall swell to flowers,
And April smiles to sunny hours.
Bright days shall be, and gentle nights
Full of soft breath and echo-lights,
As if the god of sun-time kept
His eyes half-open while he slept.
Roses shall be where roses were,
Not shadows, but reality;
As if they never perished there,
But slept in immortality:
Nature shall thrill with new delight,
And Time's relumined river run
Warm as young blood, and dazzling bright
As if its source were in the sun!

But say, hath Winter then no charms?
Is there no joy, no gladness, warms

His aged heart? no happy wiles
To cheat the hoary one to smiles?
Onward he comes — the cruel North
Pours his furious whirlwind forth
Before him — and we breathe the breath
Of famished bears that howl to death.
Onward he comes from rocks that blanch
O'er solid streams that never flow;
His tears all ice, his locks all snow,
Just crept from some huge avalanche —
A thing half-breathing and half-warm,
As if one spark began to glow
Within some statue's marble form,
Or pilgrim stiffened in the storm.
O! will not Mirth's light arrows fail
To pierce that frozen coat of mail?
O! will not joy but strive in vain
To light up those glazed eyes again?

No! take him in, and blaze the oak,
And pour the wine, and warm the ale;
His sides shall shake to many a joke,
His tongue shall thaw in many a tale,
His eyes grow bright, his heart be gay,
And even his palsy charmed away.
What heeds he then the boisterous shout
Of angry winds that scold without,
Like shrewish wives at tavern door?
What heeds he then the wild uproar
Of billows bursting on the shore?
In dashing waves, in howling breeze,
There is a music that can charm him;
When safe, and sheltered, and at ease,
He hears the storm that cannot harm him.

But hark! those shouts! that sudden din
Of little hearts that laugh within.
O! take him where the youngsters play,
And he will grow as young as they!
They come! they come! each blue-eyed Sport,
The Twelfth-Night King and all his court —
'Tis Mirth fresh crowned with mistletoe!
Music with her merry fiddles,
Joy "on light fantastic toe,"
Wit with all his jests and riddles,
Singing and dancing as they go.
And Love, young Love, among the rest,
A welcome — nor unbidden guest.

But still for Summer dost thou grieve?
Then read our poets — they shall weave
A garden of green fancies still,
Where thy wish may rove at will.
They have kept for after treats
The essences of summer sweets,
And echoes of its songs that wind
In endless music through the mind:
They have stamped in visible traces
The "thoughts that breathe," in words that shine
The flights of soul in sunny places —
To greet and company with thine.
These shall wing thee on to flowers —
The past or future that shall seem
All the brighter in thy dream
For blowing in such desert hours.
The summer never shines so bright
As thought of in a winter's night;
And the sweetest, loveliest rose
Is in the bud before it blows;

The dear one of the lover's heart
Is painted to his longing eyes,
In charms she ne'er can realize —
But when she turns again to part.
Dream thou then, and bind thy brow
With wreath of fancy roses now,
And drink of summer in the cup
Where the Muse hath mixed it up;
The "dance, and song, and sun-burnt mirth,"
With the warm nectar of the earth:
Drink! 'twill glow in every vein,
And thou shalt dream the winter through:
Then waken to the sun again,
And find thy summer vision true!

ODE: AUTUMN.

I saw old Autumn in the misty morn
Stand shadowless like silence, listening
To silence, for no lonely bird would sing
Into his hollow ear from woods forlorn,
Nor lowly hedge nor solitary thorn; —
Shaking his languid locks all dewy bright
With tangled gossamer that fell by night,
Pearling his coronet of golden corn.

Where are the songs of Summer? — With the sun,
Oping the dusky eyelids of the South,
Till shade and silence waken up as one,
And Morning sings with a warm odorous mouth.
Where are the merry birds? — Away, away,
On panting wings through the inclement skies,

Lest owls should prey
Undazzled at noon-day,
And tear with horny beak their lustrous eyes.
Where are the blooms of Summer? — In the west,
Blushing their last to the last sunny hours,
When the mild Eve by sudden Night is prest
Like tearful Proserpine, snatched from her flowers
To a most gloomy breast.
Where is the pride of Summer, — the green prime, —
The many, many leaves all twinkling? — Three
On the mossed elm; three on the naked lime
Trembling, — and one upon the old oak tree!
Where is the Dryad's immortality? —
Gone into mournful cypress and dark yew,
Or wearing the long gloomy Winter through
In the smooth holly's green eternity.
The squirrel gloats on his accomplished hoard,
The ants have brimmed their garners with ripe grain,
And honey-bees have stored
The sweets of summer in their luscious cells;
The swallows all have winged across the main;
But here the Autumn melancholy dwells,
And sighs her tearful spells
Amongst the sunless shadows of the plain.
Alone, alone,
Upon a mossy stone,
She sits and reckons up the dead and gone,
With the last leaves for a love-rosary,
Whilst all the withered world looks drearily,
Like a dim picture of the drownéd past
In the hushed mind's mysterious far away,
Doubtful what ghostly thing will steal the last
Into that distance, gray upon the gray.

O, go and sit with her, and be o'ershaded
Under the languid downfall of her hair:
She wears a coronal of flowers faded
Upon her forehead, and a face of care; —
There is enough of withered every where
To make her bower, — and enough of gloom;
There is enough of sadness to invite,
If only for the rose that died, — whose doom
Is Beauty's, — she that with the living bloom
Of conscious cheeks most beautifies the light; —
There is enough of sorrowing, and quite
Enough of bitter fruits the earth doth bear, —
Enough of chilly droppings for her bowl;
Enough of fear and shadowy despair,
To frame her cloudy prison for the soul!

SONG.

FOR MUSIC.

A LAKE and a fairy boat
To sail in the moonlight clear, —
And merrily we would float
From the dragons that watch us here!

Thy gown should be snow-white silk;
And strings of orient pearls,
Like gossamers dipped in milk,
Should twine with thy raven curls!

Red rubies should deck thy hands,
And diamonds should be thy dower —
But fairies have broke their wands,
And wishing has lost its power!

BALLAD.

SPRING it is cheery,
Winter is dreary,
Green leaves hang, but the brown must fly;
When he's forsaken,
Withered and shaken,
What can an old man do but die?

Love will not clip him,
Maids will not lip him,
Maud and Marian pass him by;
Youth it is sunny,
Age has no honey, —
What can an old man do but die?

June it was jolly,
O for its folly!
A dancing leg and a laughing eye;
Youth may be silly,
Wisdom is chilly, —
What can an old man do but die?

Friends they are scanty,
Beggars are plenty,
If he has followers, I know why;
Gold's in his clutches,
(Buying him crutches!) —
What can an old man do but die?

HYMN TO THE SUN.

GIVER of glowing light!
Though but a god of other days,
The kings and sages
Of wiser ages
Still live and gladden in thy genial rays.

King of the tuneful lyre,
Still poets' hymns to thee belong;
Though lips are cold
Whereon of old
Thy beams all turned to worshipping and song!

Lord of the dreadful bow,
None triumph now for Python's death;
But thou dost save
From hungry grave
The life that hangs upon a summer breath.

Father of rosy day,
No more thy clouds of incense rise;
But waking flowers
At morning hours
Give out their sweets to meet thee in the skies.

God of the Delphic fane,
No more thou listenest to hymns sublime;
But they will leave
On winds at eve
A solemn echo to the end of time.

AUTUMN.

THE autumn skies are flushed with gold,
And fair and bright the rivers run;
These are but streams of winter cold,
And painted mists that quench the sun.

In secret boughs no sweet birds sing,
In secret boughs no bird can shroud;
These are but leaves that take to wing,
And wintry winds that pipe so loud.

'Tis not trees' shade, but cloudy glooms
That on the cheerless valleys fall;
The flowers are in their grassy tombs,
And tears of dew are on them all.

TO A COLD BEAUTY.

LADY, wouldst thou heiress be
  To Winter's cold and cruel part?
When he sets the rivers free,
  Thou dost still lock up thy heart; —
Thou that shouldst outlast the snow
But in the whiteness of thy brow?

Scorn and cold neglect are made
  For winter gloom and winter wind,
But thou wilt wrong the summer air,
  Breathing it to words unkind, —
Breath which only should belong
To love, to sunlight, and to song!

When the little buds unclose,
  Red, and white, and pied, and blue,
And that virgin flower, the rose,
  Opes her heart to hold the dew,
Wilt thou lock thy bosom up
With no jewel in its cup?

Let not cold December sit
  Thus in Love's peculiar throne; —
Brooklets are not prisoned now,
  But crystal frosts are all agone,
And that which hangs upon the spray,
It is no snow, but flower of May!

RUTH.

She stood breast-high amid the corn,
Clasped by the golden light of morn,
Like the sweetheart of the sun,
Who many a glowing kiss had won.

On her cheek an autumn flush,
Deeply ripened; — such a blush
In the midst of brown was born,
Like red poppies grown with corn.

Round her eyes her tresses fell;
Which were blackest none could tell,
But long lashes veiled a light
That had else been all too bright.

And her hat, with shady brim,
Made her tressy forehead dim; —
Thus she stood amid the stooks,
Praising God with sweetest looks: —

Sure, I said, Heaven did not mean
Where I reap thou shouldst but glean;
Lay thy sheaf adown, and come,
Share my harvest and my home.

BALLAD.

SHE'S up and gone, the graceless girl!
And robbed my failing years;
My blood before was thin and cold,
But now 'tis turned to tears; —
My shadow falls upon my grave;
So near the brink I stand,
She might have staid a little yet,
And led me by the hand!

Ay, call her on the barren moor,
And call her on the hill, —
'Tis nothing but the heron's cry,
And plover's answer shrill;
My child is flown on wilder wings
Than they have ever spread,
And I may even walk a waste
That widened when she fled.

Full many a thankless child has been,
But never one like mine;
Her meat was served on plates of gold,
Her drink was rosy wine;
But now she'll share the robin's food,
And sup the common rill,
Before her feet will turn again
To meet her father's will!

I REMEMBER, I REMEMBER.

I REMEMBER, I remember
The house where I was born,
The little window where the sun
Came peeping in at morn;
He never came a wink too soon,
Nor brought too long a day,
But now I often wish the night
Had borne my breath away!

I remember, I remember
The roses red and white,
The violets, and the lily-cups,
Those flowers made of light!
The lilacs where the robin built,
And where my brother set
The laburnum on his birth-day,—
The tree is living yet!

I remember, I remember
Where I was used to swing,
And thought the air must rush as fresh
To swallows on the wing;
My spirit flew in feathers then,
That is so heavy now,
And summer pools could hardly cool
The fever on my brow!

I remember, I remember
The fir-trees dark and high;
I used to think their slender tops
Were close against the sky:

It was a childish ignorance,
But now 'tis little joy
To know I'm further off from heaven
Than when I was a boy.

BALLAD.

Sigh on, sad heart, for Love's eclipse
And Beauty's fairest queen,
Though 'tis not for my peasant lips
To soil her name between:
A king might lay his sceptre down,
But I am poor and nought,
The brow should wear a golden crown
That wears her in its thought.

The diamonds glancing in her hair,
Whose sudden beams surprise,
Might bid such humble hopes beware
The glancing of her eyes;
Yet looking once, I looked too long,
And if my love is sin,
Death follows on the heels of wrong,
And kills the crime within.

Her dress seemed wove of lily leaves,
It was so pure and fine,
O lofty wears, and lowly weaves,
But hoddan gray is mine;
And homely hose must step apart,
Where gartered princes stand,
But may he wear my love at heart
That wins her lily hand!

Alas! there's far from russet frieze
  To silks and satin gowns,
But I doubt if God made like degrees
  In courtly hearts and clowns.
My father wronged a maiden's mirth,
  And brought her cheeks to blame,
And all that's lordly of my birth
  Is my reproach and shame!

'Tis vain to weep, — 'tis vain to sigh,
  'Tis vain this idle speech,
For where her happy pearls do lie
  My tears may never reach;
Yet when I'm gone, e'en lofty pride
  May say of what has been,
His love was nobly born and died,
  Though all the rest was mean!

My speech is rude, — but speech is weak
  Such love as mine to tell,
Yet had I words, I dare not speak,
  So, lady, fare thee well;
I will not wish thy better state
  Was one of low degree,
But I must weep that partial fate
  Made such a churl of me.

THE WATER LADY.

Alas! the moon should ever beam
To show what man should never see! —
I saw a maiden on a stream,
And fair was she!

I staid a while, to see her throw
Her tresses back, that all beset
The fair horizon of her brow
With clouds of jet.

I staid a little while to view
Her cheek, that wore in place of red
The bloom of water, tender blue,
Daintily spread.

I staid to watch, a little space,
Her parted lips if she would sing;
The waters closed above her face
With many a ring.

And still I staid a little more;
Alas! she never comes again!
I throw my flowers from the shore,
And watch in vain.

I know my life will fade away,
I know that I must vainly pine;
For I am made of mortal clay,
But she's divine!

TO AN ABSENTEE.

O'ER hill, and dale, and distant sea,
Through all the miles that stretch between,
My thought must fly to rest on thee,
And would, though worlds should intervene.

Nay, thou art now so dear, methinks
The further we are forced apart,

Affection's firm elastic links
But bind the closer round the heart.

For now we sever each from each,
I learn what I have lost in thee;
Alas! that nothing less could teach
How great indeed my love should be!

Farewell! I did not know thy worth:
But thou art gone, and now 'tis prized:
So angels walked unknown on earth,
But when they flew were recognized!

SONG.

THE stars are with the voyager
Wherever he may sail;
The moon is constant to her time;
The sun will never fail;
But follow, follow round the world,
The green earth and the sea;
So love is with the lover's heart,
Wherever he may be.

Wherever he may be, the stars
Must daily lose their light;
The moon will veil her in the shade;
The sun will set at night.
The sun may set, but constant love
Will shine when he's away;
So that dull night is never night,
And day is brighter day.

ODE TO THE MOON.

Mother of light! how fairly dost thou go
Over those hoary crests, divinely led!—
Art thou that huntress of the silver bow
Fabled of old? Or rather dost thou tread
Those cloudy summits thence to gaze below,
Like the wild chamois from her Alpine snow,
Where hunter never climbed,—secure from dread?
How many antique fancies have I read
Of that mild presence! and how many wrought!
        Wondrous and bright,
        Upon the silver light,
Chasing fair figures with the artist, Thought!

What art thou like?—sometimes I see thee ride
A far-bound galley on its perilous way,
Whilst breezy waves toss up their silvery spray:—
        Sometimes behold thee glide,
Clustered by all thy family of stars,
Like a lone widow, through the welkin wide,
Whose pallid cheek the midnight sorrow mars;—
Sometimes I watch thee on from steep to steep,
Timidly lighted by thy vestal torch,
Till in some Latmian cave I see thee creep,
To catch the young Endymion asleep,—
Leaving thy splendor at the jagged porch!—

O, thou art beautiful, howe'er it be!
Huntress, or Dian, or whatever named;
And he, the veriest Pagan, that first framed
A silver idol, and ne'er worshipped thee!—
It is too late, or thou shouldst have my knee;

Too late now for the old Ephesian vows,
And not divine the crescent on thy brows!—
Yet, call thee nothing but the mere mild moon,
        Behind those chestnut boughs,
Casting their dappled shadows at my feet;
I will be grateful for that simple boon,
In many a thoughtful verse and anthem sweet,
And bless thy dainty face whene'er we meet.

In nights far gone,—ay, far away and dead,—
Before Care-fretted with a lidless eye,—
I was thy wooer on my little bed,
Letting the early hours of rest go by,
To see thee flood the heaven with milky light,
And feed thy snow-white swans, before I slept;
For thou wert then purveyor of my dreams,—
Thou wert the fairies' armorer, that kept
Their burnished helms, and crowns, and corselets bright,
        Their spears and glittering mails;
And ever thou didst spill in winding streams
        Sparkles and midnight gleams,
For fishes to new gloss their argent scales!—

Why sighs?—why creeping tears?—why claspéd hands?
Is it to count the boy's expended dower?
That fairies since have broke their gifted wands?
That young Delight, like any o'erblown flower,
Gave, one by one, its sweet leaves to the ground?—
Why then, fair Moon, for all thou mark'st no hour,
Thou art a sadder dial to old Time
        Than ever I have found
On sunny garden-plot, or moss-grown tower,
Mottoed with stern and melancholy rhyme.

Why should I grieve for this?—O, I must yearn,
Whilst Time, conspirator with Memory,

Keeps his cold ashes in an ancient urn,
Richly embossed with childhood's revelry,
With leaves and clustered fruits, and flowers eterne, —
(Eternal to the world, though not to me,)
Aye there will those brave sports and blossoms be,
The deathless wreath, and undecayed festoon,
When I am hearsed within, —
Less than the pallid primrose to the moon,
That now she watches through a vapor thin.

So let it be : — Before I lived to sigh,
Thou wert in Avon, and a thousand rills,
Beautiful orb ! and so, whene'er I lie
Trodden, thou wilt be gazing from thy hills.
Blest be thy loving light, where'er it spills,
And blessèd thy fair face, O mother mild!
Still shine, the soul of rivers as they run,
Still lend thy lonely lamp to lovers fond,
And blend their plighted shadows into one : —
Still smile at even on the bedded child,
And close his eyelids with thy silver wand!

TO ——.

Welcome, dear heart, and a most kind good-morrow;
The day is gloomy, but our looks shall shine : —
Flowers I have none to give thee, but I borrow
Their sweetness in a verse to speak for thine.

Here are red roses, gathered at thy cheeks, —
The white were all too happy to look white :
For love the rose, for faith the lily speaks :
It withers in false hands, but here 'tis bright!

Dost love sweet hyacinth? Its scented leaf
Curls manifold, — all love's delights blow double:
'Tis said this floweret is inscribed with grief, —
But let that hint of a forgotten trouble.

I plucked the primrose at night's dewy noon;
Like Hope, it showed its blossoms in the night; —
'Twas like Endymion, watching for the moon!
And here are sunflowers, amorous of light!

These golden buttercups are April's seal, —
The daisy stars her constellations be:
These grew so lowly, I was forced to kneel,
Therefore I pluck no daisies but for thee!

Here's daisies for the morn, primrose for gloom,
Pansies and roses for the noontide hours; —
A wight once made a dial of their bloom, —
So may thy life be measured out by flowers!

THE FORSAKEN.

THE dead are in their silent graves,
And the dew is cold above,
And the living weep and sigh
Over dust that once was love.

Once I only wept the dead,
But now the living cause my pain;
How couldst thou steal me from my tears,
To leave me to my tears again?

My mother rests beneath the sod, —
Her rest is calm and very deep:
I wished that she could see our loves, —
But now I gladden in her sleep.

Last night unbound my raven locks,
The morning saw them turned to gray,
Once they were black and well beloved,
But thou art changed, — and so are they!

The useless lock I gave thee once,
To gaze upon and think of me,
Was ta'en with smiles, — but this was torn
In sorrow that I send to thee.

AUTUMN.

THE Autumn is old,
The sere leaves are flying; —
He hath gathered up gold,
And now he is dying; —
Old age, begin sighing!

The vintage is ripe,
The harvest is heaping; —
But some that have sowed
Have no riches for reaping; —
Poor wretch, fall a weeping!

The year's in the wane,
There is nothing adorning,
The night has no eve,
And the day has no morning; —
Cold winter gives warning.

The rivers run chill,
The red sun is sinking,
And I am grown old,
And life is fast shrinking;
Here's enow for sad thinking!

ODE TO MELANCHOLY.

Come, let us set our careful breasts,
Like Philomel, against the thorn,
To aggravate the inward grief,
That makes her accents so forlorn;
The world has many cruel points,
Whereby our bosoms have been torn,
And there are dainty themes of grief,
In sadness to outlast the morn, —
True honor's dearth, affection's death,
Neglectful pride and cankering scorn,
With all the piteous tales that tears
Have watered since the world was born.

The world! — it is a wilderness,
Where tears are hung on every tree;
For thus my gloomy fantasy
Makes all things weep with me!
Come let us sit and watch the sky,
And fancy clouds where no clouds be;
Grief is enough to blot the eye,
And make heaven black with misery.
Why should birds sing such merry notes,
Unless they were more blest than we?
No sorrow ever chokes their throats,
Except sweet nightingale; for she

Was born to pain our hearts the more
With her sad melody.
Why shines the sun, except that he
Makes gloomy nooks for Grief to hide,
And pensive shades for Melancholy,
When all the earth is bright beside?
Let clay wear smiles, and green grass wave,
Mirth shall not win us back again,
Whilst man is made of his own grave,
And fairest clouds but gilded rain!

I saw my mother in her shroud,
Her cheek was cold and very pale;
And ever since I've looked on all
As creatures doomed to fail!
Why do buds ope, except to die?
Ay, let us watch the roses wither,
And think of our loves' cheeks:
And, O, how quickly time doth fly
To bring death's winter hither!
Minutes, hours, days, and weeks,
Months, years, and ages shrink to nought,
An age past is but a thought!

Ay, let us think of him a while,
That, with a coffin for a boat,
Rows daily o'er the Stygian moat,
And for our table choose a tomb:
There's dark enough in any skull
To charge with black a raven plume;
And for the saddest funeral thoughts
A winding-sheet hath ample room,
Where Death, with his keen-pointed style,
Hath writ the common doom.

How wide the yew-tree spreads its gloom,
And o'er the dead lets fall its dew,
As if in tears it wept for them,
The many human families
That sleep around its stem!
How cold the dead have made these stones,
With natural drops kept ever wet!
Lo! here the best, the worst, the world
Doth now remember or forget,
Are in one common ruin hurled,
And love and hate are calmly met;
The loveliest eyes that ever shone,
The fairest hands, and locks of jet.
Is't not enough to vex our souls,
And fill our eyes, that we have set
Our love upon a rose's leaf,
Our hearts upon a violet?
Blue eyes, red cheeks, are frailer yet;
And, sometimes, at their swift decay
Beforehand we must fret:
The roses bud and bloom again;
But love may haunt the grave of love,
And watch the mould in vain.

O clasp me, sweet, whilst thou art mine,
And do not take my tears amiss;
For tears must flow to wash away
A thought that shows so stern as this:
Forgive, if somewhile I forget,
In woe to come, the present bliss.
As frighted Proserpine let fall
Her flowers at the sight of Dis,
Even so the dark and bright will kiss.
The sunniest things throw sternest shade,

And there is even a happiness
That makes the heart afraid!
Now let us with a spell invoke
The full-orbed moon to grieve our eyes;
Not bright, not bright, but, with a cloud
Lapped all about her, let her rise
All pale and dim, as if from rest
The ghost of the late buried sun
Had crept into the skies.
The moon! she is the source of sighs,
The very face to make us sad;
If but to think in other times
The same calm, quiet look she had,
As if the world held nothing base,
Of vile and mean, of fierce and bad;
The same fair light that shone in streams,
The fairy lamp that charmed the lad;
For so it is, with spent delights
She taunts men's brains, and makes them mad.
All things are touched with melancholy,
Born of the secret soul's mistrust,
To feel her fair ethereal wings
Weighed down with vile degraded dust;
Even the bright extremes of joy
Bring on conclusions of disgust,
Like the sweet blossoms of the May,
Whose fragrance ends in must.
O, give her, then, her tribute just,
Her sighs and tears, and musings holy!
There is no music in the life
That sounds with idiot laughter solely;
There's not a string attuned to mirth,
But has its chord in Melancholy.

SONNETS.

WRITTEN IN A VOLUME OF SHAKSPEARE.

How bravely Autumn paints upon the sky
The gorgeous fame of Summer which is fled!
Hues of all flowers that in their ashes lie,
Trophied in that fair light whereon they fed,
Tulip, and hyacinth, and sweet rose red,—
Like exhalations from the leafy mould,
Look here how honor glorifies the dead,
And warms their scutcheons with a glance of gold!—
Such is the memory of poets old,
Who on Parnassus' hill have bloomed elate;
Now they are laid under their marbles cold,
And turned to clay, whereof they were create;
But god Apollo hath them all enrolled,
And blazoned on the very clouds of fate!

TO FANCY.

Most delicate Ariel! submissive thing,
Won by the mind's high magic to its hest,—
Invisible embassy, or secret guest,—
Weighing the light air on a lighter wing;—
Whether into the midnight moon, to bring
Illuminate visions to the eye of rest,—
Or rich romances from the florid West,—
Or to the sea, for mystic whispering,—
Still by thy charmed allegiance to the will
The fruitful wishes prosper in the brain,

As by the fingering of fairy skill, —
Moonlight, and waters, and soft music's strain,
Odors, and blooms, and *my* Miranda's smile,
Making this dull world an enchanted isle.

TO AN ENTHUSIAST.

YOUNG ardent soul, graced with fair Nature's truth,
Spring warmth of heart, and fervency of mind,
And still a large late love of all thy kind,
Spite of the world's cold practice and Time's tooth,
For all these gifts, I know not, in fair sooth,
Whether to give thee joy, or bid thee blind
Thine eyes with tears, — that thou hast not resigned
The passionate fire and freshness of thy youth:
For as the current of thy life shall flow,
Gilded by shine of sun or shadow-stained,
Through flowery valley or unwholesome fen,
Thrice blessèd in thy joy, or in thy woe
Thrice cursèd of thy race, — thou art ordained
To share beyond the lot of common men.

IT is not death, that sometime in a sigh
This eloquent breath shall take its speechless flight;
That sometime these bright stars, that now reply
In sunlight to the sun, shall set in night;
That this warm conscious flesh shall perish quite,
And all life's ruddy springs forget to flow;
That thoughts shall cease, and the immortal spright
Be lapped in alien clay and laid below;
It is not death to know this, — but to know

That pious thoughts, which visit at new graves
In tender pilgrimage, will cease to go
So duly and so oft, — and when grass waves
Over the past-away, there may be then
No resurrection in the minds of men.

By every sweet tradition of true hearts,
Graven by Time, in love with his own lore;
By all old martyrdoms and antique smarts,
Wherein Love died to be alive the more;
Yea, by the sad impression on the shore
Left by the drowned Leander, to endear
That coast forever, where the billows' roar
Moaneth for pity in the poet's ear;
By Hero's faith, and the foreboding tear
That quenched her brand's last twinkle in its fall;
By Sappho's leap, and the low rustling fear
That sighed around her flight; I swear by all,
The world shall find such pattern in my act,
As if Love's great examples still were lacked.

ON RECEIVING A GIFT.

Look how the golden ocean shines above
Its pebbly stones, and magnifies their girth;
So does the bright and blessèd light of love
Its own things glorify, and raise their worth.
As weeds seem flowers beneath the flattering brine,
And stones like gems, and gems as gems indeed,
Even so our tokens shine; nay, they outshine
Pebbles and pearls, and gems and coral weed;

For where be ocean waves but half so clear,
So calmly constant, and so kindly warm,
As Love's most mild and glowing atmosphere,
That hath no dregs to be upturned by storm?
Thus, sweet, thy gracious gifts are gifts of price,
And more than gold to doting Avarice.

SILENCE.

THERE is a silence where hath been no sound,
There is a silence where no sound may be,
In the cold grave — under the deep, deep sea,
Or in wide desert where no life is found,
Which hath been mute, and still must sleep profound;
No voice is hushed — no life treads silently,
But clouds and cloudy shadows wander free,
That never spoke, over the idle ground:
But in green ruins, in the desolate walls
Of antique palaces, where Man hath been,
Though the dun fox, or wild hyena, calls,
And owls, that flit continually between,
Shriek to the echo, and the low winds moan,
There the true Silence is, self-conscious and alone.

THE curse of Adam, the old curse of all
Though I inherit in this feverish life
Of worldly toil, vain wishes, and hard strife,
And fruitless thought, in Care's eternal thrall,
Yet more sweet honey than of bitter gall
I taste, through thee, my Eva, my sweet wife.

Then what was Man's lost Paradise! — how rife
Of bliss, since love is with him in his fall!
Such as our own pure passion still might frame,
Of this fair earth, and its delightful bowers,
If no fell sorrow, like the serpent, came
To trail its venom o'er the sweetest flowers: —
But, O! as many and such tears are ours,
As only should be shed for guilt and shame!

Love, dearest lady, such as I would speak,
Lives not within the humor of the eye; —
Not being but an outward fantasy,
That skims the surface of a tinted cheek —
Else it would wane with beauty, and grow weak,
As if the rose made summer, — and so lie
Amongst the perishable things that die,
Unlike the love which I would give and seek,
Whose health is of no hue — to feel decay
With cheeks' decay, that have a rosy prime.
Love is its own great loveliness alway,
And takes new lustre from the touch of time;
Its bough owns no December and no May,
But bears its blossom into Winter's clime.

THE LEE SHORE.

Sleet! and hail! and thunder!
  And ye winds that rave,
Till the sands thereunder
  Tinge the sullen wave —

Winds, that like a demon
  Howl with horrid note
Round the toiling seaman,
  In his tossing boat —

From his humble dwelling
  On the shingly shore,
Where the billows swelling
  Keep such hollow roar —

From that weeping woman,
  Seeking with her cries
Succor superhuman
  From the frowning skies —

From the urchin pining
  For his father's knee —
From the lattice shining,
  Drive him out to sea!

Let broad leagues dissever
  Him from yonder foam; —
O, God! to think man ever
  Comes too near his home!

THE DEATH-BED.

We watched her breathing through the night,
  Her breathing soft and low,
As in her breast the wave of life
  Kept heaving to and fro.

So silently we seemed to speak,
  So slowly moved about,
As we had lent her half our powers
  To eke her living out.

Our very hopes belied our fears,
  Our fears our hopes belied—
We thought her dying when she slept,
  And sleeping when she died.

For when the morn came dim and sad,
  And chill with early showers,
Her quiet eyelids closed—she had
  Another morn than ours.

LINES

ON SEEING MY WIFE AND TWO CHILDREN SLEEPING IN THE SAME CHAMBER.

AND has the earth lost its so spacious round,
The sky its blue circumference above,
That in this little chamber there is found
Both earth and heaven—my universe of love!
All that my God can give me or remove,
Here sleeping, save myself, in mimic death.
Sweet that in this small compass I behove
To live their living and to breathe their breath!
Almost I wish that with one common sigh
We might resign all mundane care and strife,
And seek together that transcendent sky,
Where father, mother, children, husband, wife,
Together pant in everlasting life!

TO MY DAUGHTER, ON HER BIRTHDAY.

Dear Fanny! nine long years ago,
While yet the morning sun was low,
And rosy with the eastern glow
   The landscape smiled;
Whilst lowed the newly-wakened herds—
Sweet as the early song of birds,
I heard those first, delightful words,
   "Thou hast a child!"

Along with that uprising dew
Tears glistened in my eyes, though few,
To hail a dawning quite as new,
   To me, as time:
It was not sorrow—not annoy—
But like a happy maid, though coy,
With grief-like welcome, even joy
   Forestalls its prime.

So mayst thou live, dear! many years,
In all the bliss that life endears,
Not without smiles, nor yet from tears
   Too strictly kept:
When first thy infant littleness
I folded in my fond caress,
The greatest proof of happiness
   Was this—I wept.

TO A CHILD EMBRACING HIS MOTHER.

Love thy mother, little one!
Kiss and clasp her neck again,—
Hereafter she may have a son

Will kiss and clasp her neck in vain.
  Love thy mother, little one!

Gaze upon her living eyes,
And mirror back her love for thee, —
Hereafter thou mayst shudder sighs
To meet them when they cannot see.
  Gaze upon her living eyes!

Press her lips the while they glow
With love that they have often told, —
Hereafter thou mayst press in woe,
And kiss them till thine own are cold.
  Press her lips the while they glow!

O, revere her raven hair!
Although it be not silver-gray;
Too early death, led on by care,
May snatch save one dear lock away.
  O! revere her raven hair!

Pray for her at eve and morn,
That heaven may long the stroke defer, —
For thou mayst live the hour forlorn
When thou wilt ask to die with her.
  Pray for her at eve and morn!

STANZAS.

Farewell life! my senses swim,
And the world is growing dim:
Thronging shadows cloud the light,
Like the advent of the night —

Colder, colder, colder still,
Upward steals a vapor chill;
Strong the earthy odor grows —
I smell the mould above the rose!

Welcome life! the spirit strives!
Strength returns and hope revives;
Cloudy fears and shapes forlorn
Fly like shadows at the morn, —
O'er the earth there comes a bloom;
Sunny light for sullen gloom,
Warm perfume for vapor cold —
I smell the rose above the mould!

April, 1845.

TO A FALSE FRIEND.

Our hands have met, but not our hearts;
Our hands will never meet again.
Friends if we have ever been,
Friends we cannot now remain:
I only know I loved you once,
I only know I loved in vain;
Our hands have met, but not our hearts;
Our hands will never meet again!

Then farewell to heart and hand!
I would our hands had never met:
Even the outward form of love
Must be resigned with some regret.
Friends we still might seem to be,
If my wrong could e'er forget
Our hands have joined, but not our hearts:
I would our hands had never met!

THE POET'S PORTION.

WHAT is a mine — a treasury — a dower —
A magic talisman of mighty power?
A poet's wide possession of the earth.
He has the enjoyment of a flower's birth
Before its budding — ere the first red streaks, —
And winter cannot rob him of their cheeks.
Look — if his dawn be not as other men's!
Twenty bright flushes — ere another kens
The first of sunlight is abroad — he sees
Its golden 'lection of the topmost trees,
And opes the splendid fissures of the morn.
When do his fruits delay, when doth his corn
Linger for harvesting? Before the leaf
Is commonly abroad, in his piled sheaf
The flagging poppies lose their ancient flame.
No sweet there is, no pleasure I can name,
But he will sip it first — before the lees.
'Tis his to taste rich honey, — ere the bees
Are busy with the brooms. He may forestall
June's rosy advent for his coronal;
Before the expectant buds upon the bough,
Twining his thoughts to bloom upon his brow.
O! blest to see the flower in its seed,
Before its leafy presence; for indeed
Leaves are but wings, on which the summer flies,
And each thing perishable fades and dies,
Escaped in thought; but his rich thinkings be
Like overflows of immortality.
So that what there is steeped shall perish never,
But live and bloom, and be a joy forever.

TIME, HOPE, AND MEMORY.

I HEARD a gentle maiden, in the spring,
Set her sweet sighs to music, and thus sing:
"Fly through the world, and I will follow thee,
Only for looks that may turn back on me;

"Only for roses that your chance may throw —
Though withered — I will wear them on my brow,
To be a thoughtful fragrance to my brain;
Warmed with such love, that they will bloom again.

"Thy love before thee, I must tread behind,
Kissing thy foot-prints, though to me unkind;
But trust not all her fondness, though it seem,
Lest thy true love should rest on a false dream.

"Her face is smiling, and her voice is sweet:
But smiles betray, and music sings deceit;
And words speak false; — yet, if they welcome prove,
I'll be their echo, and repeat their love.

"Only if wakened to sad truth, at last,
The bitterness to come, and sweetness past;
When thou art vext, then, turn again, and see
Thou hast loved Hope, but Memory loved thee."

SONG.

O LADY, leave thy silken thread
  And flowery tapestrie:
There's living roses on the bush,
  And blossoms on the tree;

Stoop where thou wilt, thy careless hand
  Some random bud will meet;
Thou canst not tread, but thou wilt find
  The daisy at thy feet.

'Tis like the birthday of the world,
  When earth was born in bloom;
The light is made of many dyes,
  The air is all perfume;
There's crimson buds, and white and blue —
  The very rainbow showers
Have turned to blossoms where they fell,
  And sown the earth with flowers.

There's fairy tulips in the east,
  The garden of the sun;
The very streams reflect the hues,
  And blossom as they run:
While Morn opes like a crimson rose,
  Still wet with pearly showers;
Then, lady, leave the silken thread
  Thou twinest into flowers!

FLOWERS.

I WILL not have the mad Clytie,
Whose head is turned by the sun;
The tulip is a courtly quean,
Whom, therefore, I will shun;
The cowslip is a country wench,
The violet is a nun; —
But I will woo the dainty rose,
The queen of every one.

The pea is but a wanton witch,
In too much haste to wed,
And clasps her rings on every hand;
The wolfsbane I should dread; —
Nor will I dreary rosemarye,
That always mourns the dead; —
But I will woo the dainty rose,
With her cheeks of tender red.

The lily is all in white, like a saint,
And so is no mate for me —
And the daisy's cheek is tipped with a blush,
She is of such low degree;
Jasmine is sweet, and has many loves,
And the broom's betrothed to the bee; —
But I will plight with the dainty rose,
For fairest of all is she.

TO ——.

STILL glides the gentle streamlet on,
With shifting current new and strange;
The water that was here is gone,
But those green shadows never change.

Serene or ruffled by the storm,
On present waves, as on the past,
The mirrored grove retains its form,
The self-same trees their semblance cast.

The hue each fleeting globule wears,
That drop bequeaths it to the next;
One picture still the surface bears,
To illustrate the murmured text.

So, love, however time may flow,
Fresh hours pursuing those that flee,
One constant image still shall show
My tide of life is true to thee.

TO ——.

I LOVE thee — I love thee!
'Tis all that I can say; —
It is my vision in the night,
My dreaming in the day;
The very echo of my heart,
The blessing when I pray:
I love thee — I love thee!
Is all that I can say.

I love thee — I love thee!
Is ever on my tongue;
In all my proudest poesy
That chorus still is sung;
It is the verdict of my eyes,
Amidst the gay and young:
I love thee — I love thee!
A thousand maids among.

I love thee — I love thee!
Thy bright and hazel glance,
The mellow lute upon those lips,
Whose tender tones entrance:
But most, dear heart of hearts, thy proofs
That still these words enhance,
I love thee — I love thee!
Whatever be thy chance.

TO ——.

LET us make a leap, my dear,
In our love of many a year,
And date it very far away,
On a bright clear summer day,
When the heart was like a sun
To itself, and falsehood none;
And the rosy lips a part
Of the very loving heart,
And the shining of the eye
But a sign to know it by; —
When my faults were all forgiven,
And my life deserved of Heaven.
Dearest, let us reckon so,
And love for all that long ago;
Each absence count a year complete,
And keep a birthday when we meet.

SERENADE.

AH, sweet, thou little knowest how
  I wake and passionate watches keep;
And yet, while I address thee now,
  Methinks thou smilest in thy sleep.
'Tis sweet enough to make me weep,
  That tender thought of love and thee,
That while the world is hushed so deep,
  Thy soul's perhaps awake to me!

Sleep on, sleep on, sweet bride of sleep!
  With golden visions for thy dower,

While I this midnight vigil keep,
  And bless thee in thy silent bower;
To me 'tis sweeter than the power
  Of sleep, and fairy dreams unfurled,
That I alone, at this still hour,
  In patient love outwatch the world.

BALLAD.

It was not in the winter
Our loving lot was cast;
It was the time of roses, —
We plucked them as we passed!

That churlish season never frowned
On early lovers yet!
O, no — the world was newly crowned
With flowers when first we met.

'Twas twilight, and I bade you go,
But still you held me fast;
It was the time of roses, —
We plucked them as we passed!

SONNETS.

TO THE OCEAN.

Shall I rebuke thee, Ocean, my old love,
That once in rage, with the wild winds at strife,
Thou darest menace my unit of a life,
Sending my clay below, my soul above,

Whilst roared thy waves, like lions when they rove
By night, and bound upon their prey by stealth?
Yet didst thou ne'er restore my fainting health? —
Didst thou ne'er murmur gently like the dove?
Nay, didst thou not against my own dear shore
Full break, last link between my land and me? —
My absent friends talk in thy very roar,
In thy waves' beat their kindly pulse I see,
And if I must not see my England more,
Next to her soil, my grave be found in thee!

Coblentz, May, 1835.

LEAR.

A POOR old king, with sorrow for my crown,
Throned upon straw, and mantled with the wind —
For pity, my own tears have made me blind,
That I might never see my children's frown;
And may be madness, like a friend, has thrown
A folded fillet over my dark mind,
So that unkindly speech may sound for kind, —
Albeit I know not. — I am childish grown —
And have not gold to purchase wit withal —
I that have once maintained most royal state —
A very bankrupt now, that may not call
My child, my child — all-beggared save in tears,
Wherewith I daily weep an old man's fate,
Foolish — and blind — and overcome with years!

SONNET TO A SONNET.

RARE composition of a poet-knight,
Most chivalrous amongst chivalric men,

Distinguished for a polished lance and pen
In tuneful contest and in tourney-fight;
Lustrous in scholarship, in honor bright,
Accomplished in all graces current then,
Humane as any in historic ken,
Brave, handsome, noble, affable, polite;
Most courteous to that race become of late
So fiercely scornful of all kind advance,
Rude, bitter, coarse, implacable in hate
To Albion, plotting ever her mischance,—
Alas, fair verse! how false and out of date
Thy phrase "sweet enemy" applied to France!

FALSE POETS AND TRUE.

LOOK how the lark soars upward and is gone,
Turning a spirit as he nears the sky!
His voice is heard, but body there is none
To fix the vague excursions of the eye.
So, poets' songs are with us, though they die
Obscured and hid by Death's oblivious shroud,
And earth inherits the rich melody,
Like raining music from the morning cloud.
Yet, few there be who pipe so sweet and loud,
Their voices reach us through the lapse of space:
The noisy day is deafened by a crowd
Of undistinguished birds, a twittering race;
But only lark and nightingale forlorn
Fill up the silences of night and morn.

TO ——.

MY heart is sick with longing, though I feed
On hope; Time goes with such a heavy pace

That neither brings nor takes from thy embrace,
As if he slept — forgetting his old speed:
For, as in sunshine only we can read
The march of minutes on the dial's face,
So in the shadows of this lonely place
There is no love, and time is dead indeed.
But when, dear lady, I am near thy heart,
Thy smile is time, and then so swift it flies,
It seems we only meet to tear apart
With aching hands and lingering of eyes.
Alas, alas! that we must learn hours' flight
By the same light of love that makes them bright!

FOR THE FOURTEENTH OF FEBRUARY.

No popular respect will I omit
To do the honor on this happy day,
When every loyal lover tasks his wit
His simple truth in studious rhymes to pay,
And to his mistress dear his hopes convey.
Rather thou knowest I would still outrun
All calendars with Love's, — whose date alway
Thy bright eyes govern better than the sun, —
For with thy favor was my life begun;
And still I reckon on from smiles to smiles,
And not by summers, for I thrive on none
But those thy cheerful countenance compiles:
O! if it be to choose and call thee mine,
Love, thou art every day my Valentine.

TO A SLEEPING CHILD.

O, 'TIS a touching thing, to make one weep,
A tender infant with its curtained eye,

Breathing as it would neither live nor die
With that unchanging countenance of sleep!
As if its silent dream, serene and deep,
Had lined its slumber with a still blue sky,
So that the passive cheeks unconscious lie,
With no more life than roses — just to keep
The blushes warm, and the mild, odorous breath.
O blossom boy! so calm is thy repose,
So sweet a compromise of life and death,
'Tis pity those fair buds should e'er unclose
For memory to stain their inward leaf,
Tinging thy dreams with unacquainted grief.

The world is with me, and its many cares,
Its woes — its wants — the anxious hopes and fears
That wait on all terrestrial affairs —
The shades of former and of future years —
Foreboding fancies and prophetic tears,
Quelling a spirit that was once elate.
Heavens! what a wilderness the world appears,
Where youth, and mirth, and health are out of date;
But no — a laugh of innocence and joy
Resounds, like music of the fairy race,
And, gladly turning from the world's annoy,
I gaze upon a little radiant face,
And bless, internally, the merry boy
Who "makes a *son-shine* in a shady place."

HUMOROUS POEMS.

HUMOROUS POEMS.

MISS KILMANSEGG AND HER PRECIOUS LEG.

A GOLDEN LEGEND.

"What is here?
Gold? yellow, glittering, precious gold?"
TIMON OF ATHENS.

Her Pedigree.

To trace the Kilmansegg pedigree,
To the very roots of the family tree,
  Were a task as rash as ridiculous:
Through antediluvian mists as thick
As London fog such a line to pick
Were enough, in truth, to puzzle Old Nick,
  Not to name Sir Harris Nicholas.

It wouldn't require much verbal strain
To trace the Kill-man, perchance, to Cain;
  But, waiving all such digressions,
Suffice it, according to family lore,
A Patriarch Kilmansegg lived of yore,
  Who was famed for his great possessions.

Tradition said he feathered his nest
Through an agricultural interest
  In the golden age of farming;
When golden eggs were laid by the geese,
And Colchian sheep wore a golden fleece,

And golden pippins — the sterling kind
Of Hesperus — now so hard to find —
Made horticulture quite charming!

A lord of land, on his own estate
He lived at a very lively rate,
But his income would bear carousing;
Such acres he had of pasture and heath,
With herbage so rich from the ore beneath,
The very ewe's and lambkin's teeth
Were turned into gold by browsing.

He gave, without any extra thrift,
A flock of sheep for a birthday gift
To each son of his loins, or daughter:
And his debts — if debts he had — at will
He liquidated by giving each bill
A dip in Pactolian water.

'Twas said that even his pigs of lead,
By crossing with some by Midas bred,
Made a perfect mine of his piggery.
And as for cattle, one yearling bull
Was worth all Smithfield-market full
Of the golden bulls of Pope Gregory.

The high-bred horses within his stud,
Like human creatures of birth and blood,
Had their golden cups and flagons:
And as for the common husbandry nags,
Their noses were tied in money-bags,
When they stopped with the carts and wagons.

Moreover, he had a golden ass,
Sometimes at stall, and sometimes at grass,
That was worth his own weight in money —

And a golden hive, on a golden bank,
Where golden bees, by alchemical prank,
  Gathered gold instead of honey.

Gold! and gold! and gold without end!
He had gold to lay by, and gold to spend,
Gold to give, and gold to lend,
  And reversions of gold *in futuro*.
In wealth the family revelled and rolled,
Himself and wife and sons so bold; —
And his daughters sang to their harps of gold
  "O bella eta del' oro!"

Such was the tale of the Kilmansegg kin
In golden text on a vellum skin,
Though certain people would wink and grin,
  And declare the whole story a parable —
That the ancestor rich was one Jacob Ghrimes,
Who held a long lease, in prosperous times,
  Of acres, pasture and arable.

That as money makes money, his golden bees
Were the Five per Cents, or which you please,
  When his cash was more than plenty —
That the golden cups were racing affairs;
And his daughters, who sung Italian airs,
  Had their golden harps of Clementi.

That the golden ass, or golden bull,
Was English John, with his pockets full,
  Then at war by land and water:
While beef, and mutton, and other meat,
Were almost as dear as money to eat,
And farmers reaped golden harvests of wheat
  At the Lord knows what per quarter!

Her Birth.

What different dooms our birthdays bring!
For instance, one little manikin thing
  Survives to wear many a wrinkle;
While death forbids another to wake,
And a son that it took nine moons to make
  Expires without even a twinkle:

Into this world we come like ships,
Launched from the docks, and stocks, and slips,
  For fortune fair or fatal;
And one little craft is cast away
In its very first trip in Babbicome Bay,
  While another rides safe at Port Natal.

What different lots our stars accord!
This babe to be hailed and wooed as a lord!
  And that to be shunned like a leper!
One, to the world's wine, honey, and corn,
Another, like Colchester native, born
  To its vinegar, only, and pepper.

One is littered under a roof
Neither wind nor water proof,—
  That's the prose of Love in a cottage,—
A puny, naked, shivering wretch,
The whole of whose birthright would not fetch,
Though Robins himself drew up the sketch,
  The bid of "a mess of pottage."

Born of Fortunatus's kin,
Another comes tenderly ushered in
  To a prospect all bright and burnished:
No tenant he for life's back slums—
He comes to the world as a gentleman comes
  To a lodging ready furnished.

And the other sex — the tender — the fair —
What wide reverses of fate are there!
Whilst Margaret, charmed by the Bulbul rare,
  In a garden of Gul reposes,
Poor Peggy hawks nosegays from street to street
Till — think of that, who find life so sweet! —
  She hates the smell of roses!

Not so with the infant Kilmansegg!
She was not born to steal or beg,
  Or gather cresses in ditches;
To plait the straw, or bind the shoe,
Or sit all day to hem and sew,
As females must, and not a few —
  To fill their insides with stitches!

She was not doomed, for bread to eat,
To be put to her hands as well as her feet —
  To carry home linen from mangles —
Or heavy-hearted, and weary-limbed,
To dance on a rope in a jacket trimmed
  With as many blows as spangles.

She was one of those who by Fortune's boon
Are born, as they say, with a silver spoon
  In her mouth, not a wooden ladle:
To speak according to poet's wont,
Plutus as sponsor stood at her font,
  And Midas rocked the cradle.

At her first *début* she found her head
On a pillow of down, in a downy bed,
  With a damask canopy over.
For although by the vulgar popular saw
All mothers are said to be "in the straw,"
  Some children are born in clover.

Her very first draught of vital air
It was not the common chameleon fare
   Of plebeian lungs and noses, —
      No — her earliest sniff
      Of this world was a whiff
   Of the genuine Otto of Roses!

When she saw the light, it was no mere ray
Of that light so common, so every-day,
   That the sun each morning launches;
But six wax tapers dazzled her eyes,
From a thing — a gooseberry-bush for size —
   With a golden stem and branches.

She was born exactly at half-past two,
As witnessed a time-piece in or-molu
   That stood on a marble table —
Showing at once the time of day,
And a team of *Gildings* running away
   As fast as they were able,
With a golden god, with a golden star,
And a golden spear, in a golden car,
   According to Grecian fable.

Like other babes, at her birth she cried;
Which made a sensation far and wide,
   Ay, for twenty miles around her;
For though to the ear 'twas nothing more
Than an infant's squall, it was really the roar
   Of a fifty-thousand pounder!
      It shook the next heir
      In his library chair,
And made him cry, "Confound her!"

Of signs and omens there was no dearth,
Any more than at Owen Glendower's birth,

Or the advent of other great people:
Two bullocks dropped dead,
As if knocked on the head,
And barrels of stout
And ale ran about,
And the village-bells such a peal rang out,
That they cracked the village steeple.

In no time at all, like mushroom spawn,
Tables sprang up all over the lawn;
Not furnished scantily or shabbily,
But on scale as vast
As that huge repast,
With its loads and cargoes
Of drink and botargoes,
At the birth of the babe in Rabelais.

Hundreds of men were turned into beasts,
Like the guests at Circe's horrible feasts,
By the magic of ale and cider:
And each country lass, and each country lad,
Began to caper and dance like mad,
And even some old ones appeared to have had
A bite from the Naples spider.

Then as night came on,
It had scared King John,
Who considered such signs not risible,
To have seen the maroons,
And the whirling moons,
And the serpents of flame,
And wheels of the same,
That according to some were "whizzable."

O, happy Hope of the Kilmanseggs!
Thrice happy in head, and body, and legs,

That her parents had such full pockets!
For had she been born of want and thrift,
For care and nursing all adrift,
It's ten to one she had had to make shift
With rickets instead of rockets!

And how was the precious baby drest?
In a robe of the East, with lace of the West,
Like one of Crœsus's issue—
Her best bibs were made
Of rich gold brocade,
And the others of silver tissue.

And when the baby inclined to nap
She was lulled on a Gros de Naples lap,
By a nurse in a modish Paris cap,
Of notions so exalted,
She drank nothing lower than Curaçoa,
Maraschino, or pink Noyau,
And on principle never malted.

From a golden boat, with a golden spoon,
The babe was fed night, morning, and noon;
And, although the tale seems fabulous,
'Tis said her tops and bottoms were gilt,
Like the oats in that stable-yard palace built
For the horse of Heliogabalus.

And when she took to squall and kick—
For pain will wring and pins will prick
E'en the wealthiest nabob's daughter—
They gave her no vulgar Dalby or gin,
But a liquor with leaf of gold therein,
Videlicet,—Dantzic Water.

In short, she was born, and bred, and nurst,
And drest in the best from the very first,
To please the genteelest censor—

And then, as soon as strength would allow,
Was vaccinated, as babes are now,
With virus ta'en from the best-bred cow
  Of Lord Althorpe's — now Earl Spencer.

Her Christening.

Though Shakspeare asks us "What's in a name?"
(As if cognomens were much the same,)
  There's really a very great scope in it.
A name? — why, wasn't there Doctor Dodd,
That servant at once of Mammon and God,
Who found four thousand pounds and odd,
  A prison — a cart — and a rope in it?

A name? — if the party had a voice,
What mortal would be a Bugg by choice?
As a Hogg, a Grubb, or a Chubb rejoice?
  Or any such nauseous blazon?
Not to mention many a vulgar name,
That would make a door-plate blush for shame,
If door-plates were not so brazen!

A name? — it has more than nominal worth,
And belongs to good or bad luck at birth —
  As dames of a certain degree know.
In spite of his page's hat and hose,
His page's jacket, and buttons in rows,
Bob only sounds like a page of prose
  Till turned into Rupertino.

Now, to christen the infant Kilmansegg,
For days and days it was quite a plague,
  To hunt the list in the lexicon:
And scores were tried, like coin, by the ring,
Ere names were found just the proper thing,
  For a minor rich as a Mexican.

Then cards were sent, the presence to beg
Of all the kin of Kilmansegg,
  White, yellow, and brown relations:
Brothers, wardens of city halls,
And uncles, rich as three golden balls
  From taking pledges of nations.

Nephews, whom Fortune seemed to bewitch,
  Rising in life like rockets —
Nieces whose doweries knew no hitch —
Aunts as certain of dying rich
  As candles in golden sockets —
Cousins German, and cousins' sons,
All thriving and opulent — some had tons
  Of Kentish hops in their pockets!

For money had stuck to the race through life
(As it did to the bushel when cash so rife
Posed Ali-Baba's brother's wife) —
  And, down to the cousins and coz-lings
The fortunate brood of the Kilmanseggs,
As if they had come out of golden eggs,
  Were all as wealthy as "goslings."

It would fill a Court Gazette to name
What east and west end people came
  To the rite of Christianity;
The lofty lord and the titled dame,
  All diamonds, plumes, and urbanity;
The Lordship, the Mayor, with his golden chain,
And two Gold Sticks, and the sheriffs twain,
Nine foreign counts, and other great men
With their orders or stars, to help M or N
  To renounce all pomp and vanity.

To paint the maternal Kilmansegg
The pen of an Eastern poet would beg,

And need no elaborate sonnet;
How she sparkled with gems whenever she stirred,
And her head niddle-noddled at every word,
And seemed so happy, a paradise bird
Had nidificated upon it.

And Sir Jacob the father strutted and bowed,
And smiled to himself, and laughed aloud,
To think of his heiress and daughter —
And then in his pockets he made a grope,
And then, in the fulness of joy and hope,
Seemed washing his hands with invisible soap
In imperceptible water.

He had rolled in money like pigs in mud,
Till it seemed to have entered into his blood
By some occult projection;
And his cheeks, instead of a healthy hue,
As yellow as any guinea grew,
Making the common phrase seem true
About a rich complexion.

And now came the nurse, and during a pause,
Her dead-leaf satin would fitly cause
A very autumnal rustle —
So full of figure, so full of fuss,
As she carried about the babe to buss,
She seemed to be nothing but bustle.

A wealthy Nabob was godpapa,
And an Indian Begum was godmamma,
Whose jewels a queen might covet;
And the priest was a vicar, and dean withal
Of that temple we see with a golden ball,
And a golden cross above it.

The font was a bowl of American gold,
Won by Raleigh in days of old,
  In spite of Spanish bravado;
And the book of prayer was so overrun
With gilt devices, it shone in the sun
Like a copy — a presentation one —
  Of Humboldt's "El Dorado."

Gold! and gold! and nothing but gold!
The same auriferous shine behold
  Wherever the eye could settle!
On the walls — the sideboard — the ceiling-sky —
On the gorgeous footmen standing by,
In coats to delight a miner's eye
  With seams of the precious metal.

Gold! and gold! and besides the gold,
The very robe of the infant told
A tale of wealth in every fold,
  It lapped her like a vapor!
So fine! so thin! the mind at a loss
Could compare it to nothing except a cross
  Of cobweb with bank-note paper.

Then her pearls — 'twas a perfect sight, forsooth,
To see them, like "the dew of her youth,"
  In such a plentiful sprinkle.
Meanwhile, the vicar read through the form,
And gave her another, not overwarm,
  That made her little eyes twinkle.

Then the babe was crossed and blessed amain;
But instead of the Kate, or Ann, or Jane,
  Which the humbler female endorses —
Instead of one name, as some people prefix,
Kilmansegg went at the tails of six,
  Like a carriage of state with its horses.

O! then the kisses she got and hugs!
The golden mugs and the golden jugs,
  That lent fresh rays to the midges!
The golden knives and the golden spoons,
The gems that sparkled like fairy boons,
It was one of the Kilmansegg's own saloons,
  But looked like Rundell and Bridge's!

Gold! and gold! the new and the old!
The company ate and drank from gold,
  They revelled, they sang, and were merry;
And one of the Gold Sticks rose from his chair
And toasted "the lass with the golden hair"
  In a bumper of golden sherry.

Gold! still gold! it rained on the nurse,
Who, unlike Danäe, was none the worse;
  There was nothing but guineas glistening!
    Fifty were given to Doctor James,
    For calling the little baby names;
    And for saying Amen!
    The clerk had ten,
  And that was the end of the Christening.

Her Childhood.

Our youth! our childhood! that spring of springs!
'Tis surely one of the blessedest things
  That nature ever invented!
When the rich are wealthy beyond their wealth,
And the poor are rich in spirits and health,
  And all with their lots contented!

There's little Phelim, he sings like a thrush,
In the self-same pair of patchwork plush,
  With the self-same empty pockets,

That tempted his daddy so often to cut
His throat, or jump in the water-butt —
But what cares Phelim? an empty nut
Would sooner bring tears to their sockets.

Give him a collar without a skirt, —
That's the Irish linen for shirt;
And a slice of bread, with a taste of dirt, —
That's poverty's Irish butter;
And what does he lack to make him blest?
Some oyster-shells, or a sparrow's nest,
A candle-end and a gutter.

But, to leave the happy Phelim alone,
Gnawing, perchance, a marrowless bone,
For which no dog would quarrel —
Turn we to little Miss Kilmansegg,
Cutting her first little toothy-peg
With a fifty guinea coral —
A peg upon which
About poor and rich
Reflection might hang a moral.

Born in wealth, and wealthily nursed,
Capped, papped, napped, and lapped from the first
On the knees of Prodigality,
Her childhood was one eternal round
Of the game of going on Tickler's ground,
Picking up gold — in reality.

With extempore carts she never played,
Or the odds and ends of a Tinker's trade,
Or little dirt pies and puddings made,
Like children happy and squalid;
The very puppet she had to pet,
Like a bait for the "Nix my Dolly" set,
Was a dolly of gold — and solid!

Gold! and gold! 'twas the burden still!
To gain the heiress's early good will
  There was much corruption and bribery;
The yearly cost of her golden toys
Would have given half London's charity-boys
And charity-girls the annual joys
  Of a holiday dinner at Highbury.

Bon-bons she ate from the gilt cornet;
And gilded queens on St. Bartlemy's day;
  Till her fancy was tinged by her presents —
And first a goldfinch excited her wish,
Then a spherical bowl with its golden fish,
  And then two golden pheasants.

Nay, once she squalled and screamed like wild —
And it shows how the bias we give to a child
  Is a thing most weighty and solemn: —
But whence was wonder or blame to spring
If little Miss K. — after such a swing —
Made a dust for the flaming gilded thing
  On the top of the Fish-street column?

Her Education.

According to metaphysical creed,
To the earliest books that children read
  For much good or much bad they are debtors —
But before with their A B C they start,
There are things in morals, as well as art,
That play a very important part —
  "Impressions before the letters."

Dame Education begins the pile,
Mayhap in the graceful Corinthian style,
  But alas for the elevation!

If the lady's maid or Gossip the nurse
With a load of rubbish, or something worse,
Have made a rotten foundation.

Even thus with little Miss Kilmansegg,
Before she learnt her E for egg,
Ere her governess came, or her masters —
Teachers of quite a different kind
Had "crammed" her beforehand, and put her mind
In a go-cart on golden castors.

Long before her A B and C,
They had taught her by heart her L. S. D.;
And as how she was born a great heiress;
And as sure as London is built of bricks,
My lord would ask her the day to fix
To ride in a fine gilt coach and six,
Like Her Worship the Lady Mayoress.

Instead of stories from Edgeworth's page,
The true golden ore for our golden age,
Or lessons from Barbauld and Trimmer,
Teaching the worth of virtue and health,
All that she knew was the virtue of wealth,
Provided by vulgar nursery stealth,
With a book of leaf-gold for a primer.

The very metal of merit they told,
And praised her for being as "good as gold!"
Till she grew as a peacock haughty;
Of money they talked the whole day round,
And weighed desert like grapes by the pound,
Till she had an idea, from the very sound,
That people with naught were naughty.

They praised — poor children with nothing at all!
Lord! how you twaddle and waddle and squall,
Like common-bred geese and ganders!

What sad little bad figures you make
To the rich Miss K , whose plainest seed-cake
  Was stuffed with corianders!

They praised her falls, as well as her walk,
Flatterers make cream cheese of chalk,
They praised — how they praised — her very small talk,
  As if it fell from a Solon!
Or the girl who at each pretty phrase let drop
A ruby comma, or pearl full-stop,
  Or an emerald semi-colon.

They praised her spirit, and now and then
The nurse brought her own little "nevy" Ben,
  To play with the future mayoress:
And when he got raps, and taps, and slaps,
Scratches and pinches, snips and snaps,
  As if from a tigress, or bearess,
They told him how lords would court that hand,
And always gave him to understand,
  While he rubbed, poor soul,
  His carrotty poll,
That his hair had been pulled by "a *hairess*."

Such were the lessons from maid and nurse,
A governess helped to make still worse,
Giving an appetite so perverse
  Fresh diet whereon to batten —
Beginning with A B C to hold
Like a royal playbill printed in gold
  On a square of pearl-white satin.

The books to teach the verbs and nouns,
And those about countries, cities and towns,
Instead of their sober drabs and browns,
  Were in crimson silk, with gilt edges; —
Her Butler, and Enfield, and Entick — in short,

Her "early lessons" of every sort,
  Looked like souvenirs, keepsakes, and pledges.

Old Johnson shone out in as fine array
As he did one night when he went to the play;
Chambaud like a beau of King Charles's day —
  Lindley Murray in like conditions;
Each weary, unwelcome, irksome task,
Appeared in a fancy dress and a mask —
If you wish for similar copies, ask
  For Howell and James's editions.

Novels she read to amuse her mind,
But always the affluent match-making kind,
  That ends with Promessi Sposi,
And a father-in-law so wealthy and grand,
He could give check-mate to Coutts in the Strand;
  So, along with a ring and posy,
He endows the bride with Golconda off-hand,
  And gives the groom Potosi.

Plays she perused — but she liked the best
Those comedy gentlefolks always possessed
  Of fortunes so truly romantic —
Of money so ready that right or wrong
It always is ready to go for a song,
Throwing it, going it, pitching it strong —
They ought to have purses as green and long
  As the cucumber called the Gigantic.

Then Eastern tales she loved for the sake
Of the purse of Oriental make,
  And the thousand pieces they put in it;
But pastoral scenes on her heart fell cold,
For Nature with her had lost its hold,
No field but the Field of the Cloth of Gold
  Would ever have caught her foot in it.

What more? She learnt to sing and dance,
To sit on a horse, although he should prance,
And to speak a French not spoken in France
  Any more than at Babel's building;
And she painted shells, and flowers, and Turks,
But her great delight was in fancy works
  That are done with gold or gilding.

Gold! still gold! — the bright and the dead,
With golden beads, and gold lace, and gold thread,
She worked in gold, as if for her bread;
  The metal had so undermined her,
Gold ran in her thoughts and filled her brain,
She was golden-headed as Peter's cane
  With which he walked behind her.

Her Accident.

The horse that carried Miss Kilmansegg,
And a better never lifted leg,
  Was a very rich bay, called Banker;
A horse of a breed and a metal so rare, —
By Bullion out of an Ingot mare, —
That for action, the best of figures, and air,
  It made many good judges hanker.

And when she took a ride in the park,
Equestrian lord, or pedestrian clerk,
  Was thrown in an amorous fever,
To see the heiress, how well she sat,
With her groom behind her, Bob or Nat,
In green, half smothered with gold, and a hat
  With more gold lace than beaver.

And then when Banker obtained a pat,
To see how he arched his neck at that!
  He snorted with pride and pleasure!
Like the steed in the fable so lofty and grand,

Who gave the poor ass to understand
That *he* didn't carry a bag of sand,
  But a burden of golden treasure.

A load of treasure? — alas! alas!
Had her horse but been fed upon English grass,
  And sheltered in Yorkshire spinneys,
Had he scoured the sand with the desert ass,
  Or where the American whinnies —
But a hunter from Erin's turf and gorse,
A regular thorough-bred Irish horse,
Why, he ran away, as a matter of course,
  With a girl worth her weight in guineas!

Mayhap 'tis the trick of such pampered nags
To shy at the sight of a beggar in rags,
  But away, like the bolt of a rabbit,
Away went the horse in the madness of fright,
And away went the horsewoman mocking the sight —
Was yonder blue flash a flash of blue light,
  Or only the skirt of her habit?

Away she flies, with the groom behind, —
It looks like a race of the Calmuck kind,
  When Hymen himself is the starter:
And the maid rides first in the four-footed strife,
Riding, striding, as if for her life,
While the lover rides after to catch him a wife,
  Although it's catching a Tartar.

But the groom has lost his glittering hat!
Though he does not sigh and pull up for that —
Alas! his horse is a tit for tat
  To sell to a very low bidder —
His wind is ruined, his shoulder is sprung;
Things, though a horse be handsome and young,
  A purchaser *will* consider.

But still flies the heiress through stones and dust;
O, for a fall, if fall she must,
  On the gentle lap of Flora!
But still, thank Heaven! she clings to her seat—
Away! away! she could ride a dead heat
With the dead who ride so fast and fleet
  In the ballad of Leonora!

Away she gallops!—it's awful work!
It's faster than Turpin's ride to York,
  On Bess, that notable clipper!
She has circled the ring!—she crosses the park!
Mazeppa, although he was stripped so stark,
  Mazeppa couldn't outstrip her!

The fields seem running away with the folks!
The elms are having a race for the oaks,
  At a pace that all jockeys disparages!
All, all is racing! the Serpentine
Seems rushing past like the "arrowy Rhine,"
The houses have got on a railway line,
  And are off like the first-class carriages!

She'll lose her life! she is losing her breath!
A cruel chase, she is chasing Death,
  As female shriekings forewarn her:
And now—as gratis as blood of Guelph—
She clears that gate, which has cleared itself
  Since then, at Hyde Park Corner!

Alas! for the hope of the Kilmanseggs!
For her head, her brains, her body, and legs,
  Her life's not worth a copper!
        Willy-nilly,
        In Piccadilly,
A hundred hearts turn sick and chilly,
  A hundred voices cry, "Stop her!"

And one old gentleman stares and stands,
Shakes his head and lifts his hands,
  And says, "How very improper!"

On and on! — what a perilous run!
The iron rails seem all mingling in one,
  To shut out the Green Park scenery!
And now the cellar its dangers reveals,
She shudders — she shrieks — she's doomed, she feels,
To be torn by powers of horses and wheels,
  Like a spinner by steam machinery!

Sick with horror she shuts her eyes,
But the very stones seem uttering cries,
  As they did to that Persian daughter,
When she climbed up the steep vociferous hill,
Her little silver flagon to fill
  With the magical golden water!

  "Batter her! shatter her!
  Throw and scatter her!"
Shouts each stony-hearted chatterer.
  "Dash at the heavy Dover!
Spill her! kill her! tear and tatter her!
Smash her! crash her!" (the stones didn't flatter her!)
"Kick her brains out! let her blood spatter her!
  Roll on her over and over!"

For so she gathered the awful sense
Of the street in its past unmacadamized tense,
  As the wild horse overran it, —
His four heels making the clatter of six,
Like a devil's tattoo, played with iron sticks
  On a kettle-drum of granite!

On! still on! she's dazzled with hints
Of oranges, ribbons, and colored prints,

A kaleidoscope jumble of shapes and tints,
And human faces all flashing,
Bright and brief as the sparks from the flints
That the desperate hoof keeps dashing!

On and on! still frightfully fast!
Dover-street, Bond-street, all are past!
But — yes — no — yes! — they're down at last!
The Furies and Fates have found them!
Down they go with a sparkle and crash,
Like a bark that's struck by the lightning flash —
There's a shriek — and a sob —
And the dense dark mob
Like a billow closes around them!

* * * * * *
* * * * * *

"She breathes!"
"She don't!"
"She'll recover!"
"She won't!"
"She's stirring! she's living, by Nemesis!"
Gold, still gold! on counter and shelf!
Golden dishes as plenty as delf!
Miss Kilmansegg's coming again to herself
On an opulent goldsmith's premises!

Gold! fine gold! — both yellow and red,
Beaten, and molten — polished, and dead —
To see the gold with profusion spread
In all forms of its manufacture!
But what avails gold to Miss Kilmansegg,
When the femoral bone of her dexter leg
Has met with a compound fracture?

Gold may soothe Adversity's smart;
Nay, help to bind up a broken heart;
But to try it on any other part
  Were as certain a disappointment,
As if one should rub the dish and plate,
Taken out of a Staffordshire crate —
In the hope of a golden service of state —
  With Singleton's "Golden Ointment."

Her Precious Leg.

"As the twig is bent, the tree's inclined,"
Is an adage often recalled to mind,
  Referring to juvenile bias:
And never so well is the verity seen,
As when to the weak, warped side we lean,
  While life's tempests and hurricanes try us.

Even thus with Miss K. and her broken limb,
By a very, very remarkable whim,
  She showed her early tuition:
While the buds of character came into blow
With a certain tinge that served to show
The nursery culture long ago,
  As the graft is known by fruition!

For the king's physician, who nursed the case,
His verdict gave with an awful face,
  And three others concurred to egg it;
That the patient, to give old Death the slip,
Like the Pope, instead of a personal trip,
  Must send her leg as a legate.

The limb was doomed, — it couldn't be saved, —
And like other people the patient behaved,
Nay, bravely that cruel parting braved,

Which makes some persons so falter,
They rather would part, without a groan,
With the flesh of their flesh, and bone of their bone,
They obtained at St. George's altar.

But when it came to fitting the stump
With a proxy limb, then flatly and plump
She spoke, in the spirit olden;
She couldn't, she shouldn't, she wouldn't — have wood!
Nor a leg of cork, if she never stood,
And she swore an oath, or something as good,
The proxy limb should be golden!

A wooden leg! what, a sort of peg,
For your common Jockeys and Jennies!
No, no, her mother might worry and plague —
Weep, go down on her knees, and beg,
But nothing would move Miss Kilmansegg!
She could — she would have a Golden Leg,
If it cost ten thousand guineas!

Wood indeed, in forest or park,
With its sylvan honors and feudal bark,
Is an aristocratical article:
But split and sawn, and hacked about town,
Serving all needs of pauper or clown,
Trod on! staggered on! Wood cut down
Is vulgar — fibre and particle!

And cork! — when the noble cork-tree shades
A lovely group of Castilian maids,
'Tis a thing for a song or sonnet! —
But cork, as it stops the bottle of gin,
Or bungs the beer — the *small* beer — in,
It pierced her heart like a corking-pin,
To think of standing upon it!

A leg of gold — solid gold throughout,
Nothing else, whether slim or stout,
  Should ever support her, God willing!
She must — she could — she would have her whim!
Her father, she turned a deaf ear to him —
  He might kill her — she didn't mind killing!
He was welcome to cut off her other limb —
  He might cut her all off with a shilling!

All other promised gifts were in vain,
Golden girdle, or golden chain,
She writhed with impatience more than pain,
  And uttered "pshaws!" and "pishes!"
But a leg of gold! as she lay in bed,
It danced before her — it ran in her head!
  It jumped with her dearest wishes!

"Gold — gold — gold! O, let it be gold!"
Asleep or awake that tale she told,
  And when she grew delirious:
Till her parents resolved to grant her wish,
If they melted down plate, and goblet, and dish,
  The case was getting so serious.

So a leg was made in a comely mould,
Of gold, fine virgin glittering gold,
  As solid as man could make it —
Solid in foot, and calf, and shank,
A prodigious sum of money it sank;
In fact, 'twas a branch of the family bank,
  And no easy matter to break it.

All sterling metal, — not half-and-half,
The goldsmith's mark was stamped on the calf, —
  'Twas pure as from Mexican barter!
And to make it more costly, just over the knee,
Where another ligature used to be,

Was a circle of jewels, worth shillings to see,
  A new-fangled badge of the garter!

'Twas a splendid, brilliant, beautiful leg,
Fit for the court of Scander-Beg,
That precious leg of Miss Kilmansegg!
  For, thanks to parental bounty,
Secure from mortification's touch,
She stood on a member that cost as much
  As a Member for all the County!

Her Fame.

To gratify stern Ambition's whims,
What hundreds and thousands of precious limbs
  On a field of battle we scatter!
Severed by sword, or bullet, or saw,
Off they go, all bleeding and raw, —
But the public seems to get the lock-jaw,
  So little is said on the matter!

Legs, the tightest that ever were seen,
The tightest, the lightest, that danced on the green,
  Cutting capers to sweet Kitty Clover;
Shattered, scattered, cut, and bowled down,
Off they go, worse off for renown,
A line in the *Times*, or a talk about town,
  Than the leg that a fly runs over!

But the precious Leg of Miss Kilmansegg,
That gowden, goolden, golden leg,
  Was the theme of all conversation!
Had it been a pillar of church and state,
Or a prop to support the whole dead weight,
It could not have furnished more debate
  To the heads and tails of the nation!

East and west, and north and south,
Though useless for either hunger or drouth,—
The Leg was in every body's mouth,
  To use a poetical figure;
Rumor, in taking her ravenous swim,
Saw, and seized on the tempting limb,
  Like a shark on the leg of a nigger.

Wilful murder fell very dead;
Debates in the House were hardly read;
In vain the police reports were fed
  With Irish riots and *rumpuses* —
The Leg! the Leg! was the great event;
Through every circle in life it went,
  Like the leg of a pair of compasses.

The last new novel seemed tame and flat;
The Leg, a novelty newer than that,
  Had tripped up the heels of fiction!
It Burked the very essays of Burke,
And, alas! how wealth over wit plays the Turk!
As a regular piece of goldsmith's work,
  Got the better of Goldsmith's diction.

"A leg of gold! what, of solid gold?"
Cried rich and poor, and young and old,
  And Master and Miss and Madam;
'Twas the talk of 'change — the alley — the bank —
And with men of scientific rank
It made as much stir as the fossil shank
  Of a lizard coëval with Adam!

Of course with Greenwich and Chelsea elves,
Men who had lost a limb themselves,
  Its interest did not dwindle;
But Bill, and Ben, and Jack, and Tom,

Could hardly have spun more yarns therefrom,
  If the leg had been a spindle.

Meanwhile the story went to and fro,
Till, gathering like the ball of snow,
By the time it got to Stratford-le-Bow,
  Through exaggeration's touches,
The heiress and hope of the Kilmanseggs
Was propped on *two* fine golden legs,
  And a pair of golden crutches!

Never had leg so great a run!
'Twas the "go" and the "kick" thrown into one:
The mode — the new thing under the sun!
  The rage — the fancy — the passion!
Bonnets were named, and hats were worn,
A la golden leg instead of Leghorn,
    And stockings and shoes
    Of golden hues
  Took the lead in the walks of fashion!

The Golden Leg had a vast career,
It was sung and danced — and to show how near
  Low folly to lofty approaches,
Down to society's very dregs,
The belles of Wapping wore "Kilmanseggs,"
And St. Giles's beaux sported golden legs
  In their pinchbeck pins and brooches!

Her first Step.

Supposing the trunk and limbs of man
Shared, on the allegorical plan,
  By the passions that mark humanity,
Whichever might claim the head, or heart,
The stomach, or any other part,
  The legs would be seized by Vanity.

There's Bardus, a six-foot column of fop,
A lighthouse without any light atop,
  Whose height would attract beholders,
If he had not lost some inches clear
By looking down at his kerseymere,
Ogling the limbs he holds so dear,
  Till he got a stoop in his shoulders.

Talk of art, of science, or books,
And down go the everlasting looks,
  To his crural beauties so wedded!
Try him, whenever you will, you find
His mind in his legs, and his legs in his mind,
All prongs and folly — in short, a kind
  Of fork — that is fiddle-headed.

What wonder, then, if Miss Kilmansegg,
With a splendid, brilliant, beautiful Leg,
Fit for the court of Scander-Beg,
Disdained to hide it, like Joan or Meg,
  In petticoats stuffed or quilted?
Not she! 'twas her convalescent whim
To dazzle the world with her precious limb,
  Nay, to go a little high-kilted.

So cards were sent for that sort of mob
Where Tartars and Africans hob-and-nob,
And the Cherokee talks of his cab and cob
  To Polish or Lapland lovers —
Cards like that hieroglyphical call
To a geographical Fancy Ball
  On the recent post-office covers.

For if lion-hunters — and great ones too —
Would mob a savage from Latakoo,
Or squeeze for a glimpse of Prince Le Boo,

That unfortunate Sandwich scion —
Hundreds of first-rate people, no doubt,
Would gladly, madly, rush to a rout,
That promised a Golden Lion!

Her Fancy Ball.

Of all the spirits of evil fame
That hurt the soul or injure the frame,
And poison what's honest and hearty,
There's none more needs a Mathew to preach
A cooling, antiphlogistic speech,
To praise and enforce
A temperate course,
Than the Evil Spirit of Party.

Go to the House of Commons, or Lords,
And they seem to be busy with simple words
In their popular sense or pedantic —
But, alas! with their cheers, and sneers, and jeers,
They're really busy, whatever appears,
Putting peas in each other's ears,
To drive their enemies frantic!

Thus Tories love to worry the Whigs,
Who treat them in turn like Schwalbach pigs,
Giving them lashes, thrashes, and digs,
With their writhing and pain delighted —
But after all that's said, and more,
The malice and spite of Party are poor
To the malice and spite of a party next door,
To a party not invited.

On with the cap and out with the light,
Weariness bids the world good-night,
At least for the usual season;
But, hark! a clatter of horses' heels;

And Sleep and Silence are broken on wheels,
  Like Wilful Murder and Treason!

Another crash — and the carriage goes —
Again poor Weariness seeks the repose
  That Nature demands imperious;
But Echo takes up the burden now,
With a rattling chorus of row-de-dow-dow,
Till Silence herself seems making a row,
  Like a Quaker gone delirious!

'Tis night — a winter night — and the stars
Are shining like winkin' — Venus and Mars
Are rolling along in their golden cars
  Through the sky's serene expansion —
But vainly the stars dispense their rays,
Venus and Mars are lost in the blaze
  Of the Kilmanseggs' luminous mansion!

Up jumps Fear in a terrible fright!
His bed-chamber windows look so bright,
  With light all the square is glutted!
Up he jumps, like a sole from the pan,
And a tremor sickens his inward man,
For he feels as only a gentleman can
  Who thinks he's being "gutted."

Again Fear settles, all snug and warm;
But only to dream of a dreadful storm
  From Autumn's sulphurous locker;
But the only electric body that falls
Wears a negative coat and positive smalls,
And draws the peal that so appalls
  From the Kilmanseggs' brazen knocker!

'Tis Curiosity's benefit night —
And perchance 'tis the English second-sight,

But whatever it be, so be it —
As the friends and guests of Miss Kilmansegg
Crowd in to look at her Golden Leg,
As many more
Mob round the door,
To see them going to see it!

In they go — in jackets and cloaks,
Plumes, and bonnets, turbans, and toques,
As if to a Congress of Nations:
Greeks and Malays, with daggers and dirks,
Spaniards, Jews, Chinese, and Turks —
Some like original foreign works,
But mostly like bad translations.

In they go, and to work like a pack,
Juan, Moses, and Shachabac,
Tom, and Jerry, and Springheeled Jack,
For some of low Fancy are lovers —
Skirting, zigzagging, casting about,
Here and there, and in and out,
With a crush, and a rush, for a full-bodied rout
In one of the stiffest of covers.

In they went, and hunted about,
Open-mouthed like chub and trout,
And some with the upper lip thrust out,
Like that fish for routing, a barbel —
While Sir Jacob stood to welcome the crowd,
And rubbed his hands, and smiled aloud,
And bowed, and bowed, and bowed, and bowed,
Like a man who is sawing marble.

For princes were there, and noble peers;
Dukes descended from Norman spears;
Earls that dated from early years;

And lords in vast variety —
Besides the gentry both new and old —
For people who stand on legs of gold
Are sure to stand well with society.

"But where — where — where?" with one accord
Cried Moses and Mufti, Jack and my Lord,
Wang-Fong and Il Bondocani —
When slow, and heavy, and dead as a dump,
They heard a foot begin to stump,
Thump! lump!
Lump! thump!
Like the spectre in "Don Giovanni!"

And, lo! the heiress, Miss Kilmansegg,
With her splendid, brilliant, beautiful leg,
In the garb of a goddess olden —
Like chaste Diana going to hunt,
With a golden spear — which of course was blunt,
And a tunic looped up to a gem in front,
To show the Leg that was Golden!

Gold! still gold! her Crescent behold,
That should be silver, but would be gold;
And her robe's auriferous spangles!
Her golden stomacher — how she would melt!
Her golden quiver and golden belt,
Where a golden bugle dangles!

And her jewelled garter? O, sin! O, shame!
Let Pride and Vanity bear the blame,
That brings such blots on female fame!
But to be a true recorder,
Besides its thin transparent stuff,
The tunic was looped quite high enough
To give a glimpse of the Order!

But what have sin or shame to do
With a Golden Leg — and a stout one, too?
Away with all Prudery's panics!
That the precious metal, by thick and thin,
Will cover square acres of land or sin,
Is a fact made plain
Again and again,
In morals as well as mechanics.

A few, indeed, of her proper sex,
Who seemed to feel her foot on their necks,
And feared their charms would meet with checks
From so rare and splendid a blazon —
A few cried "fie!" — and "forward" — and "bold!"
And said of the Leg it might be gold,
But to them it looked like brazen!

'Twas hard, they hinted, for flesh and blood,
Virtue, and beauty, and all that's good,
To strike to mere dross their topgallants —
But what were beauty, or virtue, or worth,
Gentle manners, or gentle birth,
Nay, what the most talented head on earth
To a Leg worth fifty Talents!

But the men sang quite another hymn
Of glory and praise to the precious limb —
Age, sordid age, admired the whim,
And its indecorum pardoned —
While half of the young — ay, more than half —
Bowed down and worshipped the Golden Calf,
Like the Jews when their hearts were hardened.

A Golden Leg! what fancies it fired!
What golden wishes and hopes inspired!
To give but a mere abridgment —

What a leg to leg-bail Embarrassment's serf!
What a leg for a leg to take on the turf!
  What a leg for a marching regiment!

A Golden Leg! — whatever Love sings,
'Twas worth a bushel of "plain gold rings,"
  With which the romantic wheedles.
'Twas worth all the legs in stockings and socks —
'Twas a leg that might be put in the stocks,
  N. B. — Not the parish beadle's!

And Lady K. nid-nodded her head,
Lapped in a turban fancy-bred,
Just like a love-apple, huge and red,
  Some Mussul-womanish mystery;
    But whatever she meant
      To represent,
She talked like the Muse of History.

She told how the filial leg was lost;
And then how much the gold one cost;
  With its weight to a Trojan fraction:
And how it took off, and how it put on;
And called on Devil, Duke, and Don,
Mahomet, Moses, and Prester John,
  To notice its beautiful action.

And then of the Leg she went in quest;
And led it where the light was best;
And made it lay itself up to rest
  In postures for painters' studies:
It cost more tricks and trouble, by half,
Than it takes to exhibit a six-legged calf
  To a boothful of country cuddies.

Nor yet did the heiress herself omit
The arts that help to make a hit,

And preserve a prominent station.
She talked and laughed far more than her share;
And took a part in "Rich and Rare
Were the Gems she wore" — and the gems were there,
Like a song with an illustration.

She even stood up with a count of France
To dance — alas! the measures we dance
When Vanity plays the piper!
Vanity, Vanity, apt to betray,
And lead all sorts of legs astray,
Wood, or metal, or human clay, —
Since Satan first played the viper!

But first she doffed her hunting gear,
And favored Tom Tug with her golden spear,
To row with down the river —
A Bonze had her golden bow to hold;
A Hermit her belt and bugle of gold;
And an Abbot her golden quiver.

And then a space was cleared on the floor,
And she walked the Minuet de la Cour,
With all the pomp of a Pompadour;
But, although she began *andante*,
Conceive the faces of all the rout,
When she finished off with a whirligig bout,
And the Precious Leg stuck stiffly out
Like the leg of a *figuranté*!

So the courtly dance was goldenly done,
And golden opinions, of course, it won
From all different sorts of people —
Chiming, ding-dong, with flattering phrase,
In one vociferous peal of praise,
Like the peal that rings on royal days
From Loyalty's parish steeple.

And yet, had the leg been one of those
That dance for bread in flesh-colored hose,
  With Rosina's pastoral bevy,
The jeers it had met, — the shouts! the scoff!
The cutting advice to "take itself off,"
  For sounding but half so heavy.

Had it been a leg like those, perchance,
That teach little girls and boys to dance,
To set, poussette, recede, and advance,
  With the steps and figures most proper, —
Had it hopped for a weekly or quarterly sum,
How little of praise or grist would have come
  To a mill with such a hopper!

But the leg was none of those limbs forlorn —
Bartering capers and hops for corn —
That meet with public hisses and scorn,
  Or the morning journal denounces —
Had it pleased to caper from morn till dusk,
There was all the music of "Money Musk"
  In its ponderous bangs and bounces.

But hark! — as slow as the strokes of a pump,
    Lump, thump!
    Thump, lump!
As the Giant of Castle Otranto might stump
  To a lower room from an upper —
Down she goes with a noisy dint,
For, taking the crimson turban's hint,
A noble lord at the head of the Mint
  Is leading the Leg to supper!

But the supper, alas! must rest untold,
With its blaze of light and its glitter of gold,
  For to paint that scene of glamour,

It would need the great Enchanter's charm,
Who waves over palace, and cot, and farm,
An arm like the goldbeater's golden arm
  That wields a golden hammer.

He — only HE — could fitly state
THE MASSIVE SERVICE OF GOLDEN PLATE,
  With the proper phrase and expansion —
The Rare Selection of FOREIGN WINES —
The ALPS OF ICE and MOUNTAINS OF PINES,
The punch in OCEANS and sugary shrines,
The TEMPLE OF TASTE from GUNTER'S DESIGNS —
In short, all that WEALTH with A FEAST combines,
  In a SPLENDID FAMILY MANSION.

Suffice it each masked outlandish guest
Ate and drank of the very best,
  According to critical conners —
And then they pledged the hostess and host,
But the Golden Leg was the standing toast,
    And, as somebody swore,
    Walked off with more
  Than its share of the "hips!" and honors!

    "Miss Kilmansegg! —
    Full glasses I beg! —
Miss Kilmansegg and her Precious Leg!"
  And away went the bottle careering!
Wine in bumpers! and shouts in peals!
Till the Clown didn't know his head from his heels,
The Mussulman's eyes danced two-some reels,
  And the Quaker was hoarse with cheering!

Her Dream.

Miss Kilmansegg took off her Leg,
And laid it down like a cribbage-peg,

For the rout was done and the riot:
The square was hushed; not a sound was heard;
The sky was gray, and no creature stirred,
Except one little precocious bird,
That chirped — and then was quiet.

So still without, — so still within; —
It had been a sin
To drop a pin —
So intense is silence after a din,
It seemed like Death's rehearsal!
To stir the air no eddy came;
And the taper burnt with as still a flame,
As to flicker had been a burning shame,
In a calm so universal.

The time for sleep had come, at last;
And there was the bed, so soft, so vast,
Quite a field of Bedfordshire clover;
Softer, cooler, and calmer, no doubt,
From the piece of work just ravelled out,
For one of the pleasures of having a rout
Is the pleasure of having it over.

No sordid pallet, or truckle mean,
Of straw, and rug, and tatters unclean;
But a splendid, gilded, carved machine,
That was fit for a royal chamber.
On the top was a gorgeous golden wreath;
And the damask curtains hung beneath,
Like clouds of crimson and amber.

Curtains, held up by two little plump things,
With golden bodies and golden wings, —
Mere fins for such solidities —

Two Cupids, in short,
Of the regular sort,
But the housemaid called them "Cupidities."

No patchwork quilt, all seams and scars,
But velvet, powdered with golden stars,
A fit mantle for *Night*-commanders!
And the pillow, as white as snow undimmed,
And as cool as the pool that the breeze has skimmed,
Was cased in the finest cambric, and trimmed
With the costliest lace of Flanders.

And the bed — of the eider's softest down,
'Twas a place to revel, to smother, to drown
In a bliss inferred by the poet;
For if ignorance be indeed a bliss,
What blessed ignorance equals this,
To sleep — and not to know it?

O, bed! O, bed! delicious bed!
That heaven upon earth to the weary head;
But a place that to name would be ill-bred,
To the head with a wakeful trouble —
'Tis held by such a different lease!
To one, a place of comfort and peace,
All stuffed with the down of stubble geese,
To another with only the stubble!

To one a perfect halcyon nest,
All calm, and balm, and quiet, and rest,
And soft as the fur of the cony —
To another, so restless for body and head,
That the bed seems borrowed from Nettlebed,
And the pillow from Stratford the Stony!

To the happy, a first-class carriage of ease,
To the Land of Nod, or where you please;

But alas! for the watchers and weepers,
Who turn, and turn, and turn again,
But turn, and turn, and turn in vain,
With an anxious brain,
And thoughts in a train
That does not run upon *sleepers!*

Wide awake as the mousing owl,
Night-hawk, or other nocturnal fowl, —
But more profitless vigils keeping, —
Wide awake in the dark they stare,
Filling with phantoms the vacant air,
As if that crook-backed tyrant Care
Had plotted to kill them sleeping.

And O! when the blessed diurnal light
Is quenched by the providential night,
To render our slumber more certain,
Pity, pity the wretches that weep,
For they must be wretched who cannot sleep
When God himself draws the curtain!

The careful Betty the pillow beats,
And airs the blankets, and smooths the sheets,
And gives the mattress a shaking;
But vainly Betty performs her part,
If a ruffled head and a rumpled heart
As well as the couch want making.

There's Morbid, all bile, and verjuice, and nerves,
Where other people would make preserves,
He turns his fruits into pickles:
Jealous, envious, and fretful by day,
At night, to his own sharp fancies a prey,
He lies like a hedgehog rolled up the wrong way,
Tormenting himself with his prickles.

But a child — that bids the world good-night,
In downright earnest, and cuts it quite —
  A cherub no art can copy, —
'Tis a perfect picture to see him lie
As if he had supped on dormouse pie,
(An ancient classical dish, by the by)
  With sauce of syrup of poppy.

O, bed! bed! bed! delicious bed!
That heaven upon earth to the weary head,
  Whether lofty or low its condition!
But, instead of putting our plagues on shelves,
In our blankets how often we toss ourselves,
Or are tossed by such allegorical elves
  As Pride, Hate, Greed, and Ambition!

The independent Miss Kilmansegg
Took off her independent Leg
  And laid it beneath her pillow,
And then on the bed her frame she cast;
The time for repose had come at last,
But long, long after the storm is past
  Rolls the turbid, turbulent billow.

No part she had in vulgar cares
That belong to common household affairs —
Nocturnal annoyances such as theirs
  Who lie with a shrewd surmising
That while they are couchant (a bitter cup!)
Their bread and butter are getting up,
  And the coals — confound them! — are rising.

No fear she had her sleep to postpone,
Like the crippled widow who weeps alone,
And cannot make a doze her own,

For the dread that mayhap on the morrow,
The true and Christian reading to balk,
A broker will take up her bed and walk,
By way of curing her sorrow.

No cause like these she had to bewail:
But the breath of applause had blown a gale,
And winds from that quarter seldom fail
To cause some human commotion;
But whenever such breezes coincide
With the very spring-tide
Of human pride,
There's no such swell on the ocean!

Peace, and ease, and slumber lost,
She turned, and rolled, and tumbled, and tossed,
With a tumult that would not settle:
A common case, indeed, with such
As have too little, or think too much,
Of the precious and glittering metal.

Gold! — she saw at her golden foot
The peer whose tree had an olden root,
The proud, the great, the learned to boot,
The handsome, the gay, and the witty —
The man of science — of arms — of art,
The man who deals but at Pleasure's mart,
And the man who deals in the city.

Gold, still gold — and true to the mould!
In the very scheme of her dream it told;
For, by magical transmutation,
From her Leg through her body it seemed to go,
Till, gold above, and gold below,
She was gold, all gold, from her little gold toe
To her organ of Veneration!

And still she retained, through Fancy's art,
The golden bow, and the golden dart,
With which she had played a goddess's part
 In her recent glorification.
And still, like one of the self-same brood,
On a plinth of the self-same metal she stood
 For the whole world's adoration.

And hymns of incense around her rolled,
From golden harps and censers of gold, —
For Fancy in dreams is as uncontrolled
 As a horse without a bridle:
What wonder, then, from all checks exempt,
If, inspired by the Golden Leg, she dreamt
 She was turned to a golden idol?

Her Courtship.

When, leaving Eden's happy land,
The grieving angel led by the hand
 Our banished father and mother,
Forgotten, amid their awful doom,
The tears, the fears, and the future's gloom,
On each brow was a wreath of Paradise bloom,
 That our parents had twined for each other.

It was only while sitting like figures of stone,
For the grieving angel had skyward flown,
As they sat, those two, in the world alone,
 With disconsolate hearts nigh cloven,
That, scenting the gust of happier hours,
They looked around for the precious flowers,
And, lo! — a last relic of Eden's dear bowers —
 The chaplet that Love had woven!

And still, when a pair of lovers meet,
There's a sweetness in air, unearthly sweet,

That savors still of that happy retreat
  Where Eve by Adam was courted:
Whilst the joyous thrush, and the gentle dove,
Wooed their mates in the boughs above,
  And the serpent, as yet, only sported.

Who hath not felt that breath in the air,
A perfume and freshness strange and rare,
A warmth in the light, and a bliss every where,
  When young hearts yearn together?
All sweets below, and all sunny above,
O! there's nothing in life like making love,
  Save making hay in fine weather!

Who hath not found amongst his flowers
A blossom too bright for this world of ours,
  Like a rose among snows of Sweden?
But, to turn again to Miss Kilmansegg,
Where must Love have gone to beg,
If such a thing as a Golden Leg
  Had put its foot in Eden?

And yet — to tell the rigid truth —
Her favor was sought by age and youth —
  For the prey will find a prowler!
She was followed, flattered, courted, addressed,
Wooed, and cooed, and wheedled, and pressed,
By suitors from North, South, East, and West,
  Like that heiress, in song, Tibbie Fowler!

But, alas! alas! for the woman's fate,
Who has from a mob to choose a mate!
  'Tis a strange and painful mystery!
But the more the eggs, the worse the hatch;
The more the fish, the worse the catch;
The more the sparks, the worse the match;
  Is a fact in woman's history.

Give her between a brace to pick,
And, mayhap, with luck to help the trick,
She will take the Faustus, and leave the Old Nick —
  But, her future bliss to baffle,
Amongst a score let her have a voice,
And she'll have as little cause to rejoice
As if she had won the "man of her choice"
  In a matrimonial raffle!

Thus, even thus, with the heiress and hope,
Fulfilling the adage of too much rope,
  With so ample a competition,
She chose the least worthy of all the group,
Just as the vulture makes a stoop,
And singles out from the herd or troop
  The beast of the worst condition.

A foreign count — who came incog.,
Not under a cloud, but under a fog,
  In a Calais packet's fore-cabin,
To charm some lady British-born,
With his eyes as black as the fruit of the thorn,
And his hooky nose, and his beard half-shorn,
  Like a half-converted Rabbin.

And because the sex confess a charm
In the man who has slashed a head or arm,
  Or has been a throat's undoing,
He was dressed like one of the glorious trade,
At least when glory is off parade,
With a stock, and a frock, well trimmed with braid,
  And frogs — that went a-wooing.

Moreover, as counts are apt to do,
On the left-hand side of his dark surtout,
At one of those holes that buttons go through,

(To be a precise recorder,)
A ribbon he wore, or rather a scrap,
About an inch of ribbon mayhap,
That one of his rivals, a whimsical chap,
Described as his "Retail Order."

And then — and much it helped his chance —
He could sing, and play first fiddle, and dance,
Perform charades and proverbs of France —
Act the tender, and do the cruel;
For amongst his other killing parts,
He had broken a brace of female hearts,
And murdered three men in duel!

Savage at heart, and false of tongue,
Subtle with age, and smooth to the young,
Like a snake in his coiling and curling —
Such was the count — to give him a niche —
Who came to court that heiress rich,
And knelt at her foot — one needn't say which —
Besieging her castle of *Sterling*.

With prayers and vows he opened his trench,
And plied her with English, Spanish, and French,
In phrases the most sentimental!
And quoted poems in high and low Dutch,
With now and then an Italian touch,
Till she yielded, without resisting much,
To homage so continental.

And then, the sordid bargain to close,
With a miniature sketch of his hooky nose,
And his dear dark eyes, as black as sloes,
And his beard and whiskers as black as those,
The lady's consent he requited —
And instead of the lock that lovers beg,
The count received from Miss Kilmansegg

A model, in small, of her Precious Leg —
And so the couple were plighted!

But, O! the love that gold must crown!
Better — better, the love of the clown,
Who admires his lass in her Sunday gown,
As if all the fairies had dressed her!
Whose brain to no crooked thought gives birth,
Except that he never will part on earth
With his true love's crooked tester!

Alas! for the love that's linked with gold!
Better — better a thousand times told —
More honest, happy, and laudable,
The downright loving of pretty Cis,
Who wipes her lips, though there's nothing amiss,
And takes a kiss, and gives a kiss,
In which her heart is audible!

Pretty Cis, so smiling and bright,
Who loves as she labors, with all her might,
And without any sordid leaven!
Who blushes as red as haws and hips,
Down to her very finger-tips,
For Roger's blue ribbons — to her, like strips
Cut out of the azure of heaven!

Her Marriage.

'Twas morn — a most auspicious one!
From the golden East the golden sun
Came forth his glorious race to run,
Through clouds of most splendid tinges;
Clouds that lately slept in shade,
But now seemed made
Of gold brocade,
With magnificent golden fringes.

Gold above, and gold below,
The earth reflected the golden glow,
  From river, and hill, and valley;
Gilt by the golden light of morn,
The Thames — it looked like the Golden Horn,
And the barge that carried coal or corn
  Like Cleopatra's galley!

Bright as a cluster of golden-rod,
Suburban poplars began to nod,
  With extempore splendor furnished;
While London was bright with glittering clocks,
Golden dragons, and golden cocks,
    And above them all,
    The dome of St. Paul,
With its golden cross and its golden ball,
  Shone out as if newly burnished!

And, lo! for golden hours and joys,
Troops of glittering golden boys
Danced along with a jocund noise,
  And their gilded emblems carried!
In short, 'twas the year's most golden day,
By mortals called the first of May,
    When Miss Kilmansegg,
    Of the Golden Leg,
  With a golden ring was married!

And thousands of children, women, and men,
Counted the clock from eight till ten,
  From St. James's sonorous steeple;
For, next to that interesting job,
The hanging of Jack, or Bill, or Bob,
There's nothing so draws a London mob
  As the noosing of very rich people.

And a treat it was for a mob to behold
The bridal carriage that blazed with gold!
And the footmen tall, and the coachman bold,
  In liveries so resplendent —
Coats you wondered to see in place,
They seemed so rich with golden lace,
  That they might have been independent.

Coats that made those menials proud
Gaze with scorn on the dingy crowd,
  From their gilded elevations;
Not to forget that saucy lad,
(Ostentation's favorite cad,)
The page, who looked, so splendidly clad,
  Like a page of the "Wealth of Nations."

But the coachman carried off the state,
With what was a Lancashire body of late
  Turned into a Dresden Figure;
With a bridal nosegay of early bloom,
About the size of a birchen broom,
And so huge a white favor, had Gog been groom,
  He need not have worn a bigger.

And then to see the groom! the count!
With foreign orders to such an amount,
  And whiskers so wild — nay, bestial;
He seemed to have borrowed the shaggy hair
As well as the stars of the Polar Bear,
  To make him look celestial!

And then — Great Jove — the struggle, the crush,
The screams, the heaving, the awful rush,
  The swearing, the tearing, and fighting, —
The hats and bonnets smashed like an egg, —
To catch a glimpse of the Golden Leg,

Which, between the steps and Miss Kilmansegg,
  Was fully displayed in alighting!

From the golden ankle up to the knee
There it was for the mob to see!
A shocking act had it chanced to be
  A crooked leg or a skinny:
But although a magnificent veil she wore,
Such as never was seen before,
In case of blushes, she blushed no more
  Than George the First on a guinea!

Another step, and, lo! she was launched!
All in white, as brides are *blanched*,
  With a wreath of most wonderful splendor —
Diamonds, and pearls, so rich in device,
That, according to calculation nice,
Her head was worth as royal a price
  As the head of the Young Pretender.

Bravely she shone — and shone the more
As she sailed through the crowd of squalid and poor,
  Thief, beggar, and tatterdemalion —
Led by the count, with his sloe-black eyes
Bright with triumph, and some surprise,
Like Anson on making sure of his prize
  The famous Mexican galleon!

Anon came Lady K., with her face
Quite made up to act with grace,
  But she cut the performance shorter,
For instead of pacing stately and stiff,
At the stare of the vulgar she took a miff,
And ran, full speed, into church, as if
  To get married before her daughter.

But Sir Jacob walked more slowly, and bowed
Right and left to the gaping crowd,
  Wherever a glance was seizable;
For Sir Jacob thought he bowed like a Guelph,
And therefore bowed to imp and elf,
And would gladly have made a bow to himself,
  Had such a bow been feasible.

And last — and not the least of the sight,
Six "Handsome Fortunes" all in white,
Came to help in the marriage rite,
  And rehearse their own hymeneals;
And then, the bright procession to close,
They were followed by just as many beaux,
  Quite fine enough for ideals.

Glittering men and splendid dames,
Thus they entered the porch of St. James',
  Pursued by a thunder of laughter;
For the beadle was forced to intervene,
For Jim the Crow, and his May-day Queen,
With her gilded ladle, and Jack i' the Green,
  Would fain have followed after!

Beadle-like he hushed the shout;
But the temple was full "inside and out,"
And a buzz kept buzzing all round about
  Like bees when the day is sunny —
A buzz universal that interfered
With the rite that ought to have been revered,
As if the couple already were smeared
  With Wedlock's treacle and honey!

Yet wedlock's a very awful thing!
'Tis something like that feat in the ring
  Which requires good nerve to do it —

When one of a "Grand Equestrian Troop"
Makes a jump at a gilded hoop,
Not certain at all
Of what may befall
After his getting through it!

But the count he felt the nervous work
No more than any polygamous Turk,
Or bold piratical skipper,
Who, during his buccaneering search,
Would as soon engage "a hand" in church
As a hand on board his clipper!

And how did the bride perform her part?
Like any bride who is cold at heart,
Mere snow with the ice's glitter;
What but a life of winter for her!
Bright but chilly, alive without stir,
So splendidly comfortless, — just like a fir
When the frost is severe and bitter.

Such were the future man and wife!
Whose bale or bliss to the end of life
A few short words were to settle —
Wilt thou have this woman?
I will — and then,
Wilt thou have this man?
I will, and Amen —
And those two were one flesh, in the angels' ken,
Except one Leg — that was metal.

Then the names were signed — and kissed the kiss
And the bride, who came from her coach a miss,
As a countess walked to her carriage —
Whilst Hymen preened his plumes like a dove,
And Cupid fluttered his wings above,

In the shape of a fly — as little a Love
   As ever looked in at a marriage!

Another crash — and away they dashed,
And the gilded carriage and footmen flashed
   From the eyes of the gaping people —
Who turned to gaze at the toe and heel
Of the golden boys beginning a reel,
To the merry sound of a wedding-peal
   From St. James's musical steeple.

Those wedding-bells! those wedding-bells!
How sweetly they sound in pastoral dells
   From a tower in an ivy-green jacket!
But town-made joys how dearly they cost!
And after all are tumbled and tost,
Like a peal from a London steeple, and lost
   In town-made riot and racket.

The wedding-peal, how sweetly it peals
With grass or heather beneath our heels, —
   For bells are Music's laughter!
But a London peal, well mingled, be sure,
With vulgar noises and voices impure,
What a harsh and discordant overture
   To the harmony meant to come after!

But hence with Discord — perchance, too soon
To cloud the face of the honeymoon
   What a dismal occultation! —
Whatever Fate's concerted trick,
The countess and count, at the present nick,
Have a chicken and not a crow to pick
   At a sumptuous cold collation.

A breakfast — no unsubstantial mess,
But one in the style of good Queen Bess,

Who — hearty as hippocampus —
Broke her fast with ale and beef,
Instead of toast and the Chinese leaf,
And in lieu of anchovy — grampus!

A breakfast of fowl, and fish, and flesh,
Whatever was sweet, or salt, or fresh,
With wines the most rare and curious —
Wines, of the richest flavor and hue;
With fruits from the worlds both Old and New;
And fruits obtained before they were due
At a discount most usurious.

For wealthy palates there be, that scout
What is *in* season, for what is *out*,
And prefer all precocious savor;
For instance, early green peas, of the sort
That costs some four or five guineas a quart;
Where the *Mint* is the principal flavor.

And many a wealthy man was there,
Such as the wealthy city could spare,
To put in a portly appearance —
Men whom their fathers had helped to gild:
And men who had had their fortunes to build,
And — much to their credit — had richly filled
Their purses by *pursy-verance*.

Men, by popular rumor at least,
Not the last to enjoy a feast!
And truly they were not idle!
Luckier far than the chestnut tits,
Which, down at the door, stood champing their bits,
At a different sort of bridle.

For the time was come — and the whiskered count
Helped his bride in the carriage to mount,
And fain would the Muse deny it,

But the crowd, including two butchers in blue,
(The regular killing Whitechapel hue,)
Of her Precious Calf had as ample a view,
As if they had come to buy it!

Then away! away! with all the speed
That golden spurs can give to the steed, —
Both yellow boys and guineas, indeed,
Concurred to urge the cattle, —
Away they went, with favors white,
Yellow jackets, and pannels bright,
And left the mob, like a mob at night,
Agape at the sound of a rattle.

Away! away! they rattled and rolled,
The count, and his bride, and her Leg of Gold —
That faded charm to the charmer!
Away, — through Old Brentford rang the din,
Of wheels and heels, on their way to win
That hill, named after one of her kin
The Hill of the Golden Farmer!

Gold, still gold — it flew like dust!
It tipped the post-boy, and paid the trust;
In each open palm it was freely thrust;
There was nothing but giving and taking!
And if gold could insure the future hour,
What hopes attended that bride to her bower;
But, alas! even hearts with a four-horse power
Of opulence end in breaking!

Her Honeymoon.

The moon — the moon, so silver and cold,
Her fickle temper has oft been told,
Now shady — now bright and sunny —
But, of all the lunar things that change,
The one that shows most fickle and strange,

And takes the most eccentric range,
  Is the moon — so called — of honey!

To some a full-grown orb revealed,
As big and as round as Norval's shield,
  And as bright as a burner Bude-lighted;
To others as dull, and dingy, and damp,
As any oleaginous lamp,
Of the regular old parochial stamp,
  In a London fog benighted.

To the loving, a bright and constant sphere,
That makes earth's commonest scenes appear
  All poetic, romantic, and tender;
Hanging with jewels a cabbage-stump,
And investing a common post, or a pump,
A currant-bush or a gooseberry clump,
  With a halo of dreamlike splendor.

A sphere such as shone from Italian skies,
In Juliet's dear, dark, liquid eyes,
  Tipping trees with its argent braveries —
And to couples not favored with Fortune's boons
One of the most delightful of moons,
For it brightens their pewter platters and spoons
  Like a silver service of Savory's!

For all is bright, and beauteous, and clear,
And the meanest thing most precious and dear,
  When the magic of love is present:
Love, that lends a sweetness and grace
To the humblest spot and the plainest face —
That turns Wilderness Row into Paradise Place,
  And Garlic Hill to Mount Pleasant!

Love that sweetens sugarless tea,
And makes contentment and joy agree

With the coarsest boarding and bedding;
Love, that no golden ties can attach,
But nestles under the humblest thatch,
And will fly away from an emperor's match
To dance at a penny wedding!

O, happy, happy, thrice happy state,
When such a bright planet governs the fate
Of a pair of united lovers!
'Tis theirs, in spite of the serpent's hiss,
To enjoy the pure primeval kiss
With as much of the old original bliss
As mortality ever recovers!

There's strength in double joints, no doubt,
In double X Ale, and Dublin Stout,
That the single sorts know nothing about —
And a fist is strongest when doubled —
And double aqua-fortis, of course,
And double soda-water, perforce,
Are the strongest that ever bubbled!

There's double beauty whenever a swan
Swims on a lake, with her double thereon;
And ask the gardener, Luke or John,
Of the beauty of double-blowing —
A double dahlia delights the eye;
And it's far the loveliest sight in the sky
When a double rainbow is glowing!

There's warmth in a pair of double soles;
As well as a double allowance of coals —
In a coat that is double-breasted —
In double windows and double doors;
And a double U wind is blest by scores
For its warmth to the tender-chested.

There's two-fold sweetness in double-pipes;
And a double barrel and double snipes
  Give the sportsman a duplicate pleasure:
There's double safety in double locks;
And double letters bring cash for the box;
And all the world knows that double knocks
  Are gentility's double measure.

There's a double sweetness in double rhymes,
And a double at whist and a double Times
  In profit are certainly double —
By doubling, the hare contrives to escape:
And all seamen delight in a doubled cape,
  And a double-reefed topsail in trouble.

There's a double chuck at a double chin,
And of course there's a double pleasure therein,
  If the parties are brought to telling:
And, however our Dennises take offence,
A double meaning shows double sense;
    And if proverbs tell truth,
    A double tooth
  Is Wisdom's adopted dwelling!

But double wisdom, and pleasure, and sense,
Beauty, respect, strength, comfort, and thence
  Through whatever the list discovers,
They are all in the double blessedness summed
Of what was formerly double-drummed,
  The marriage of two true lovers!

Now the Kilmansegg moon — it must be told —
Though instead of silver it tipped with gold —
Shone rather wan, and distant, and cold,
  And, before its days were at thirty,
Such gloomy clouds began to collect,

With an ominous ring of ill effect,
As gave but too much cause to expect
 Such weather as seamen call dirty!

And yet the moon was the "young May moon,"
And the scented hawthorn had blossomed soon,
 And the thrush and the blackbird were singing—
The snow-white lambs were skipping in play,
And the bee was humming a tune all day
To flowers as welcome as flowers in May,
 And the trout in the stream was springing!

But what were the hues of the blooming earth,
Its scents—its sounds—or the music and mirth,
 Or its furred or its feathered creatures,
To a pair in the world's last sordid stage,
Who had never looked into Nature's page,
And had strange ideas of a Golden Age,
 Without any Arcadian features?

And what were joys of the pastoral kind
To a bride—town-made—with a heart and mind
 With simplicity ever at battle?
A bride of an ostentatious race,
Who, thrown in the Golden Farmer's place,
Would have trimmed her shepherds with golden lace,
 And gilt the horns of her cattle.

She could not please the pigs with her whim,
And the sheep wouldn't cast their eyes at a limb
 For which she had been such a martyr:
The deer in the park, and the colts at grass,
And the cows, unheeded let it pass;
And the ass on the common was such an ass,
  That he wouldn't have swapped
  The thistle he cropped
 For her Leg, including the Garter!

She hated lanes, and she hated fields —
She hated all that the country yields —
  And barely knew turnips from clover:
She hated walking in any shape,
And a country stile was an awkward scrape,
Without the bribe of a mob to gape
  At the Leg in clambering over!

O blessed Nature, "O rus! O rus!"
Who cannot sigh for the country thus,
  Absorbed in a worldly torpor —
Who does not yearn for its meadow-sweet breath,
Untainted by care, and crime, and death,
And to stand sometimes upon grass or heath —
  That soul, spite of gold, is a pauper!

But to hail the pearly advent of Morn,
And relish the odor fresh from the thorn,
  She was far too pampered a madam —
Or to joy in the daylight waxing strong,
While, after ages of sorrow and wrong,
The scorn of the proud, the misrule of the strong,
And all the woes that to man belong,
The lark still carols the self-same song
  That he did to the uncurst Adam!

The Lark! she had given all Leipsic's flocks
For a Vauxhall tune in a musical box;
  And as for the birds in the thicket,
Thrush or ousel in leafy niche,
The linnet or finch, she was far too rich
To care for a morning concert to which
  She was welcome without any ticket.

Gold, still gold, her standard of old,
All pastoral joys were tried by gold,
  Or by fancies golden and crural —

Till ere she had passed one week unblest,
As her agricultural uncle's guest,
Her mind was made up and fully imprest
  That felicity could not be rural.

And the count? — to the snow-white lambs at play,
And all the scents and the sights of May,
  And the birds that warbled their passion,
His ears, and dark eyes, and decided nose
Were as deaf and as blind and as dull as those
That overlook the Bouquet de Rose,
      The Huile Antique,
      And Parfum Unique,
  In a barber's Temple of Fashion.

To tell, indeed, the true extent
Of his rural bias, so far it went
  As to covet estates in ring fences —
And for rural lore he had learned in town
That the country was green turned up with brown,
And garnished with trees that a man might cut down,
  Instead of his own expenses.

And yet, had that fault been his only one,
The pair might have had few quarrels or none,
  For their tastes thus far were in common;
But faults he had that a haughty bride
With a Golden Leg could hardly abide —
Faults that would even have roused the pride
  Of a far less metalsome woman!

It was early days indeed for a wife,
In the very spring of her married life,
  To be chilled by its wintry weather —
But, instead of sitting as love-birds do,
Or Hymen's turtles that bill and coo —

Enjoying their "moon and honey for two,"
  They were scarcely seen together!

In vain she sat with her Precious Leg
A little exposed, *à la* Kilmansegg,
  And rolled her eyes in their sockets!
He left her in spite of her tender regards,
And those loving murmurs described by bards,
For the rattling of dice and the shuffling of cards,
  And the poking of balls into pockets!

Moreover he loved the deepest stake
And the heaviest bets the players would make;
  And he drank — the reverse of sparely, —
And he used strange curses that made her fret;
And when he played with herself at piquet,
    She found, to her cost,
    For she always lost,
  That the count did not count quite fairly.

And then came dark mistrust and doubt,
Gathered by worming his secrets out,
  And slips in his conversations —
Fears, which all her peace destroyed,
That his title was null — his coffers were void —
And his French château was in Spain, or enjoyed
  The most airy of situations.

But still his heart — if he had such a part —
She — only she — might possess his heart,
  And hold his affections in fetters —
Alas! that hope, like a crazy ship,
Was forced its anchor and cable to slip,
When, seduced by her fears, she took a dip
  In his private papers and letters.

Letters that told of dangerous leagues;
And notes that hinted as many intrigues
  As the count's in the "Barber of Seville"—
In short, such mysteries came to light,
That the countess-bride, on the thirtieth night,
Woke and started up in affright,
And kicked and screamed with all her might,
And finally fainted away outright,
  For she dreamt she had married the Devil!

Her Misery.

Who hath not met with home-made bread,
A heavy compound of putty and lead—
And home-made wines that rack the head,
  And home-made liqueurs and waters?
Home-made pop that will not foam,
And home-made dishes that drive one from home,
    Not to name each mess,
    For the face or dress,
  Home-made by the homely daughters?

Home-made physic, that sickens the sick;
Thick for thin and thin for thick;—
In short, each homogeneous trick
  For poisoning domesticity?
And since our Parents, called the First,
A little family squabble nurst,
Of all our evils the worst of the worst
  Is home-made infelicity.

There's a golden bird that claps its wings,
And dances for joy on its perch, and sings
  With a Persian exultation:
For the sun is shining into the room,
And brightens up the carpet-bloom,

As if it were new, bran-new from the loom,
  Or the lone nun's fabrication.

And thence the glorious radiance flames
On pictures in massy gilded frames —
Enshrining, however, no painted dames,
  But portraits of colts and fillies —
Pictures hanging on walls which shine,
In spite of the bard's familiar line,
  With clusters of "gilded lilies."

And still the flooding sunlight shares
Its lustre with gilded sofas and chairs,
  That shine as if freshly burnished —
And gilded tables, with glittering stocks
Of gilded china, and golden clocks,
Toy, and trinket, and musical box,
  That Peace and Paris have furnished.

And, lo! with the brightest gleam of all
The glowing sunbeam is seen to fall
  On an object as rare as splendid —
The golden foot of the Golden Leg
Of the countess — once Miss Kilmansegg —
  But there all sunshine is ended.

Her cheek is pale, and her eye is dim,
And downward cast, yet not at the limb,
Once the centre of all speculation;
  But downward drooping in comfort's dearth,
As gloomy thoughts are drawn to the earth —
Whence human sorrows derive their birth —
  By a moral gravitation.

Her golden hair is out of its braids,
And her sighs betray the gloomy shades
  That her evil planet revolves in —

And tears are falling that catch a gleam
So bright as they drop in the sunny beam,
That tears of *aqua regia* they seem,
  The water that gold dissolves in!

Yet, not in filial grief were shed
  Those tears for a mother's insanity;
Nor yet because her father was dead,
For the bowing Sir Jacob had bowed his head
  To Death — with his usual urbanity;
The waters that down her visage rilled
Were drops of unrectified spirit distilled
  From the limbec of Pride and Vanity.

Tears that fell alone and uncheckt,
Without relief, and without respect,
Like the fabled pearls that the pigs neglect,
  When pigs have that opportunity —
And of all the griefs that mortals share,
The one that seems the hardest to bear
  Is the grief without community.

How blessed the heart that has a friend
A sympathizing ear to lend
  To troubles too great to smother!
For as ale and porter, when flat, are restored
Till a sparkling, bubbling head they afford,
So sorrow is cheered by being poured
  From one vessel into another.

But friend or gossip she had not one
To hear the vile deeds that the count had done,
  How night after night he rambled;
And how she had learned by sad degrees
That he drank, and smoked, and, worse than these,
  That he "swindled, intrigued, and gambled."

How he kissed the maids, and sparred with John;
And came to bed with his garments on;
  With other offences as heinous —
And brought *strange* gentlemen home to dine,
That he said were in the Fancy line,
And they fancied spirits instead of wine,
  And called her lap-dog "Wenus!"

Of "making a book" how he made a stir,
But never had written a line to her,
  Once his idol and Cara Sposa:
And how he had stormed, and treated her ill,
Because she refused to go down to a mill,
She didn't know where, but remembered still
  That the miller's name was Mendoza.

How often he waked her up at night,
And oftener still by the morning light,
  Reeling home from his haunts unlawful;
Singing songs that shouldn't be sung,
Except by beggars and thieves unhung —
Or volleying oaths, that a foreign tongue
  Made still more horrid and awful!

How oft, instead of otto of rose,
With vulgar smells he offended her nose,
  From gin, tobacco, and onion!
And then how wildly he used to stare!
And shake his fist at nothing, and swear, —
And pluck by the handful his shaggy hair,
Till he looked like a study of Giant Despair
  For a new edition of Bunyan!

For dice will run the contrary way,
As well is known to all who play,
  And cards will conspire as in treason:
And what with keeping a hunting-box,

Following fox —
Friends in flocks,
Burgundies, Hocks,
From London Docks;
Stultz's frocks,
Manton and Nock's
Barrels and locks,
Shooting blue rocks,
Trainers and jocks,
Buskins and socks,
Pugilistical knocks,
And fighting-cocks,
If he found himself short in funds and stocks,
These rhymes will furnish the reason!

His friends, indeed, were falling away —
Friends who insist on play or pay —
And he feared at no very distant day
To be cut by Lord and by Cadger,
As one who was gone or going to smash,
For his checks no longer drew the cash,
Because, as his comrades explained in flash,
"He had overdrawn his badger."

Gold! gold — alas! for the gold
Spent where souls are bought and sold,
In Vice's Walpurgis revel!
Alas! for muffles, and bulldogs, and guns,
The leg that walks, and the leg that runs,
All real evils, though Fancy ones,
When they lead to debt, dishonor, and duns,
Nay, to death, and perchance the Devil!

Alas! for the last of a Golden race!
Had she cried her wrongs in the market-place,
She had warrant for all her clamor —

For the worst of rogues, and brutes, and rakes,
Was breaking her heart by constant aches,
With as little remorse as the pauper who breaks
A flint with a parish hammer!

Her Last Will.

Now the Precious Leg, while cash was flush,
Or the count's acceptance worth a rush,
Had never excited dissension;
But no sooner the stocks began to fall,
Than, without any ossification at all,
The limb became what people call
A perfect bone of contention.

For altered days brought altered ways,
And instead of the complimentary phrase,
So current before her bridal—
The countess heard, in language low,
That her Precious Leg was precious slow,
A good 'un to look at, but bad to go,
And kept quite a sum lying idle.

That instead of playing musical airs,
Like Colin's foot in going up-stairs—
As the wife in the Scottish ballad declares—
It made an infernal stumping.
Whereas a member of cork, or wood,
Would be lighter and cheaper, and quite as good,
Without the unbearable thumping.

Perhaps she thought it a decent thing
To show her calf to cobbler and king,
But nothing could be absurder—
While none but the crazy would advertise
Their gold before their servants' eyes,

Who of course some night would make it a prize,
  By a shocking and barbarous murder.

But spite of hint, and threat, and scoff,
  The Leg kept its situation:
For legs are not to be taken off
  By a verbal amputation.
And mortals when they take a whim,
The greater the folly the stiffer the limb
  That stands upon it or by it —
So the countess, then Miss Kilmansegg,
At her marriage refused to stir a peg,
Till the lawyers had fastened on her leg,
  As fast as the law could tie it.

Firmly then — and more firmly yet —
With scorn for scorn, and with threat for threat,
  The proud one confronted the cruel:
And loud and bitter the quarrel arose,
Fierce and merciless — one of those,
With spoken daggers, and looks like blows,
  In all but the bloodshed a duel!

Rash, and wild, and wretched, and wrong,
Were the words that came from weak and strong,
  Till, maddened for desperate matters,
Fierce as tigress escaped from her den,
She flew to her desk — 'twas opened — and then,
In the time it takes to try a pen,
Or the clerk to utter his slow Amen,
  Her Will was in fifty tatters!

But the count, instead of curses wild,
Only nodded his head and smiled,
As if at the spleen of an angry child;

But the calm was deceitful and sinister!
A lull like the lull of the treacherous sea —
For Hate in that moment had sworn to be
The Golden Leg's sole Legatee,
And that very night to administer!

Her Death.

'Tis a stern and startling thing to think
How often mortality stands on the brink
Of its grave without any misgiving:
And yet, in this slippery world of strife,
In the stir of human bustle so rife
There are daily sounds to tell us that Life
Is dying, and Death is living!

Ay, Beauty the girl, and Love the boy,
Bright as they are with hope and joy,
How their souls would sadden instanter,
To remember that one of those wedding bells,
Which ring so merrily through the dells,
Is the same that knells
Our last farewells,
Only broken into a canter!

But breath and blood set doom at nought —
How little the wretched countess thought,
When at night she unloosed her sandal,
That the Fates had woven her burial-cloth,
And that Death, in the shape of a death's head moth,
Was fluttering round her candle!

As she looked at her clock of or-molu,
For the hours she had gone so wearily through
At the end of a day of trial —
How little she saw in her pride of prime

The dart of death in the hand of Time —
  That hand which moved on the dial!

As she went with her taper up the stair,
How little her swollen eye was aware
  That the Shadow which followed was double!
Or when she closed her chamber door,
It was shutting out, and forevermore,
  The world — and its worldly trouble.

Little she dreamt, as she laid aside
Her jewels — after one glance of pride —
  They were solemn bequests to Vanity —
Or when her robes she began to doff,
That she stood so near to the putting off
  Of the flesh that clothes humanity.

And when she quenched the taper's light,
How little she thought, as the smoke took flight,
That her day was done — and merged in a night
  Of dreams and duration uncertain —
    Or, along with her own,
    That a hand of bone
  Was closing mortality's curtain!

But life is sweet, and mortality blind,
And youth is hopeful, and Fate is kind
  In concealing the day of sorrow;
And enough is the present tense of toil —
For this world is, to all, a stiffish soil —
And the mind flies back with a glad recoil
  From the debts not due till to-morrow.

Wherefore else does the spirit fly
And bid its daily cares good-by,
  Along with its daily clothing?
Just as the felon condemned to die —

With a very natural loathing —
Leaving the sheriff to dream of ropes,
From his gloomy cell in a vision elopes,
To caper on sunny greens and slopes,
Instead of the dance upon nothing.

Thus, even thus, the countess slept,
While Death still nearer and nearer crept,
Like the Thane who smote the sleeping —
But her mind was busy with early joys,
Her golden treasures and golden toys,
That flashed a bright
And golden light
Under lids still red with weeping.

The golden doll that she used to hug!
Her coral of gold, and the golden mug!
Her godfather's golden presents!
The golden service she had at her meals,
The golden watch, and chain, and seals,
Her golden scissors, and thread, and reels,
And her golden fishes and pheasants!

The golden guineas in silken purse —
And the golden legends she heard from her nurse,
Of the Mayor in his gilded carriage —
And London streets that were paved with gold —
And the golden eggs that were laid of old —
With each golden thing
To the golden ring
At her own auriferous marriage!

And still the golden light of the sun
Through her golden dream appeared to run,
Though the night that roared without was one
To terrify seamen or gypsies —

While the moon, as if in malicious mirth,
Kept peeping down at the ruffled earth,
As though she enjoyed the tempest's birth,
  In revenge of her old eclipses.

But vainly, vainly the thunder fell,
For the soul of the sleeper was under a spell
  That time had lately embittered —
The count, as once at her foot he knelt —
That foot which now he wanted to melt!
But — hush! — 'twas a stir at her pillow she felt —
  And some object before her glittered.

'Twas the Golden Leg! — she knew its gleam!
And up she started, and tried to scream, —
  But even in the moment she started —
Down came the limb with a frightful smash,
And, lost in the universal flash
That her eyeballs made at so mortal a crash,
  The spark, called Vital, departed!

*   *   *   *   *

Gold, still gold! hard, yellow, and cold,
For gold she had lived, and she died for gold —
  By a golden weapon — not oaken;
In the morning they found her all alone —
Stiff, and bloody, and cold as stone —
But her Leg, the Golden Leg, was gone,
  And the "golden bowl was broken!"

Gold — still gold! it haunted her yet —
At the Golden Lion the inquest met —
  Its foreman, a carver and gilder —
And the jury debated from twelve till three
What the verdict ought to be,

And they brought it in as Felo-de-Se,
  "Because her own leg had killed her!"

Her Moral.

Gold! gold! gold! gold!
Bright and yellow, hard and cold,
Molten, graven, hammered and rolled;
Heavy to get, and light to hold;
Hoarded, bartered, bought, and sold,
Stolen, borrowed, squandered, doled:
Spurned by the young, but hugged by the old
To the very verge of the church-yard mould;
Price of many a crime untold:
Gold! gold! gold! gold!
Good or bad a thousand-fold!
  How widely its agencies vary —
To save — to ruin — to curse — to bless —
As even its minted coins express,
Now stamped with the image of good Queen Bess,
  And now of a Bloody Mary.

A MORNING THOUGHT.

No more, no more will I resign
  My couch so warm and soft,
To trouble trout with hook and line,
  That will not spring aloft.

With larks appointments one may fix
  To greet the dawning skies,
But hang the getting up at six
  For fish that will not *rise!*

LOVE AND LUNACY.

THE Moon — who does not love the silver moon,
In all her fantasies and all her phases?
Whether full-orbed in the nocturnal noon,
Shining in all the dew-drops on the daisies,
To light the tripping Fairies in their mazes,
While stars are winking at the pranks of Puck;
Or huge and red, as on brown sheaves she gazes;
Or new and thin when coin is turned for luck;—
Who will not say that Dian is a Duck?

But, O! how tender, beautiful and sweet,
When in her silent round, serene, and clear,
By assignation loving fancies meet,
To recompense the pangs of absence drear!
So Ellen, dreaming of Lorenzo, dear,
But distant from the city mapped by Mogg,
Still saw his image in that silver sphere,
Plain as the Man with lantern, bush, and dog,
That used to set our ancestors a-gog.

And so she told him in a pretty letter,
That came to hand exactly as Saint Meg's
Was striking ten — eleven had been better;
For then he might have eaten six more eggs,
And both of the bedevilled turkey-legs,
With relishes from East, West, North, and South,
Draining, beside, the teapot to the dregs.
Whereas a man whose heart is in his mouth,
Is rather spoilt for hunger and for drouth.

And so the kidneys, broiling hot, were wasted;
The brawn — it never entered in his thought;

The grated Parmesan remained untasted;
  The potted shrimps were left as they were bought,
  The capelings stood as merely good for nought,
The German sausage did not tempt him better,
  Whilst Juno, licking her poor lips, was taught
There's neither bone nor skin about a letter,
Gristle, nor scalp, that one can give a setter.

Heaven bless the man who first devised a mail!
  Heaven bless that public pile which stands concealing
The Goldsmiths' front with such a solid veil!
  Heaven bless the Master, and Sir Francis Freeling,
  The drags, the nags, the leading or the wheeling,
The whips, the guards, the horns, the coats of scarlet,
  The boxes, bags, those evening bells a-pealing!
Heaven bless, in short, each posting thing, and varlet,
That helps a Werter to a sigh from Charlotte.

So felt Lorenzo as he oped the sheet,
  Where, first, the darling signature he kissed,
And then, recurring to its contents sweet
  With thirsty eyes, a phrase I must enlist,
  He *gulped* the words, to hasten to their gist;
In mortal ecstasy his soul was bound—
  When, lo! with features all at once a-twist,
He gave a whistle, wild enough in sound
To summon Faustus's Infernal Hound!

Alas! what little miffs and tiffs in love,
  A snubbish word, or pouting look mistaken,
Will loosen screws with sweethearts hand and glove,
  O! love, rock firm when chimney-pots were shaken,
  A pettish breath will into huffs awaken,
To spit like hump-backed cats, and snarling Towzers!
  Till hearts are wrecked and foundered, and forsaken,

As ships go to Old Davy, Lord knows how, sirs,
While heaven is blue enough for Dutchmen's trousers!

"The moon's at full, love, and I think of you" —
Who would have thought that such a kind P. S.
Could make a man turn white, then red, then blue,
Then black, and knit his eyebrows and compress
His teeth, as if about to effervesce
Like certain people when they lose at whist!
So looked the chafed Lorenzo, ne'ertheless,
And, in a trice, the paper he had kissed
Was crumpled like a snowball in his fist!

Ah! had he been less versed in scientifics —
More ignorant, in short, of what is what —
He ne'er had flared up in such calorifics;
But he *would* seek societies, and trot
To Clubs — Mechanics' Institutes — and got
With Birkbeck — Bartley — Combe — George Robins — Rennie,
And other lecturing men. And had he not
That work, of weekly parts, which sells so many,
The Copper-bottomed Magazine — or "Penny?"

But, of all learnéd pools whereon, or in,
Men dive like dabchicks, or like swallows skim,
Some hardly damped, some wetted to the skin,
Some drowned like pigs when they attempt to swim,
Astronomy was most Lorenzo's whim,
('Tis studied by a Prince among the Burmans);
He loved those heavenly bodies which, the Hymn
Of Addison declares, preach solemn sermons,
While waltzing on their pivots like young Germans.

Night after night, with telescope in hand,
Supposing that the night was fair and clear,

Aloft, on the house-top, he took his stand,
  Till he obtained to know each twinkling sphere
  Better, I doubt, than Milton's "Starry Vere;"
Thus, reading through poor Ellen's fond epistle,
  He soon espied the flaw — the lapse so sheer
That made him raise his hair in such a bristle,
And like the Boatswain of the Storm-Ship, whistle.

"The moon's at full, love, and I think of thee," —
  "Indeed! I'm very much her humble debtor,
But not the moon-calf she would have me be.
  Zounds! does she fancy that I know no better?"
  Herewith, at either corner of the letter
He gave a most ferocious, rending pull; —
  "O woman! woman! that no vows can fetter,
A moon to stay for three weeks at the full!
By Jove! a very pretty cock-and-bull!

"The moon at full! 'twas very finely reckoned!
  Why so she wrote me word upon the first,
The twelfth, and now upon the twenty-second —
  Full! — yes — it must be full enough to burst!
  But let her go — of all vile jilts the worst" —
Here with his thumbs he gave contemptuous snaps,
  Anon he blubbered like a child that's nursed,
And then he hit the table frightful raps,
And stamped till he had broken both his straps.

"The moon's at full — and I am in her thought —
  No doubt: I do believe it in my soul!"
Here he threw up his head, and gave a snort
  Like a young horse first harnessed to a pole;
  "The moon is full — ay, so is this d—d bowl!"
And, grinning like the sourest of curmudgeons,
  Globe — water — fishes — he dashed down the whole,

Strewing the carpet with the gasping gudgeons;
Men do the strangest things in such love-dudgeons.

"I fill her thoughts — her memory's vicegerent?
  No, no — some paltry puppy — three weeks old —
And round as Norval's shield" — thus incoherent
  His fancies grew as he went on to scold;
  So stormy waves are into breakers rolled,
Worked up at last to mere chaotic wroth —
  This — that — heads — tails — thoughts jumbled uncontrolled,
As onions, turnips, meat, in boiling broth,
By turns bob up, and splutter in the froth.

"Fool that I was to let a baby face —
  A full one — like a hunter's — round and red —
Ass that I am, to give her more a place
  Within this heart" — and here he struck his head.
  "'Sdeath! are the almanac-compilers dead?
But no — 'tis all an artifice — a trick,
  Some newer face — some dandy underbred —
Well — be it so — of all the sex I'm sick!"
Here Juno wondered why she got a kick.

"'The moon is full' — where's her infernal scrawl?
  'And you are in my thought: that silver ray
Will ever your dear image thus recall' —
  My image? Mine! She'd barter it away
  For Pretty Poll's on an Italian's tray!
Three weeks, full weeks — it is too plain — too bad —
  Too gross and palpable! O cursèd day!
My senses have not crazed — but if they had —
Such moons would worry a Mad Doctor mad!

"O Nature! wherefore did you frame a lip
  So fair for falsehood? Wherefore have you dressed

Deceit so angel-like?" With sudden rip
He tore six new buff buttons from his vest,
And groped with hand impetuous at his breast,
As if some flea from Juno's fleecy curls
Had skipped to batten on a human chest;
But no — the hand comes forth, and down it hurls
A lady's miniature beset with pearls.

Yet long upon the floor it did not tarry,
Before another outrage could be planned:
Poor Juno, who had learned to fetch and carry,
Picked up and brought it to her master's hand,
Who seized it, and the mimic features scanned;
Yet not with the old loving ardent drouth,
He only saw in that fair face, so bland,
Look how he would at it, East, West, North, South,
A moon, a full one, with eyes, nose, and mouth.

"I'll go to her;" — herewith his hat he touched,
And gave his arm a most heroic brandish;
"But no — I'll write" — and here a spoon he clutched,
And rammed it with such fury in the standish,
A sable flood, like Niger the outlandish,
Came rushing forth. O Antics and Buffoons!
Ye never danced a caper so ran-tan-dish;
He jumped, thumped, tore — swore — more than ten dragoons,
At all nights, noons, moons, spoons, and pantaloons

But soon ashamed, or weary, of such dancing,
Without a Collinet's or Weippert's band,
His rampant arms and legs left off their prancing,
And down he sat again, with pen in hand,
Not fiddle-headed, or King's pattern grand,
But one of Bramah's patent Caligraphics;

And many a sheet it spoiled before he planned
A likely letter. Used to pure seraphics,
Philippics sounded strangely after Sapphics.

Long while he rocked like Yankee in his chair,
Staring as he would stare the wainscot through,
And then he thrust his fingers in his hair,
And set his crest up like a cockatoo;
And trampled with his hoofs, a mere Yahoo:
At last, with many a tragic frown and start,
He penned a billet, very far from doux,
'Twas sour, severe — but think of a man's smart
Writing with lunar caustic on his heart!

The letter done and closed, he lit his taper,
And sealing, as it were, his other mocks,
He stamped a grave device upon the paper,
No Cupid toying with his Psyche's locks,
But some stern head of the old Stoic stocks —
Then, fiercely striding through the staring streets,
He dropped the bitter missive in a box,
Beneath the cakes, and tarts, and sugared treats
In Mrs. Smelling's window-full of sweets.

Soon sped the letter — thanks to modern plans,
Our English mails run little in the style
Of those great German wild-beast caravans,
Eil-wagens — though they do not "go like *ile*," —
But take a good twelve minutes to the mile —
On Monday morning, just at ten o'clock,
As Ellen hummed "The Young May Moon" the while,
Her ear was startled by that double knock
Which thrills the nerves like an electric shock!

Her right hand instantly forgot its cunning,
And down into the street it dropped, or flung,

Right on the hat and wig of Mr. Gunning,
  The jug that o'er her ten-weeks-stocks had hung;
  Then down the stairs by twos and threes she sprung,
And through the passage like a burglar darted.
  Alas! how sanguine are the fond and young —
She little thought, when with the coin she parted,
She paid a sixpence to be broken-hearted!

Too dear at any price; had she but paid
  Nothing, and taken discount, it was dear;
Yet, worthless as it was, the sweet-lipped maid
  Oft kissed the letter in her brief career
  Between the lower and the upper sphere,
Where, seated in a study bistre-brown,
  She tried to pierce a mystery as clear
As *that* I once saw puzzling a young clown —
"Reading Made Easy," but turned upside down.

Yet Ellen, like most misses in the land,
  Had sipped sky blue through certain of her teens,
At one of those establishments which stand
  In highways, byways, squares, and village greens;
  'Twas called "The Grove," a name that always means
Two poplars stand like sentries at the gate —
  Each window had its close Venetian screens
And Holland blind, to keep in a cool state
The twenty-four Young Ladies of Miss Bate.

But when the screens were left unclosed by chance,
  The blinds not down, as if Miss B. were dead,
Each upper window to a passing glance
  Revealed a little dimity white bed;
  Each lower one a cropped or curly head;
And thrice a week, for soul's and health's economies,
  Along the road the twenty-four were led,

Like coupled hounds, whipped in by two she-dominies
With faces rather graver than Melpomene's.

And thus their studies they pursued: — On Sunday,
  Beef, collects, batter, texts from Dr. Price;
Mutton, French, pancakes, grammar — of a Monday;
  Tuesday — hard dumplings, globes, Chapone's Advice;
  Wednesday — fancy-work, rice-milk (no spice);
Thursday — pork, dancing, currant-bolsters, reading;
  Friday — beef, Mr. Butler, and plain rice:
Saturday — scraps, short lessons and short feeding,
Stocks, back-boards, hash, steel-collars, and good breeding.

From this repertory of female learning
  Came Ellen once a quarter, always fatter!
To gratify the eyes of parents yearning.
  'Twas evident in bolsters, beef, and batter,
  Hard dumplings, and rice-milk, she did not smatter,
But heartily, as Jenkins says, "demollidge;"
  But as for any learning, not to flatter,
As often happens when girls leave their college,
She had done nothing but grow out of knowledge.

At Long Division sums she had no chance,
  And History was quite as bad a balk;
Her French it was too small for Petty France
  And Priscian suffered in her English talk:
  Her drawing might be done with cheese or chalk;
As for the globes — the use of the terrestrial
  She knew when she went out to take a walk,
Or take a ride; but touching the celestial,
Her knowledge hardly soared above the bestial.

Nothing she learned of Juno, Pallas, Mars;
  Georgium, for what she knew, might stand for Burgo,

Sidus, for Master: then, for northern stars,
The Bear she fancied did in sable fur go,
The Bull was Farmer Giles's bull, and, ergo,
The Ram the same that butted at her brother;
As for the Twins, she only guessed that Virgo
From coming after them, must be their mother;
The Scales weighed soap, tea, figs, like any other.

As ignorant as donkeys in Gallicia,
She thought that Saturn, with his Belt, was but
A private, may be, in the Kent Militia:
That Charles's Wain would stick in a deep rut,
That Venus was a real West End slut —
O, gods and goddesses of Greek Theogony!
That Bernice's Hair would curl and cut,
That Cassiopëia's Chair was good Mahogany,
Nicely French-polished — such was her cosmogony!

Judge, then, how puzzled by the scientifics
Lorenzo's letter came now to dispense;
A lizard, crawling over hieroglyphics,
Knows quite as much of their Egyptian sense;
A sort of London fog, opaque and dense,
Hung over verbs, nouns, genitives, and datives.
In vain she pored and pored, with eyes intense,
As well is known to oyster-operatives,
Mere looking at the shells won't open natives.

Yet mixed with the hard words, so called, she found
Some easy ones that gave her heart the staggers;
Words giving tongue against her, like a hound
At picking out a fault — words speaking daggers
The very letters seemed, in hostile swaggers,
To lash their tails, but not as horses do,
Nor like the tails of spaniels, gentle waggers,

But like a lion's, ere he tears in two
A black, to see if he is black all through.

With open mouth, and eyeballs at full stretch,
  She gazed upon the paper sad and sorry,
No sound — no stir — quite petrified, poor wretch!
  As when Apollo, in old allegory,
  Down-stooping like a falcon, made his quarry
Of Niobe, just turned to Purbeck stone;
  In fact, since Cupid got into a worry,
Judge if a suing lover, let alone
A lawyer, ever wrote in such a tone.

" Ellen, I will no longer call you mine,
  That time is past, and ne'er can come again;
However other lights undimmed may shine,
  And undiminishing, one truth is plain,
  Which I, alas! have learned — that love can wane.
The dream has passed away, the veil is rent,
  Your heart was not intended for my reign;
A sphere so full, I feel, was never meant
With one poor man in it to be content.

" It must, no doubt, be pleasant beyond measure,
  To wander underneath the whispering bough
With Dian, a perpetual round of pleasure.
  Nay, fear not — I absolve of every vow —
  Use — use your own celestial pleasure now,
Your apogee and perigee arrange.
  Herschel might aptly stare and wonder how,
To me that constant disk has nothing strange —
A counterfeit is something hard to change.

" O Ellen! I once little thought to write
  Such words unto you, with so hard a pen;
Yet outraged love will change its nature quite,

And turn like tiger hunted to its den —
How Falsehood trips in her deceits on men!
And stands abashed, discovered, and forlorn!
Had it been only cusped — but gibbous — then
It had gone down — but Faith drew back in scorn,
And would not swallow it — without a horn!

"I am in occultation — that is plain:
My culmination's past — that's quite as clear.
But think not I will suffer your disdain
To hang a lunar rainbow on a tear.
Whate'er my pangs, they shall be buried here;
No murmur — not a sigh — shall thence exhale:
Smile on — and for your own peculiar sphere
Choose some eccentric path — you cannot fail,
And pray stick on a most portentous tail!

"Farewell! I hope you are in health and gay;
For me, I never felt so well and merry —
As for the bran-new idol of the day,
Monkey or man, I am indifferent — very!
Nor even will ask who is the Happy Jerry;
My jealousy is dead, or gone to sleep,
But let me hint that you will want a wherry,
Three weeks spring-tide, and not a chance of neap,
Your parlors will be flooded six feet deep!

"O Ellen! how delicious was that light
Wherein our plighted shadows used to blend,
Meanwhile the melancholy bird of night —
No more of that — the lover's at an end.
Yet if I may advise you, as a friend,
Before you next pen sentiments so fond,
Study your cycles — I would recommend

Our Airy — and let South be duly conned,
And take a dip, I beg, in the great Pond.

"Farewell again! it is farewell forever!
  Before your lamp of night be lit up thrice,
I shall be sailing, haply, for Swan River,
  Jamaica, or the Indian land of rice,
  Or Boothia Felix — happy clime of ice!
For Trebizond, or distant Scanderoon,
  Ceylon, or Java redolent of spice,
Or settling, neighbor of the Cape baboon,
Or roaming o'er — The Mountains of the Moon!

"What matters where? my world no longer owns
  That dear meridian spot from which I dated
Degrees of distance, hemispheres, and zones,
  A globe all blank and barren and belated.
  What matters where my future life be fated?
With Lapland hordes, or Koords or Afric peasant,
  A squatter in the western woods located,
What matters where? My bias, at the present,
Leans to the country that reveres the Crescent!

"Farewell! and if forever, fare thee well!
  As wrote another of my fellow-martyrs:
I ask no sexton for his passing-bell,
  I do not ask your tear-drops to be starters,
  However I may die, transfixed by Tartars,
By Cobras poisoned, by Constrictors strangled,
  By shark or cayman snapt above the garters,
By royal tiger or Cape lion mangled,
Or starved to death in the wild woods entangled,

"Or tortured slowly at an Indian stake,
  Or smothered in the sandy hot simoom,

Or crushed in Chili by earth's awful quake,
  Or baked in lava, a Vesuvian tomb,
  Or dirged by syrens and the billows' boom,
Or stiffened to a stock 'mid Alpine snows,
  Or stricken by the plague with sudden doom,
Or sucked by Vampyres to a last repose,
Or self-destroyed, impatient of my woes.

"Still fare you well, however I may fare,
  A fare perchance to the Lethean shore,
Caught up by rushing whirlwinds in the air,
  Or dashed down cataracts with dreadful roar:
  Nay, this warm heart, once yours unto the core,
This hand you should have claimed in church or minster,
  Some cannibal may gnaw" — she read no more —
Prone on the carpet fell the senseless spinster,
Losing herself, as 'twere, in Kidderminster!

Of course of such a fall the shock was great;
  In rushed the father, panting from the shop,
In rushed the mother, without cap or tête,
  Pursued by Betty Housemaid with her mop;
  The cook to change her apron did not stop,
The charwoman next scrambled up the stair —
  All help to lift, to haul, to seat, to prop,
And then they stand and smother round the chair,
Exclaiming in a chorus, "Give her air!"

One sears her nostrils with a burning feather,
  Another rams a phial up her nose;
A third crooks all her finger-joints together,
  A fourth rips up her laces and her bows,
  While all by turns keep trampling on her toes,
And, when she gasps for breath, they pour in plump,
  A sudden drench that down her thorax goes,

As if in fetching her — some wits so jump —
She must be fetched with water like a pump!

No wonder that thus drenched, and wrenched, and galled,
  As soon as possible, from syncope's fetter
Her senses had the sense to be recalled,
  "I'm better — that will do — indeed I'm better."
  She cried to each importunate besetter;
Meanwhile escaping from the stir and smother,
  The prudent parent seized the lover's letter,
(Daughters should have no secrets with a Mother,)
And read it through from one end to the other

From first to last, she never skipped a word —
  For young Lorenzo of all youths was one
So wise, so good, so moral she averred,
  So clever, quite above the common run —
  She made him sit by her, and called him son.
No matrimonial suit, e'en Duke's or Earl's,
  So flattered her maternal feelings — none!
For mothers always think young men are pearls
Who come and throw themselves before their girls.

And now, at warning signal from her finger,
  The servants most reluctantly withdrew,
But listening on the stairs contrived to linger;
  For Ellen, gazing round with eyes of blue,
  At last the features of her parent knew,
And summoning her breath and vocal powers,
  "O, mother!" she exclaimed — "O, is it true —
Our dear Lorenzo" — the dear name drew showers —
"*Ours*," cried the mother, "pray don't call him ours!

"I never liked him, never, in my days!"
  ["O yes — you did" — said Ellen with a sob,]

"There always *was* a something in his ways —
  [" So sweet — so kind," said Ellen, with a throb,]
  " His very face was what I call a snob,
And, spite of West End coats and pantaloons,
  He had a sort of air of the swell mob;
I'm sure when he has come of afternoons
To tea, I've often thought — I'll watch my spoons!"

"The spoons!" cried Ellen, almost with a scream,
  " O cruel — false as cruel — and unjust!
He that once stood so high in your esteem!"
  " He!" cried the dame, grimacing her disgust,
  " I like him? — yes — as any body must
An infidel that scoffs at God and Devil:
  Didn't he bring you Bonaparty's bust?
Lord! when he calls I hardly can be civil —
My favorite was always Mr. Neville.

" Lorenzo? — I should like, of earthly things,
  To see him hanging forty cubits high;
Doesn't he write like Captain Rocks and Swings?
  Nay, in this very letter bid you try
  To make yourself particular, and tie
A tail on — a prodigious tail! — O, daughter!
  And don't he ask you down his area — fie!
And recommend to cut your being shorter,
With brick-bats round your neck in ponds of water?"

Alas! to think how readers thus may vary
  A writer's sense! — What mortal would have thought
Lorenzo's hints about Professor Airy
  And Pond to such a likeness could be brought!
  Who would have dreamed the simple way he taught
To make a comet of poor Ellen's moon,
  Could furnish forth an image so distraught,

As Ellen, walking Regent Street at noon,
Tailed — like a fat Cape sheep, or a raccoon!

And yet, whate'er absurdity the brains
  May hatch, it ne'er wants wet-nurses to suckle it;
Or dry ones, like a hen, to take the pains
  To lead the nudity abroad, and chuckle it;
  No whim so stupid but some fool will buckle it
To jingle bell-like on his empty head,
  No mental mud—but some will knead and knuckle it,
And fancy they are making fancy-bread; —
No ass has written, but some ass has read.

No dolts could lead if others did not follow 'em.
  No Hahnémann could give decillionth drops
If any man could not be got to swallow 'em;
  But folly never comes to such full stops.
  As soon, then, as the Mother made such swaps
Of all Lorenzo's meanings, heads and tails,
  The Father seized upon her malaprops —
"My girl down areas — of a night! 'Ods nails!
  I'll stick the scoundrel on his area-rails!

"I will! — as sure as I was christened John!
  A girl — well born — and bred — and schooled at Ditton —
Accomplished — handsome — with a tail stuck on!
  And chucked — Zounds! chucked in horseponds like a kitten;
  I wish I had been by when that was written!" —
And doubling to a fist each ample hand,
  The empty air he boxed with, à la Britton,
As if in training for a fight long planned,
With Nobody — for love — at No Man's Land!

"I'll pond — I'll tail him!" In a voice of thunder
He recommenced his fury and his fuss,
Loud, open-mouthed, and wedded to his blunder,
Like one of those great guns that end in buss.
"I'll teach him to write ponds and tails to us!"
But while so menacing this-that-and-t'others,
His wife broke in with certain truths, as thus:
"Men are not women — fathers can't be mothers —
Females are females" — and a few such others.

So saying, with rough nudges, willy-nilly,
She hustled him outside the chamber-door,
Looking, it must be owned, a little silly;
And then she did as the Carinthian boor
Serves (Goldsmith says) the traveller that's poor:
Id est, she shut him in the outer space,
With just as much apology — no more —
As Boreas would present in such a case,
For slamming the street door right in your face.

And now the secrets of the sex thus kept,
What passed in that important tête-à-tête
'Twixt dam and daughter, nobody except
Paul Pry, or his Twin Brother, could narrate —
So turn we to Lorenzo, left of late
In front of Mrs. Snelling's sugared snacks,
In such a very waspish stinging state —
But now at the Old Dragon, stretched on racks,
Fretting, and biting down his nails to tacks;

Because that new fast four-inside — the Comet,
Instead of keeping its appointed time,
But deviated some few minutes from it,
A thing with all astronomers a crime,
And he had studied in that lore sublime;

Nor did his heat get any less or shorter
  For pouring upon passion's unslacked lime
A well-grown glass of Cogniac and water,
Mixed stiff as starch by the Old Dragon's daughter.

At length, " Fair Ellen " sounding with a flourish,
  The Comet came all bright, bran new, and smart:
Meanwhile the melody conspired to nourish
  The hasty spirit in Lorenzo's heart,
  And soon upon the roof he "topped his part,"
Which never had a more impatient man on,
  Wishing devoutly that the steeds would start
Like lightning greased — or, as at Ballyshannon
Sublimed, " greased lightning shot out of a cannon!"

For, ever since the letter left his hand,
  His mind had been in vascillating motion,
Dodge-dodging like a flustered crab on land,
  That cannot ask its way, and has no notion
  If right or left leads to the German Ocean —
Hatred and Love by turns enjoyed monopolies,
  Till, like a Doctor following his own potion,
Before a learned pig could spell Acropolis,
He went and booked himself for our metropolis.

"O, for a horse," or rather four — "with wings!"
  For so he put his wish into the plural —
No relish he retained for country things,
  He could not join felicity with rural,
  His thoughts were all with London and the mural,
Where architects — not paupers — heap and *pile* stones:
  Or with the horses' muscles, called the crural,
How fast they could macadamize the milestones
Which passed as tediously as gall or bile stones.

Blind to the picturesque, he ne'er perceived
  In Nature one artistical fine stroke;
For instance, how that purple hill relieved
  The beggar-woman in the gypsy-poke,
  And how the red cow carried off her cloak;
Or how the aged horse, so gaunt and gray,
  Threw off a noble mass of beech and oak!
Or how the tinker's ass, beside the way,
Came boldly out from a white cloud — to bray!

Such things have no delight for worried men,
  That travel full of care and anxious smart:
Coachmen and horses are your artists then;
  Just try a team of draughtsmen with the Dart,
  Take Shee, for instance, Etty, Jones, and Hart,
Let every neck be put into its noose,
  Then tip 'em on the flank to make 'em start,
And see how they will draw! — Four screws let loose
Would make a difference — or I'm a goose —

Nor cared he more about the promised crops,
  If oats were looking up, or wheat was laid,
For flies in turnips, or a blight in hops,
  Or how the barley prospered or decayed;
  In short, no items of the farming trade,
Peas, beans, tares, 'taters, could his mind beguile;
  Nor did he answer to the servant-maid,
That always asked at every other mile,
"Where do we change, sir?" with her sweetest smile.

Nor more he listened to the Politician,
  Who lectured on his left, a formal prig,
Of Belgium's, Greece's, Turkey's sad condition,
  Not worth a cheese, an olive, or a fig;
  Nor yet unto the critic, fierce and big,

Who, holding forth, all lonely, in his glory,
  Called one a sad bad Poet — and a Whig,
And one, a first-rate proser — and a Tory;
So critics judge, now, of a song or story.

Nay, when the coachman spoke about the 'Leger,
  Of Popsy, Mopsy, Bergamotte, and Civet,
Of breeder, trainer, owner, backer, hedger,
  And nags as right, or righter than a trivet,
  The theme his cracked attention could not rivet;
Though leaning forward to the man of whips,
  He seemed to give an ear — but did not give it,
For Ellen's moon (that saddest of her slips)
Would not be hidden by a "new Eclipse."

If any thought e'er flitted in his head
  Belonging to the sphere of Bland and Crocky,
It was to wish the team all thorough-bred,
  And every buckle on their backs a jockey:
  When spinning down a steep descent, or rocky,
He never watched the wheel, and longed to lock it,
  He liked the bolters that set off so cocky,
Nor did it shake a single nerve or shock it,
Because the Comet raced against the Rocket.

Thanks to which rivalry, at last the journey
  Finished an hour and a quarter under time,
Without a case for surgeon or attorney,
  Just as St. James's rang its seventh chime.
And now, descending from his seat sublime,
  Behold Lorenzo, weariest of wights,
  In that great core of brick, and stone, and lime,
Called England's Heart — but which, as seen of nights,
Has rather more the appearance of its lights.

Away he scudded — elbowing, perforce,
  Through cads, and lads, and many a Hebrew worrier,
With fruit, knives, pencils — all dirt cheap, of course,
  Coachmen, and hawkers, of the Globe and "Currier;"
  Away! the cookmaid is not such a skurrier,
When, fit to split her gingham as she goes,
  With six just striking on the clock to hurry her,
She strides along with one of her three beaux,
To get well placed at "Ashley's" — now Ducrow's.

"I wonder if the moon is full to-night!"
  He muttered, jealous as a Spanish Don,
When, lo! to aggravate that inward spite,
  In glancing at a board he spied thereon
  A play-bill for dramatic folks to con,
In letters such as those may read, who run,
  "'KING JOHN' — O yes — I recollect King John!
'My Lord, they say five moons' — *five* moons! well done!
I wonder Ellen was content with one!

"Five moons — all full! and all at once in heaven!
  She should have lived in that prolific reign!"
Here he arrived in front of number seven,
  The abode of all his joy and all his pain;
  A sudden tremor shot through every vein,
He wished he'd come up by the heavy wagon,
  And felt an impulse to turn back again,
O, that he ne'er had quitted the Old Dragon!
Then came a sort of longing for a flagon.

His tongue and palate seemed so parched with drouth —
  The very knocker filled his soul with dread,
As if it had a living lion's mouth,
  With teeth so terrible, and tongue so red,
  In which he had engaged to put his head.

The bell-pull turned his courage into vapor,
 As though 'twould cause a shower-bath to shed
Its thousand shocks, to make him sigh and caper —
He looked askance, and did not like the scraper.

"What business have I here? (he thought) a dunce
 A hopeless passion thus to fan and foster,
Instead of putting out its wick at once:
 She's gone — it's very evident I've lost her —
 And to the wanton wind I should have tossed her —
Pish! I will leave her with her moon, at ease,
 To toast and eat it, like a single Gloster,
Or cram some fool with it, as good green cheese,
Or make a honey-moon, if so she please.

"Yes — here I leave her;" and as thus he spoke,
 He plied the knocker with such needless force,
It almost split the pannel of sound oak;
 And then he went as wildly through a course
 Of ringing, till he made abrupt divorce
Between the bell and its dumbfounded handle;
 While up ran Betty, out of breath and hoarse,
And thrust into his face her blown-out candle,
To recognize the author of such scandal.

Who, presto! cloak, and carpet-bag to boot,
 Went stumbling, rumbling, up the dark one pair,
With other noise than his whose "very foot
 Had music in't as he came up the stair:"
 And then with no more manners than a bear,
His hat upon his head, no matter how,
 No modest tap his presence to declare,
He bolted in a room, without a bow,
And there sat Ellen, with a marble brow!

Like fond Medora, watching at her window,
  Yet not of any Corsair bark in search —
The jutting lodging-house of Mrs. Lindo,
  "The Cheapest House in Town" of Todd and Sturch.
  The private house of Reverend Doctor Birch,
The public-house, closed nightly at eleven,
  And then that house of prayer, the parish church,
Some roofs and chimneys, and a glimpse of heaven,
Made up the whole look-out of Number Seven.

Yet something in the prospect so absorbed her,
  She seemed quite drowned and dozing in a dream;
As if her own beloved full moon still orbed her,
  Lulling her fancy in some lunar scheme,
  With lost Lorenzo, may be, for its theme —
Yet when Lorenzo touched her on the shoulder,
  She started up with an abortive scream,
As if some midnight ghost, from regions colder,
Had come within his bony arms to fold her.

"Lorenzo!" — "Ellen!" — then came "Sir!" and "Madam!"
  They tried to speak, but hammered at each word,
As if it were a flint for great MacAdam;
  Such broken English never else was heard,
  For like an aspen leaf each nerve was stirred,
A chilly tremor thrilled them through and through,
  Their efforts to be stiff were quite absurd,
They shook like jellies made without a due
  And proper share of common joiner's glue.

"Ellen! I'm come — to bid you — fare — farewell;"
  They thus began to fight their verbal duel;
"Since some more hap — hap — happy man must dwell — "
  "Alas — Loren — Lorenzo! — cru — cru — cruel!"

For so they split their words like grits for gruel.
At last the Lover, as he long had planned,
Drew out that once inestimable jewel,
Her portrait, which was erst so fondly scanned,
And thrust poor Ellen's face into her hand.

"There — take it, Madam — take it back, I crave,
The face of one — but I must now forget her;
Bestow it on whatever hapless slave
Your art has last enticed into your fetter —
And there are your epistles — there! each letter!
I wish no record of your vows' infractions;
Send them to South — or Children — you had better —
They will be novelties — rare benefactions
To shine in Philosophical Transactions!

"Take them — pray take them — I resign them quite!
And there's the glove you gave me leave to steal —
And there's the handkerchief, so pure and white,
Once sanctified by tears, when Miss O'Neill —
But no — you did not — cannot — do not feel
A Juliet's faith, that time could only harden!
Fool that I was, in my mistaken zeal!
I should have led you — by your leave and pardon —
To Bartley's Orrery, not Covent Garden!

"And here's the birth-day ring — nor man nor devil
Should once have torn it from my living hand;
Perchance 'twill look as well on Mr. Neville;
And that — and that is all — and now I stand
Absolved of each dissevered tie and band —
And so farewell, till Time's eternal sickle
Shall reap our lives; in this, or foreign land
Some other may be found for truth to stickle,
Almost as fair, and not so false and fickle!"

And there he ceased, as truly it was time;
  For of the various themes that left his mouth,
One half surpassed her intellectual climb:
  She knew no more than the old Hill of Howth
  About that "Children of a larger growth,"
Who notes proceedings of the F. R. S.'s;
  Kit North was just as strange to her as South,
Except the South the weathercock expresses;
Nay, Bartley's Orrery defied her guesses.

Howbeit some notion of his jealous drift
  She gathered from the simple outward fact
That her own lap contained each slighted gift;
  Though quite unconscious of his cause to act
  So like Othello, with his face unblacked;
"Alas!" she sobbed, "your cruel course I see
  These faded charms no longer can attract;
Your fancy palls, and you would wander free,
And lay your own apostasy on me!

"*I* false! — unjust Lorenzo! — and to *you!*
  O, all ye holy gospels that incline
The soul to truth, bear witness I am true!
  By all that lives, of earthly or divine —
  So long as this poor throbbing heart is mine —
I false! — the world shall change its course as soon
  True as the streamlet to the stars that shine —
True as the dial to the sun at noon,
True as the tide to 'yonder blessed moon'!"

And as she spoke, she pointed through the window,
  Somewhere above the houses' distant tops,
Betwixt the chimney-pots of Mrs. Lindo,
  And Todd and Sturch's cheapest of all shops
  For ribbons, laces, muslins, silks, and fops; —

Meanwhile, as she upraised her face so Grecian,
  And eyes suffused with scintillating drops,
Lorenzo looked, too, o'er the blinds Venetian,
To see the sphere so troubled with repletion.

"The Moon!" he cried, and an electric spasm
  Seemed all at once his features to distort,
And fixed his mouth, a dumb and gaping chasm —
  His faculties benumbed and all amort —
  At last his voice came, of most shrilly sort,
Just like a sea-gull's wheeling round a rock —
  "Speak! — Ellen! — is your sight indeed so short!
The Moon! — Brute! savage that I am, and block!
The Moon! (O, ye Romantics, what a shock!)
Why, that's the new Illuminated Clock!"

MORNING MEDITATIONS.

Let Taylor preach, upon a morning breezy,
How well to rise while nights and larks are flying;
For my part, getting up seems not so easy
        By half as *lying*.

What if the lark does carol in the sky,
Soaring beyond the sight to find him out —
Wherefore am I to rise at such a fly?
        I'm not a trout.

Talk not to me of bees and such-like hums,
The smell of sweet herbs at the morning prime;
Only lie long enough, and bed becomes
        A bed of *time*.

To me Dan Phœbus and his car are nought,
His steeds that paw impatiently about;
Let them enjoy, say I, as horses ought,
The first turn-out!

Right beautiful the dewy meads appear,
Besprinkled by the rosy-fingered girl;
What then, — if I prefer my pillow-beer
To early pearl?

My stomach is not ruled by other men's,
And, grumbling for a reason, quaintly begs
Wherefore should master rise before the hens
Have laid their eggs?

Why from a comfortable pillow start
To see faint flushes in the east awaken?
A fig, say I, for any streaky part,
Excepting bacon.

An early riser Mr. Gray has drawn,
Who used to haste the dewy grass among,
"To meet the sun upon the upland lawn," —
Well — he died young.

With charwomen such early hours agree,
And sweeps that earn betimes their bit and sup;
But I'm no climbing boy, and need not be
All up — all up!

So here I lie, my morning calls deferring,
Till something nearer to the stroke of noon; —
A man that's fond precociously of *stirring*,
Must be a spoon.

A TALE OF A TRUMPET.

"Old woman, old woman, will you go a-shearing?
Speak a little louder, for I'm very hard of hearing."
OLD BALLAD.

Of all old women hard of hearing,
The deafest, sure, was Dame Eleanor Spearing!
On her head, it is true,
Two flaps there grew,
That served for a pair of gold rings to go through;
But for any purpose of ears in a parley,
They heard no more than ears of barley.

No hint was needed from D. E. F.
You saw in her face that the woman was deaf:
From her twisted mouth to her eyes so peery,
Each queer feature asked a query;
A look that said, in a silent way,
"Who? and What? and How? and Eh?
I'd give my ears to know what you say!"
And well she might! for each auricular
Was deaf as a post — and that post in particular
That stands at the corner of Dyott-street now,
And never hears a word of a row!

Ears that might serve her now and then
As extempore racks for an idle pen;
Or to hang with hoops from jewellers' shops,
With coral, ruby, or garnet drops;
Or, provided the owner so inclined,
Ears to stick a blister behind;
But as for hearing wisdom or wit,
Falsehood, or folly, or tell-tale-tit,

Or politics, whether of Fox or Pitt,
Sermon, lecture, or musical bit,
Harp, piano, fiddle, or kit,
They might as well, for any such wish,
Have been buttered, done brown, and laid in a dish!
She was deaf as a post, — as said before, —
And as deaf as twenty similes more,
Including the adder, that deafest of snakes,
Which never hears the coil it makes.

She was deaf as a house — which modern tricks
Of language would call as deaf as bricks —
  For her all human kind were dumb;
  Her drum, indeed, was so muffled a drum,
  That none could get a sound to come,
Unless the Devil who had Two Sticks!
She was deaf as a stone — say one of the stones
Demosthenes sucked to improve his tones;
And surely deafness no further could reach
Than to be in his mouth without hearing his speech!
She was deaf as a nut — for nuts, no doubt,
Are deaf to the grub that's hollowing out —
As deaf, alas! as the dead and forgotten —
(Gray has noticed the waste of breath
In addressing the "dull, cold ear of death,")
Or the Felon's ear, that was stuffed with Cotton —
Or Charles the First, *in statue quo;*
Or the still-born figures of Madame Tussaud,
With their eyes of glass, and their hair of flax,
That only stare, whatever you "ax,"
For their ears, you know, are nothing but wax.

She was deaf as the ducks that swam in the pond,
And wouldn't listen to Mrs. Bond, —

As deaf as any Frenchman appears,
When he puts his shoulders into his ears:
And — whatever the citizen tells his son —
As deaf as Gog and Magog at one!
Or, still to be a simile-seeker,
As deaf as dog's-ears to Enfield's Speaker!

She was deaf as any tradesman's dummy,
Or as Pharaoh's mother's mother's mummy;
Whose organs, for fear of our modern sceptics,
Were plugged with gums and antiseptics.

She was deaf as a nail — that you cannot hammer
A meaning into, for all your clamor —
There never *was* such a deaf old Gammer!
    So formed to worry
    Both Lindley and Murray,
By having no ear for music or grammar!

Deaf to sounds, as a ship out of soundings,
Deaf to verbs, and all their compoundings,
Adjective, noun, and adverb, and particle,
Deaf to even the definite article —
No verbal message was worth a pin,
Though you hired an earwig to carry it in!

In short, she was twice as deaf as Deaf Burke,
Or all the deafness in Yearsley's Work,
Who, in spite of his skill in hardness of hearing,
    Boring, blasting, and pioneering,
    To give the dunny organ a clearing,
Could never have cured Dame Eleanor Spearing.

Of course the loss was a great privation,
For one of her sex — whatever her station —
And none the less that the dame had a turn

For making all families one concern,
And learning whatever there was to learn
In the prattling, tattling village of Tringham —
As who wore silk? and who wore gingham?
And what the Atkins's shop might bring 'em?
How the Smiths contrived to live? and whether
The fourteen Murphys all pigged together?
The wages per week of the Weavers and Skinners,
And what they boiled for their Sunday dinners?
What plates the Bugsbys had on the shelf,
Crockery, china, wooden, or delf?
And if the parlor of Mrs. O'Grady
Had a wicked French print, or Death and the Lady?
Did Snip and his wife continue to jangle?
Had Mrs. Wilkinson sold her mangle?
What liquor was drunk by Jones and Brown?
And the weekly score they ran up at the Crown?
If the cobbler could read, and believed in the Pope?
And how the Grubbs were off for soap?
If the Snobbs had furnished their room up stairs,
And how they managed for tables and chairs,
Beds, and other household affairs,
Iron, wooden, and Staffordshire wares;
   And if they could muster a whole pair of bellows?
In fact she had much of the spirit that lies
Perdu in a notable set of Paul Prys,
   By courtesy called Statistical Fellows —
A prying, spying, inquisitive clan,
Who had gone upon much of the self-same plan,
   Jotting the laboring class's riches;
And after poking in pot and pan,
   And routing garments in want of stitches,
Have ascertained that a working man
   Wears a pair and a quarter of average breeches!

But this, alas! from her loss of hearing
Was all a sealed book to Dame Eleanor Spearing;
  And often her tears would rise to their founts —
Supposing a little scandal at play
'Twixt Mrs. O'Fie and Mrs. Au Fait —
  That she couldn't audit the gossips' accounts.
'Tis true, to her cottage still they came,
And ate her muffins just the same,
And drank the tea of the widowed dame,
    And never swallowed a thimble the less
    Of something the reader is left to guess,
    For all the deafness of Mrs. S.,
Who *saw* them talk, and chuckle, and cough,
    But to *see* and not share in the social flow,
    She might as well have lived, you know,
    In one of the houses in Owen's Row,
Near the New River Head, with its water cut off!

    And yet the almond-oil she had tried,
    And fifty infallible things beside,
    Hot, and cold, and thick, and thin,
    Dabbed, and dribbled, and squirted in:
But all remedies failed; and though some it was clear
    (Like the brandy and salt
    We now exalt)
  Had made a noise in the public ear,
  She was just as deaf as ever, poor dear.

At last — one very fine day in June —
    Suppose her sitting,
    Busily knitting,
And humming she didn't quite know what tune,
  For nothing she heard but a sort of a whizz,
Which, unless the sound of a circulation,
Or of thoughts in the process of fabrication,

By a spinning-jennyish operation,
  It's hard to say what buzzing it is.
However, except that ghost of a sound,
She sat in a silence most profound —
The cat was purring about the mat,
But her mistress heard no more of that
Than if it had been a boatswain's cat;
And as for the clock the moments nicking,
The dame only gave it credit for ticking.
The bark of her dog she did not catch;
Nor yet the click of the lifted latch;
Nor yet the creak of the opening door;
Nor yet the fall of the foot on the floor —
But she saw the shadow that crept on her gown,
And turned its skirt of a darker brown.

And, lo! a man! a pedler? ay, marry,
With a little back-shop that such tradesmen carry,
Stocked with brooches, ribbons, and rings,
Spectacles, razors, and other odd things,
For lad and lass, as Autolycus sings;
A chapman for goodness and cheapness of ware
Held a fair dealer enough at a fair,
But deemed a piratical sort of invader
By him we dub the "regular trader,"
Who, luring the passengers in as they pass
By lamps, gay panels, and mouldings of brass,
And windows with only one huge pane of glass,
And his name in gilt characters, German or Roman,
If he isn't a pedler, at least is a showman!

However, in the stranger came,
And, the moment he met the eyes of the dame,
Threw her as knowing a nod as though
He had known her fifty long years ago;

And, presto! before she could utter "Jack" —
Much less "Robinson" — opened his pack —
  And then from amongst his portable gear,
With even more than a pedler's tact, —
(Slick himself might have envied the act) —
Before she had time to be deaf, in fact,
  Popped a trumpet into her ear.

"There, ma'am! try it!
You needn't buy it —
The last new patent — and nothing comes nigh it
For affording the deaf, at little expense,
The sense of hearing, and hearing of sense!
A real blessing — and no mistake,
Invented for poor humanity's sake;
For what can be a greater privation
Than playing dummy to all creation,
And only looking at conversation —
Great philosophers talking like Platos,
And members of Parliament moral as Catos,
And your ears as dull as waxy potatoes!
Not to name the mischievous quizzers,
Sharp as knives, but double as scissors,
Who get you to answer quite by guess
Yes for no, and no for yes."
("That's very true," says Dame Eleanor S.)

"Try it again! No harm in trying —
I'm sure you'll find it worth your buying.
A little practice — that is all —
And you'll hear a whisper, however small,
Through an Act of Parliament party wall, —
Every syllable clear as day,
And even what people are going to say —

I wouldn't tell a lie, I wouldn't,
But my trumpets have heard what Solomon's couldn't;
And as for Scott, he promises fine,
But can he warrant his horns, like mine,
Never to hear what a lady shouldn't?—
Only a guinea — and can't take less."
("That's very dear," says Dame Eleanor S.)

"Dear! — O dear, to call it dear!
Why it isn't a horn you buy, but an ear;
Only think, and you'll find on reflection
You're bargaining, ma'am, for the Voice of Affection;
For the language of Wisdom, and Virtue, and Truth,
And the sweet little innocent prattle of youth;
Not to mention the striking of clocks —
Cackle of hens — crowing of cocks —
Lowing of cow, and bull, and ox —
Bleating of pretty pastoral flocks —
Murmur of waterfall over the rocks —
Every sound that Echo mocks —
Vocals, fiddles, and musical-box —
And, zounds! to call such a concert dear!
But I mustn't swear with my horn in your ear.
Why, in buying that trumpet you buy all those
That Harper, or any trumpeter, blows
At the Queen's levees, or the Lord Mayor's shows,
At least as far as the music goes,
Including the wonderful lively sound
Of the Guards' key-bugles all the year round.
Come — suppose we call it a pound!
Come," said the talkative man of the pack,
"Before I put my box on my back,
For this elegant, useful conductor of sound,
Come — suppose we call it a pound!

"Only a pound! it's only the price
Of hearing a concert once or twice,
It's only the fee
You might give Mr. C.,
And after all not hear his advice,
But common prudence would bid you stump it;
For, not to enlarge,
It's the regular charge
At a fancy fair for a penny trumpet.
Lord! what's a pound to the blessing of hearing!"
("A pound's a pound," said Dame Eleanor Spearing.)

"Try it again! no harm in trying!
A pound's a pound, there's no denying;
But think what thousands and thousands of pounds
We pay for nothing but hearing sounds;
Sounds of equity, justice, and law,
Parliamentary jabber and jaw,
Pious cant and moral saw,
Hocus-pocus, and Nong-tong-paw,
And empty sounds not worth a straw;
Why, it costs a guinea, as I'm a sinner,
To hear the sounds at a public dinner;
One-pound-one thrown into the puddle,
To listen to fiddle, faddle and fuddle!
Not to forget the sounds we buy
From those who sell their sounds so high,
That, unless the managers pitch it strong,
To get a signora to warble a song
You must fork out the blunt with a haymaker's prong.

"It's not the thing for me — I know it —
To crack my own trumpet up and blow it;
But it is the best, and time will show it.

There was Mrs. F.
So very deaf,
That she might have worn a percussion-cap,
And been knocked on the head without hearing it snap.
Well, I sold her a horn, and the very next day
She heard from her husband at Botany Bay!
Come — eighteen shillings — that's very low,
You'll save the money as shillings go, —
And I never knew so bad a lot, —
By hearing whether they ring or not!
Eighteen shillings! it's worth the price,
Supposing you're delicate-minded and nice,
To have the medical man of your choice,
Instead of the one with the strongest voice —
Who comes and asks you how's your liver,
And where you ache, and whether you shiver,
And as to your nerves so apt to quiver,
As if he was hailing a boat on the river!
And then, with a shout, like Pat in a riot,
Tells you to keep yourself perfectly quiet!

"Or a tradesman comes — as tradesmen will —
Short and crusty about his bill,
Of patience, indeed, a perfect scorner,
And because you're deaf and unable to pay,
Shouts whatever he has to say,
In a vulgar voice, that goes over the way,
Down the street and round the corner!
Come — speak your mind — it's 'No or Yes.'"
("I've half a mind," said Dame Eleanor S.)

"Try it again — no harm in trying;
Of course you hear me, as easy as lying;
No pain at all, like a surgical trick,
To make you squall, and struggle, and kick,

Like Juno, or Rose,
Whose ear undergoes
Such horrid tugs at membrane and gristle,
For being as deaf as yourself to a whistle!

"You may go to surgical chaps, if you choose,
Who will blow up your tubes like copper flues,
Or cut your tonsils right away,
As you'd shell out your almonds for Christmas-day;
And after all a matter of doubt,
Whether you ever would hear the shout
Of the little blackguards that bawl about,
'There you go with your tonsils out!'
Why, I knew a deaf Welshman who came from Glamorgan
On purpose to try a surgical spell,
And paid a guinea, and might as well
Have called a monkey into his organ!
For the Aurist only took a mug,
And poured in his ear some acoustical drug,
That, instead of curing, deafened him rather,
As Hamlet's uncle served Hamlet's father!
That's the way with your surgical gentry!
And happy your luck
If you don't get stuck
Through your liver and lights at a royal entry,
Because you never answered the sentry!

"Try it again, dear madam, try it!
Many would sell their beds to buy it.
I warrant you often wake up in the night,
Ready to shake to a jelly with fright,
And up you must get to strike a light,
And down you go in you know not what,
Whether the weather is chilly or not,—

That's the way a cold is got,—
To see if you heard a noise or not!

"Why, bless you, a woman with organs like yours
Is hardly safe to step out of doors!
Just fancy a horse that comes full pelt,
But as quiet as if he was 'shod with felt,'
Till he rushes against you with all his force,
And then I needn't describe, of course,
While he kicks you about without remorse,
How awkward it is to be groomed by a horse!
Or a bullock comes, as mad as King Lear,
And you never dream that the brute is near,
Till he pokes his horn right into your ear,
Whether you like the thing or lump it,—
And all for want of buying a trumpet!

"I'm not a female to fret and vex,
But if I belonged to the sensitive sex,
Exposed to all sorts of indelicate sounds,
I wouldn't be deaf for a thousand pounds.
Lord! only think of chucking a copper
To Jack or Bob with a timber limb,
Who looks as if he was singing a hymn,
Instead of a song that's very improper!
Or just suppose in a public place
You see a great fellow a-pulling a face,
With his staring eyes and his mouth like an O,—
And how is a poor deaf lady to know—
The lower orders are up to such games—
If he's calling 'Green Peas,' or calling her names?"
("They're tenpence a peck!" said the deafest of dames.)

"'Tis strange what very strong advising,
By word of mouth or advertising,

By chalking on walls, or placarding on vans,
With fifty other different plans,
The very high pressure, in fact, of pressing,
It needs to persuade one to purchase a blessing!
Whether the Soothing American Syrup,
A Safety Hat or a Safety Stirrup, —
Infallible Pills for the human frame,
Or Rowland's O-don't-o (an ominous name!)
A Doudney's suit which the shape so hits
That it beats all others into *fits;*
A Mechi's razor for beards unshorn,
Or a Ghost-of-a-Whisper-Catching Horn!

"Try it again, ma'am, only try!"
Was still the voluble pedler's cry;
"It's a great privation, there's no dispute,
To live like the dumb unsociable brute,
And to hear no more of the *pro* and *con,*
And how society's going on,
Than Mumbo Jumbo or Prester John,
And all for want of this *sine quâ non;*
  Whereas, with a horn that never offends,
You may join the genteelest party that is,
And enjoy all the scandal, and gossip, and quiz,
  And be certain to hear of your absent friends; —
Not that elegant ladies, in fact,
In genteel society ever detract,
Or lend a brush when a friend is blacked,
At least as a mere malicious act, —
But only talk scandal for fear some fool
Should think they were bred at *charity* school.
  Or, maybe, you like a little flirtation,
Which even the most Don Juanish rake
Would surely object to undertake
  At the same high pitch as an altercation.

It's not for me, of course, to judge
How much a deaf lady ought to begrudge;
But half-a-guinea seems no great matter —
Letting alone more rational patter —
Only to hear a parrot chatter;
Not to mention that feathered wit,
The starling, who speaks when his tongue is slit;
The pies and jays that utter words,
And other Dicky Gossips of birds,
That talk with as much good sense and decorum
As many *Beaks* who belong to the quorum.

"Try it — buy it — say ten-and-six,
The lowest price a miser could fix:
I don't pretend with horns of mine,
Like some in the advertising line,
To '*magnify sounds*' on such marvellous scales,
That the sounds of a cod seem as big as a whale's;
But popular rumors, right or wrong, —
Charity sermons, short or long, —
Lecture, speech, concerto, or song,
All noises and voices, feeble or strong,
From the hum of a gnat to the clash of a gong,
This tube will deliver, distinct and clear;
    Or supposing by chance
    You wish to dance,
Why, it's putting a *Horn-pipe* into your ear!
    Try it — buy it!
    Buy it — try it!
The last new patent, and nothing comes nigh it,
  For guiding sounds to proper tunnel:
Only try till the end of June,
And if you and the trumpet are out of tune,
  I'll turn it gratis into a funnel!"

In short, the pedler so beset her, —
Lord Bacon couldn't have gammoned her better, —
With flatteries plump and indirect,
And plied his tongue with such effect, —
A tongue that could almost have buttered a crumpet, —
The deaf old woman bought the trumpet.

* * * * * *

* * * * * *

The pedler was gone. With the horn's assistance,
She heard his steps die away in the distance;
And then she heard the tick of the clock,
The purring of puss, and the snoring of Shock!
And she purposely dropt a pin that was little,
And heard it fall as plain as a skittle!

'Twas a wonderful horn, to be but just!
Nor meant to gather dust, must, and rust:
So in half a jiffy, or less than that,
In her scarlet cloak and her steeple hat,
Like old Dame Trot, but without her Cat,
The gossip was hunting all Tringham thorough,
As if she meant to canvass the borough,
  Trumpet in hand, or up to the cavity: —
And, sure, had the horn been one of those
The wild rhinoceros wears on his nose
  It couldn't have ripped up more depravity!

Depravity! mercy shield her ears!
'Twas plain enough that her village peers
  In the ways of vice were no raw beginners;
For whenever she raised the tube to her drum,
Such sounds were transmitted as only come
  From the very brass band of human sinners!

Ribald jest and blasphemous curse,
(Bunyan never vented worse,)

With all those weeds, not flowers, of speech
Which the seven Dialecticians teach;
Filthy conjunctions, and dissolute nouns,
And particles picked from the kennels of towns,
With irregular verbs for irregular jobs,
Chiefly active in rows and mobs,
Picking possessive pronouns' fobs,
And interjections as bad as a blight,
Or an Eastern blast, to the blood and the sight;
Fanciful phrases for crime and sin,
And smacking of vulgar lips where gin,
Garlic, tobacco, and offals go in —
A jargon so truly adapted, in fact,
To each thievish, obscene, and ferocious act,
So fit for the brute with the human shape,
Savage baboon, or libidinous ape,
From their ugly mouths it will certainly come
Should they ever get weary of shamming dumb!

Alas! for the voice of Virtue and Truth,
And the sweet little innocent prattle of youth!
The smallest urchin whose tongue could tang
Shocked the dame with a volley of slang,
Fit for Fagin's juvenile gang;
While the charity chap,
With his muffin cap,
His crimson coat and his badge so garish,
Playing at dumps, or pitch in the hole,
Cursed his eyes, limbs, body, and soul,
As if they didn't belong to the parish!
'Twas awful to hear, as she went along,
The wicked words of the popular song;
Or supposing she listened — as gossips will —
At a door ajar, or a window agape,
To catch the sounds they allowed to escape,

Those sounds belonged to Depravity still!
The dark allusion, or bolder brag
Of the dexterous " dodge," and the lots of " swag,"
The plundered house — or the stolen nag —
The blazing rick, or the darker crime
That quenched the spark before its time —
The wanton speech of the wife immoral —
The noise of drunken or deadly quarrel, —
With savage menaces, which threatened the life,
Till the heart seemed merely a strop " for the knife ; "
The human liver, no better than that
Which is sliced and thrown to an old woman's cat ;
And the head, so useful for shaking and nodding,
To be punched into holes, like a " shocking bad hat "
That is only fit to be punched into wadding!

In short, wherever she turned the horn,
To the highly bred or the lowly born,
The working man who looked over the hedge,
Or the mother nursing her infant pledge,
The sober Quaker, averse to quarrels,
Or the governess pacing the village through,
With her twelve young ladies, two and two,
Looking, as such young ladies do,
Trussed by Decorum and stuffed with morals —
Whether she listened to Hob or Bob,
Nob or Snob,
The Squire on his cob,
Or Trudge and his ass at a tinkering job,
To the saint who expounded at " Little Zion " —
Or the " sinner who kept the Golden Lion " —
The man teetotally weaned from liquor —
The beadle, the clerk, or the reverend vicar —
Nay, the very pie in its cage of wicker —
She gathered such meanings, double or single,

That, like the bell
With muffins to sell,
Her ear was kept in a constant tingle!

But this was nought to the tales of shame,
The constant runnings of evil fame,
Foul, and dirty, and black as ink,
That her ancient cronies, with nod and wink,
Poured in her horn like slops in a sink:
While sitting in conclave, as gossips do,
With their Hyson or Howqua, black or green,
And not a little of feline spleen
Lapped up in "Catty packages," too,
To give a zest to the sipping and supping;
For still, by some invisible tether,
Scandal and tea are linked together,
As surely as scarification and cupping;
Yet never since Scandal drank Bohea—
Or sloe, or whatever it happened to be,
For some grocerly thieves
Turn over new leaves
Without much amending their lives or their tea—
No, never since cup was filled or stirred,
Were such vile and horrible anecdotes heard,
As blackened their neighbors of either gender,
Especially that which is called the Tender,
But instead of the softness we fancy therewith,
As hardened in vice as the vice of a smith.

Women! the wretches! had soiled and marred
Whatever to womanly nature belongs;
For the marriage tie they had no regard,
Nay, sped their mates to the sexton's yard,
(Like Madame Laffarge, who with poisonous pinches
Kept cutting off her L by inches)
And as for drinking, they drank so hard

That they drank their flat-irons, pokers, and tongs!
The men — they fought and gambled at fairs;
And poached — and didn't respect gray hairs —
Stole linen, money, plate, poultry, and corses;
And broke in houses as well as horses;
Unfolded folds to kill their own mutton,
And would their own mothers and wives for a button —
But not to repeat the deeds they did,
Backsliding in spite of all moral skid,
If all were true that fell from the tongue,
There was not a villager, old or young,
But deserved to be whipped, imprisoned, or hung,
Or sent on those travels which nobody hurries
To publish at Colburn's, or Longmans', or Murray's.

Meanwhile the trumpet, *con amore*,
Transmitted each vile diabolical story;
And gave the least whisper of slips and falls,
As that gallery does in the dome of St. Paul's,
Which, as all the world knows, by practice or print,
Is famous for making the most of a hint.
Not a murmur of shame,
Or buzz of blame,
Not a flying report that flew at a name,
Not a plausible gloss, or significant note,
Not a word in the scandalous circles afloat
Of a beam in the eye or diminutive mote,
But vortex-like that tube of tin
Sucked the censorious particle in;
And, truth to tell, for as willing an organ
As ever listened to serpent's hiss,
Nor took the viperous sound amiss,
On the snaky head of an ancient Gorgon!

The dame, it is true, would mutter "Shocking!"
And give her head a sorrowful rocking,

And make a clucking with palate and tongue,
Like the call of Partlet to gather her young, —
A sound, when human, that always proclaims
At least a thousand pities and shames,
  But still the darker the tale of sin,
Like certain folks when calamities burst
Who find a comfort in "hearing the worst,"
  The further she poked the trumpet in.
Nay, worse, whatever she heard, she spread
  East, and West, and North, and South,
Like the ball which, according to Captain Z.,
  Went in at his ear, and came out at his mouth.

What wonder, between the horn and the dame,
Such mischief was made wherever they came,
That the parish of Tringham was all in a flame!
  For although it requires such loud discharges,
Such peals of thunder as rumbled at Lear,
To turn the smallest of table beer,
A little whisper breathed into the ear
  Will sour a temper "as sour as varges."
In fact, such very ill blood there grew,
  From this private circulation of stories,
That the nearest neighbors, the village through,
Looked at each other as yellow and blue
As any electioneering crew
  Wearing the colors of Whigs and Tories.

Ah! well the poet said, in sooth,
That "whispering tongues can poison Truth,"
Yea, like a dose of oxalic acid,
Wrench and convulse poor Peace, the placid,
And rack dear Love with internal fuel,
Like arsenic pastry, or, what is as cruel,
Sugar of lead, that sweetens gruel;

At least such torments began to wring 'em
From the very morn
When that mischievous horn
Caught the whisper of tongues in Tringham.

The Social Clubs dissolved in huffs,
And the Sons of Harmony came to cuffs,
While feuds arose, and family quarrels,
That discomposed the mechanics of morals,
For screws were loose between brother and brother,
While sisters fastened their nails on each other:
Such wrangles, and jangles, and miff, and tiff,
And spar, and jar — and breezes as stiff
As ever upset a friendship or skiff!
The plighted lovers, who used to walk,
Refused to meet, and declined to talk;
And wished for *two* moons to reflect the sun,
That they mightn't look together on one;
While wedded affection ran so low,
That the oldest John Anderson snubbed his Jo —
And instead of the toddle adown the hill,
Hand in hand,
As the song has planned,
Scratched her, penniless, out of his will!

In short, to describe what came to pass
In a true, though somewhat theatrical way,
Instead of "Love in a Village" — alas!
The piece they performed was "The Devil to Pay!"

However, as secrets are brought to light,
And mischief comes home like chickens at night;
And rivers are tracked throughout their course,
And forgeries traced to their proper source; —
And the sow that ought
By the ear is caught, —

And the sin to the sinful door is brought;
And the cat at last escapes from the bag —
And the saddle is placed on the proper nag;
And the fog blows off, and the key is found —
And the faulty scent is picked out by the hound —
And the fact turns up like a worm from the ground
And the matter gets wind to waft it about;
And a hint goes abroad and the murder is out —
And the riddle is guessed — and the puzzle is known —
So the truth was sniffed, and the trumpet was *blown!*

* * * * *

'Tis a day in November — a day of fog —
But the Tringham people are all agog;
  Fathers, mothers, and mothers' sons, —
  With sticks, and staves, and swords, and guns, —
As if in pursuit of a rabid dog;
But their voices — raised to the highest pitch —
Declare that the game is "a Witch! — a Witch!"
Over the green and along by the George —
Past the stocks, and the church, and the forge,
And round the pound, and skirting the pond,
Till they come to the whitewashed cottage beyond,
And there at the door they muster and cluster,
And thump, and kick, and bellow, and bluster —
Enough to put old Nick in a fluster!
A noise, indeed, so loud and long,
And mixed with expressions so very strong,
That supposing, according to popular fame,
"Wise Woman" and Witch to be the same,
No hag with a broom would unwisely stop,
But up and away through the chimney-top;
Whereas, the moment they burst the door,
Planted fast on her sanded floor,

With her trumpet up to her organ of hearing,
Lo and behold! — Dame Eleanor Spearing!

O! then arises the fearful shout —
Bawled and screamed, and bandied about —
" Seize her! — drag the old Jezebel out!"
While the beadle — the foremost of all the band —
Snatches the horn from her trembling hand,
And after a pause of doubt and fear,
Puts it up to his sharpest ear.

" Now silence — silence — one and all!"
For the clerk is quoting from Holy Paul!
    But before he rehearses
    A couple of verses,
The beadle lets the trumpet fall;
For instead of the words so pious and humble,
He hears a supernatural grumble.

Enough, enough! and more than enough; —
Twenty impatient hands and rough,
By arm, and leg, and neck, and scruff,
Apron, 'kerchief, gown of stuff —
Cap, and pinner, sleeve, and cuff —
Are clutching the Witch wherever they can,
With the spite of woman and fury of man;
And then — but first they kill her cat,
And murder her dog on the very mat —
And crush the infernal trumpet flat; —
And then they hurry her through the door
She never, never, will enter more!

Away! away! down the dusty lane
They pull her and haul her, with might and main:
And happy the hawbuck, Tom or Harry,
Dandy, or Sandy, Jerry, or Larry,

Who happens to get a "leg to carry!"
And happy the foot that can give her a kick,
And happy the hand that can find a brick —
And happy the fingers that hold a stick —
Knife to cut, or pin to prick —
And happy the boy who can lend her a lick; —
Nay, happy the urchin — charity-bred —
Who can shy very nigh to her wicked old head!

Alas! to think how people's creeds
Are contradicted by people's deeds!
  But though the wishes that Witches utter
Can play the most diabolical rigs —
Send styes in the eye — and measle the pigs —
  Grease horses' heels — and spoil the butter;
Smut and mildew the corn on the stalk —
And turn new milk to water and chalk, —
Blight apples — and give the chickens the pip —
And cramp the stomach — and cripple the hip —
And waste the body — and addle the eggs —
And give a baby bandy legs;
Though in common belief a Witch's curse
Involves all these horrible things and worse —
As ignorant bumpkins all profess —
No bumpkin makes a poke the less
At the back or the ribs of old Eleanor S.!
  As if she were only a sack of barley;
Or gives her credit for greater might
Than the powers of darkness confer at night
  On that other old woman, the parish Charley;
Ay, now's the time for a witch to call
On her imps and suckings one and all —
Newes, Pyewacket, or Peck in the Crown,
(As Matthew Hopkins has handed them down)
Dick, and Willet, and Sugar-and-Sack,

Greedy Grizel, Jarmara the Black,
Vinegar Tom and the rest of the pack —
Ay, now's the nick for her friend Old Harry
To come "with his tail" like the bold Glengarry,
And drive her foes from their savage job
As a mad Black Bullock would scatter a mob: —
 But no such matter is down in the bond;
And spite of her cries that never cease,
But scare the ducks and astonish the geese,
 The dame is dragged to the fatal pond!

And now they come to the water's brim —
And in they bundle her — sink or swim;
Though it's twenty to one that the wretch must drown,
With twenty sticks to hold her down;
Including the help to the self-same end,
Which a travelling pedler stops to lend.
A pedler! — Yes! — The same! — the same!
Who sold the horn to the drowning dame!
And now is foremost amid the stir,
With a token only revealed to her;
A token that makes her shudder and shriek,
And point with her finger, and strive to speak —
But before she can utter the name of the Devil,
Her head is under the water level!

Moral.

There are folks about town — to name no names —
Who much resemble that deafest of dames;
 And over their tea, and muffins, and crumpets,
Circulate many a scandalous word,
And whisper tales they could only have heard
 Through some such Diabolical Trumpets!

NO!

No sun — no moon!
No morn — no noon —
No dawn — no dusk — no proper time of day —
No sky — no earthly view —
No distance looking blue —
No road — no street — no "t'other side the way" —
No end to any Row —
No indications where the Crescents go —
No top to any steeple —
No recognitions of familiar people —
No courtesies for showing 'em —
No knowing 'em!
No travelling at all — no locomotion,
No inkling of the way — no notion —
"No go" — by land or ocean —
No mail — no post —
No news from any foreign coast —
No park — no ring — no afternoon gentility —
No company — no nobility —
No warmth, no cheerfulness, no healthful ease,
No comfortable feel in any member —
No shade, no shine, no butterflies, no bees,
No fruits, no flowers, no leaves, no birds,
November!

THE IRISH SCHOOLMASTER.

ALACK! 'tis melancholy theme to think
How Learning doth in rugged states abide,
And, like her bashful owl, obscurely blink,

In pensive glooms and corners, scarcely spied;
Not, as in Founders' Halls and domes of pride,
Served with grave homage, like a tragic queen,
But with one lonely priest compelled to hide,
In midst of foggy moors and mosses green,
In that clay cabin hight the College of Kilreen!

This college looketh South and West alsoe,
Because it hath a cast in windows twain;
Crazy and cracked they be, and wind doth blow
Thorough transparent holes in every pane,
Which Dan, with many paines, makes whole again
With nether garments, which his thrift doth teach
To stand for glass, like pronouns, and when rain
Stormeth, he puts, "once more unto the breach,"
Outside and in, though broke, yet so he mendeth each.

And in the midst a little door there is,
Whereon a board that doth congratulate
With painted letters, red as blood I wis,
Thus written, "Chyldren taken in to Bate;"
And oft, indeed, the inward of that gate,
Most ventriloque, doth utter tender squeak,
And moans of infants that bemoan their fate
In midst of sounds of Latin, French, and Greek,
Which, all i'the Irish tongue, he teacheth them to speak.

For some are meant to right illegal wrongs,
And some for Doctors of Divinitie,
Whom he doth teach to murder the dead tongues,
And soe win academical degree;
But some are bred for service of the sea,
Howbeit, their store of learning is but small,
For mickle waste he counteth it would be

To stock a head with bookish wares at all,
Only to be knocked off by ruthless cannon-ball.

Six babes he sways, — some little and some big,
Divided into classes six ; — alsoe,
He keeps a parlor boarder of a pig,
That in the college fareth to and fro,
And picketh up the urchins' crumbs below, —
And eke the learned rudiments they scan,
And thus his A, B, C, doth wisely know, —
Hereafter to be shown in caravan,
And raise the wonderment of many a learned man.

Alsoe, he schools some tame familiar fowls,
Whereof, above his head, some two or three
Sit darkly squatting, like Minerva's owls,
But on the branches of no living tree,
And overlook the learned family ;
While, sometimes, Partlet, from her gloomy perch,
Drops feather on the nose of Dominie,
Meanwhile, with serious eye, he makes research
In leaves of that sour tree of knowledge — now a birch.

No chair he hath, the awful pedagogue,
Such as would magisterial hams imbed,
But sitteth lowly on a beechen log,
Secure in high authority and dread :
Large, as a dome for learning, seems his head,
And like Apollo's, all beset with rays,
Because his locks are so unkempt and red,
And stand abroad in many several ways : —
No laurel crown he wears, howbeit his cap is baize,

And, underneath, a pair of shaggy brows
O'erhang as many eyes of gizzard hue,
That inward giblet of a fowl, which shows

A mongrel tint, that is ne brow ne blue;
His nose, — it is a coral to the view;
Well nourished with Pierian potheen, —
For much he loves his native mountain dew; —
But to depict the dye would lack, I ween,
A bottle-red, in terms, as well as bottle-green.

As for his coat, 'tis such a jerkin short
As Spenser had, ere he composed his Tales;
But underneath he hath no vest, nor aught,
So that the wind his airy breast assails;
Below, he wears the nether garb of males,
Of crimson plush, but non-plushed at the knee: —
Thence further down the native red prevails,
Of his own naked fleecy hosierie: —
Two sandals, without soles, complete his cap-a-pie.

Nathless, for dignity, he now doth lap
His function in a magisterial gown,
That shows more countries in it than a map, —
Blue tinct, and red, and green, and russet brown,
Besides some blots, standing for country-town;
And eke some rents, for streams and rivers wide;
But, sometimes, bashful when he looks adown,
He turns the garment of the other side,
Hopeful that so the holes may never be espied!

And soe he sits, amidst the little pack,
That look for shady or for sunny noon,
Within his visage, like an almanack, —
His quiet smile foretelling gracious boon:
But when his mouth droops down, like rainy moon,
With horrid chill each little heart unwarms,
Knowing that infant showers will follow soon,

And with forebodings of near wrath and storms
They sit, like timid hares, all trembling on their forms.

Ah! luckless wight, who cannot then repeat
"Corduroy Colloquy," — or "Ki, Kæ, Kod," —
Full soon his tears shall make his turfy seat
More sodden, though already made of sod,
For Dan shall whip him with the word of God, —
Severe by rule, and not by nature mild,
He never spoils the child and spares the rod,
But spoils the rod and never spares the child,
And soe with holy rule deems he is reconciled.

But surely the just sky will never wink
At men who take delight in childish throe,
And stripe the nether-urchin like a pink
Or tender hyacinth, inscribed with woe;
Such bloody pedagogues, when they shall know,
By useless birches, that forlorn recess,
Which is no holiday, in Pit below,
Will hell not seem designed for their distress, —
A melancholy place, that is all bottomlesse?

Yet would the Muse not chide the wholesome use
Of needful discipline, in due degree.
Devoid of sway, what wrongs will time produce!
Whene'er the twig untrained grows up a tree,
This shall a Carder, that a Whiteboy be,
Ferocious leaders of atrocious bands,
And Learning's help be used for infamie,
By lawless clerks, that, with their bloody hands,
In murdered English write Rock's murderous commands.

But, ah! what shrilly cry doth now alarm
The sooty fowls that dozed upon the beam,

All sudden fluttering from the brandished arm
And cackling chorus with the human scream;
Meanwhile the scourge plies that unkindly seam
In Phelim's brogues, which bares his naked skin,
Like traitor gap in warlike fort, I deem,
That falsely lets the fierce besieger in,
Nor seeks the pedagogue by other course to win.

No parent dear he hath to heed his cries; —
Alas! his parent dear is far aloof,
And deep in Seven-Dial cellar lies,
Killed by kind cudgel-play, or gin of proof,
Or climbeth, catwise, on some London roof,
Singing, perchance, a lay of Erin's Isle,
Or, whilst he labors, weaves a fancy-woof,
Dreaming he sees his home, — his Phelim smile;
Ah, me! that luckless imp, who weepeth all the while!

Ah! who can paint that hard and heavy time,
When first the scholar lists in Learning's train,
And mounts her rugged steep enforced to climb,
Like sooty imp, by sharp posterior pain,
From bloody twig, and eke that Indian cane,
Wherein, alas! no sugared juices dwell?
For this, the while one stripling's sluices drain,
Another weepeth over chilblains fell,
Always upon the heel, yet never to be well!

Anon a third, for his delicious root,
Late ravished from his tooth by elder chit,
So soon is human violence afoot,
So hardly is the harmless biter bit!
Meanwhile, the tyrant, with untimely wit.
And mouthing face, derides the small one's moan,
Who, all lamenting for his loss, doth sit,

Alack, — mischance comes seldomtimes alone,
But ay the worried dog must rue more curs than one.

For, lo! the pedagogue, with sudden drub,
Smites his scald head, that is already sore, —
Superfluous wound, — such is Misfortune's rub!
Who straight makes answer with redoubled roar,
And sheds salt tears twice faster than before,
That still with backward fist he strives to dry;
Washing with brackish moisture, o'er and o'er,
His muddy cheek, that grows more foul thereby,
Till all his rainy face looks grim as rainy sky.

So Dan, by dint of noise, obtains a peace,
And with his natural untender knack,
By new distress, bids former grievance cease,
Like tears dried up with rugged huckaback,
That sets the mournful visage all awrack;
Yet soon the childish countenance will shine
Even as thorough storms the soonest slack,
For grief and beef in adverse ways incline,
This keeps, and that decays, when duly soaked in brine.

Now, all is hushed, and, with a look profound,
The Dominie lays ope the learned page;
(So be it called) although he doth expound
Without a book, both Greek and Latin sage;
Now telleth he of Rome's rude infant age,
How Romulus was bred in savage wood,
By wet-nurse wolf, devoid of wolfish rage,
And laid foundation-stone of walls of mud,
But watered it, alas! with warm fraternal blood.

Anon, he turns to that Homeric war,
How Troy was sieged like Londonderry town;

And stout Achilles, at his jaunting-car,
Dragged mighty Hector with a bloody crown:
And eke the bard, that sung of their renown,
In garb of Greece most beggar-like and torn,
He paints, with colly, wandering up and down:
Because, at once, in seven cities born;
And so, of parish rights, was, all his days, forlorn.

Anon, through old Mythology he goes,
Of gods defunct, and all their pedigrees,
But shuns their scandalous amours, and shows
How Plato wise, and clear-eyed Socrates,
Confessed not to those heathen he's and she's;
But through the clouds of the Olympic cope
Beheld St. Peter with his holy keys,
And owned their love was nought, and bowed to Pope,
Whilst all their purblind race in Pagan mist did grope.

From such quaint themes he turns, at last, aside,
To new philosophies, that still are green,
And shows what railroads have been tracked to guide
The wheels of great political machine;
If English corn should grow abroad, I ween,
And gold be made of gold, or paper sheet;
How many pigs be born to each spalpeen;
And, ah! how man shall thrive beyond his meat, —
With twenty souls alive to one square sod of peat!

Here he makes end; and all the fry of youth,
That stood around with serious look intense,
Close up again their gaping eyes and mouth,
Which they had opened to his eloquence,
As if their hearing were a three-fold sense.
But now the current of his words is done,
And whether any fruits shall spring from thence

In future time, with any mother's son!
It is a thing, God wot! that can be told by none.

Now by the creeping shadows of the noon,
The hour is come to lay aside their lore;
The cheerful pedagogue perceives it soon,
And cries "Begone!" unto the imps, — and four
Snatch their two hats and struggle for the door,
Like ardent spirits vented from a cask,
All blithe and boisterous, — but leave two more,
With Reading made Uneasy for a task,
To weep, whilst all their mates in merry sunshine bask.

Like sportive Elfins, on the verdant sod,
With tender moss so sleekly overgrown,
That doth not hurt, but kiss, the sole unshod,
So soothly kind is Erin to her own!
And one, at Hare and Hound, plays all alone, —
For Phelim's gone to tend his step-dame's cow;
Ah! Phelim's step-dame is a cankered crone!
Whilst other twain play at an Irish row,
And, with shillelah small, break one another's brow!

But careful Dominie, with ceaseless thrift,
Now changeth ferula for rural hoe;
But, first of all, with tender hand doth shift
His college gown, because of solar glow,
And hangs it on a bush, to scare the crow:
Meanwhile, he plants in earth the dappled bean,
Or trains the young potatoes all a-row,
Or plucks the fragrant leek for pottage green,
With that crisp curly herb, called Kale in Aberdeen.

And so he wisely spends the fruitful hours,
Linked each to each by labor, like a bee,

Or rules in Learning's hall, or trims her bowers;
Would there were many more such wights as he,
To sway each capital academie
Of Cam and Isis; for, alack! at each
There dwells, I wot, some dronish Dominie,
That does no garden work, nor yet doth teach,
But wears a floury head, and talks in flowery speech!

TO ——.

COMPOSED AT ROTTERDAM.

I GAZE upon a city, — a city new and strange;
Down many a watery vista my fancy takes a range:
From side to side I saunter, and wonder where I am;
And can *you* be in England, and *I* at Rotterdam!

Before me lie dark waters, in broad canals and deep,
Whereon the silver moonbeams sleep, restless in their
sleep;
A sort of vulgar Venice reminds me where I am;
Yes, yes, you are in England, and I'm at Rotterdam.

Tall houses with quaint gables, where frequent windows
shine,
And quays that lead to bridges, and trees in formal line,
And masts of spicy vessels from western Surinam,
All tell me you're in England, but I'm in Rotterdam.

Those sailors, how outlandish the face and form of each!
They deal in foreign gestures, and use a foreign speech;
A tongue not learned near Isis, or studied by the Cam,
Declares that you're in England, and I'm at Rotterdam.

And now across a market my doubtful way I trace,
Where stands a solemn statue, the Genius of the place;
And to the great Erasmus I offer my salaam,
Who tells me you're in England, but I'm at Rotterdam.

The coffee-room is open — I mingle in its crowd —
The dominos are noisy — the hookahs raise a cloud;
The flavor now of Fearon's, that mingles with my dram,
Reminds me you're in England, and I'm at Rotterdam.

Then here it goes, a bumper — the toast it shall be mine,
In scheidam, or in sherry, tokay, or hock of Rhine;
It well deserves the brightest, where sunbeam ever swam —
"The Girl I love in England" I drink at Rotterdam!

March, 1835.

LOVE.

O, Love! what art thou, Love? the ace of hearts,
  Trumping earth's kings and queens, and all its suits;
A player, masquerading many parts
  In life's odd carnival; — a boy that shoots,
From ladies' eyes, such mortal woundy darts;
  A gardener, pulling heart's-ease up by the roots;
The Puck of Passion — partly false — part real —
A marriageable maiden's "beau ideal"?

O, Love! what art thou, Love? a wicked thing,
  Making green misses spoil their work at school;
A melancholy man, cross-gartering!
  Grave ripe-faced Wisdom made an April fool?
A youngster, tilting at a wedding-ring?
  A sinner, sitting on a cuttie-stool?
A Ferdinand de Something in a hovel,
Helping Matilda Rose to make a novel?

O, Love! what art thou, Love? one that is bad
  With palpitations of the heart — like mine —
A poor bewildered maid, making so sad
  A necklace of her garters — fell design!
A poet, gone unreasonably mad,
  Ending his sonnets with a hempen line?
O, Love! — but whither, now? forgive me, pray;
I'm not the first that Love hath led astray.

THE SEASON.

SUMMER's gone and over!
  Fogs are falling down;
And with russet tinges
  Autumn's doing brown.

Boughs are daily rifled
  By the gusty thieves,
And the Book of Nature
  Getteth short of leaves.

Round the tops of houses,
  Swallows, as they flit,
Give, like yearly tenants,
  Notices to quit.

Skies, of fickle temper,
  Weep by turns, and laugh —
Night and Day together
  Taking half-and-half.

So September endeth —
  Cold, and most perverse —
But the month that follows
  Sure will pinch us worse!

FAITHLESS SALLY BROWN.

AN OLD BALLAD.

YOUNG Ben he was a nice young man,
  A carpenter by trade;
And he fell in love with Sally Brown,
  That was a lady's maid.

But as they fetched a walk one day,
  They met a press-gang crew;
And Sally she did faint away,
  Whilst Ben he was brought to.

The boatswain swore with wicked words,
  Enough to shock a saint,
That though she did seem in a fit,
  'Twas nothing but a feint.

"Come, girl," said he, "hold up your head,
  He'll be as good as me;
For when your swain is in our boat,
  A boatswain he will be."

So when they'd made their game of her,
  And taken off her elf,
She roused, and found she only was
  A coming to herself.

"And is he gone, and is he gone?"
  She cried, and wept outright:
"Then I will to the water side,
  And see him out of sight."

A waterman came up to her, —
  " Now, young woman," said he,
" If you weep on so, you will make
  Eye-water in the sea."

" Alas ! they've taken my beau, Ben,
  To sail with old Benbow ; "
And her woe began to run afresh,
  As if she'd said, Gee woe !

Says he, " They've only taken him
  To the Tender-ship, you see ; "
" The Tender-ship," cried Sally Brown,
  " What a hard-ship that must be !

" O ! would I were a mermaid now,
  For then I'd follow him ;
But, O ! — I'm not a fish-woman,
  And so I cannot swim.

" Alas ! I was not born beneath
  The virgin and the scales,
So I must curse my cruel stars,
  And walk about in Wales."

Now Ben had sailed to many a place
  That's underneath the world ;
But in two years the ship came home,
  And all her sails were furled.

But when he called on Sally Brown,
  To see how she got on,
He found she'd got another Ben,
  Whose Christian name was John.

"O, Sally Brown, O, Sally Brown,
  How could you serve me so?
I've met with many a breeze before,
  But never such a blow!"

Then reading on his 'bacco-box,
  He heaved a heavy sigh,
And then began to eye his pipe,
  And then to pipe his eye.

And then he tried to sing "All's Well,"
  But could not, though he tried;
His head was turned, and so he chewed
  His pigtail till he died.

His death, which happened in his berth,
  At forty-odd befell:
They went and told the sexton, and
  The sexton tolled the bell.

BIANCA'S DREAM.

A VENETIAN STORY.

BIANCA! — fair Bianca! — who could dwell
  With safety on her dark and hazel gaze,
Nor find there lurked in it a witching spell,
  Fatal to balmy nights and blessèd days?
The peaceful breath that made the bosom swell
  She turned to gas, and set it in a blaze;
Each eye of hers had Love's Eupyrion in it,
That he could light his link at in a minute.

So that, wherever in her charms she shone,
  A thousand breasts were kindled into flame;

Maidens who cursed her looks forgot their own,
  And beaux were turned to flambeaux where she came;
All hearts indeed were conquered but her own,
  Which none could ever temper down or tame:
In short, to take our haberdasher's hints,
She might have written over it, — "From Flints."

She was, in truth, the wonder of her sex,
  At least in Venice — where with eyes of brown,
Tenderly languid, ladies seldom vex
  An amorous gentle with a needless frown;
Where gondolas convey guitars by pecks,
  And love at casements climbeth up and down,
Whom, for his tricks and custom in that kind,
Some have considered a Venetian blind.

Howbeit, this difference was quickly taught,
  Amongst more youths who had this cruel jailer,
To hapless Julio — all in vain he sought
  With each new moon his hatter and his tailor;
In vain the richest padusoy he bought,
  And went in bran-new beaver to assail her —
As if to show that Love had made him *smart*
All over — and not merely round his heart.

In vain he labored through the sylvan park
  Bianca haunted in — that where she came
Her learned eyes in wandering might mark
  The twisted cipher of her maiden name,
Wholesomely going through a course of bark:
  No one was touched or troubled by his flame,
Except the Dryads, those old maids that grow
In trees, — like wooden dolls in embryo.

In vain complaining elegies he writ,
  And taught his tuneful instrument to grieve,

And sang in quavers how his heart was split,
  Constant beneath her lattice with each eve;
She mocked his wooing with her wicked wit,
  And slashed his suit so that it matched his sleeve,
Till he grew silent at the vesper star,
And, quite despairing, hamstringed his guitar.

Bianca's heart was coldly frosted o'er
  With snows unmelting — an eternal sheet;
But his was red within him, like the core
  Of old Vesuvius, with perpetual heat;
And oft he longed internally to pour
  His flames and glowing lava at her feet,
But when his burnings he began to spout,
She stopped his mouth, and put the *crater* out.

Meanwhile he wasted in the eyes of men,
  So thin, he seemed a sort of skeleton-key
Suspended at Death's door — so pale — and then
  He turned as nervous as an aspen-tree;
The life of man is three-score years and ten,
  But he was perishing at twenty-three,
For people truly said, as grief grew stronger,
" It could not shorten his poor life — much longer."

For why, he neither slept, nor drank, nor fed,
  Nor relished any kind of mirth below;
Fire in his heart, and frenzy in his head,
  Love had become his universal foe,
Salt in his sugar — nightmare in his bed,
  At last, no wonder wretched Julio,
A sorrow-ridden thing, in utter dearth
Of hope, — made up his mind to cut her girth!

For hapless lovers always died of old,
  Sooner than chew reflection's bitter cud;

So Thisbe stuck herself, what time 'tis told
  The tender-hearted mulberries wept blood :
And so poor Sappho, when her boy was cold,
  Drowned her salt tear-drops in a salter flood,
Their fame still breathing, though their breath be past,
For those old *suitors* lived beyond their last.

So Julio went to drown, — when life was dull,
  But took his corks, and merely had a bath ;
And once, he pulled a trigger at his skull,
  But merely broke a window in his wrath ;
And once, his hopeless being to annul,
  He tied a pack-thread to a beam of lath,
A line so ample, 'twas a query whether
'Twas meant to be a halter or a tether.

Smile not in scorn, that Julio did not thrust
  His sorrows through — 'tis horrible to die ;
And come down with our little all of dust,
  That dun of all the duns to satisfy ;
To leave life's pleasant city as we must,
  In Death's most dreary sponging-house to lie,
Where even all our personals must go
To pay the debt of nature that we owe !

So Julio lived : — 'twas nothing but a pet
  He took at life — a momentary spite ;
Besides, he hoped that time would some day get
  The better of love's flame, however bright.
A thing that time has never compassed yet,
  For love, we know, is an immortal light.
Like that old fire, that, quite beyond a doubt,
Was always in, — for none have found it out.

Meanwhile, Bianca dreamed — 'twas once when night
  Along the darkened plain began to creep,

Like a young Hottentot, whose eyes are bright,
  Although in skin as sooty as a sweep:
The flowers had shut their eyes — the zephyr light
  Was gone, for it had rocked the leaves to sleep,
And all the little birds had laid their heads
Under their wings — sleeping in feather beds.

Lone in her chamber sate the dark-eyed maid,
  By easy stages jaunting through her prayers,
But listening side long to a serenade,
  That robbed the saints a little of their shares;
For Julio underneath the lattice played
  His Deh Vieni, and such amorous airs,
Born only underneath Italian skies,
Where every fiddle has a Bridge of Sighs.

Sweet was the tune — the words were even sweeter,
  Praising her eyes, her lips, her nose, her hair,
With all the common tropes wherewith in metre
  The hackney poets overcharge their fair.
Her shape was like Diana's, but completer;
  Her brow with Grecian Helen's might compare.
Cupid, alas! was cruel Sagittarius,
Julio — the weeping waterman Aquarius.

Now, after listing to such laudings rare,
  'Twas very natural indeed to go —
What if she did postpone one little prayer! —
  To ask her mirror "if it was not so?"
'Twas a large mirror, none the worse for wear,
  Reflecting her at once from top to toe:
And there she gazed upon that glossy track,
That showed her front face, though it "gave her back."

And long her lovely eyes were held in thrall,
  By that dear page where first the woman reads:

That Julio was no flatterer, none at all,
  She told herself — and then she told her beads
Meanwhile, the nerves insensibly let fall
  Two curtains fairer than the lily breeds;
For sleep had crept and kissed her unawares,
Just at the half-way milestone of her prayers.

Then like a drooping rose so bended she,
  Till her bowed head upon her hand reposed;
But still she plainly saw, or seemed to see,
  That fair reflection, though her eyes were closed,
A beauty bright, as it was wont to be,
  A portrait Fancy painted while she dozed:
'Tis very natural, some people say,
To dream of what we dwell on in the day.

Still shone her face — yet not, alas! the same,
  But 'gan some dreary touches to assume,
And sadder thoughts with sadder changes came —
  Her eyes resigned their light, her lips their bloom,
Her teeth fell out, her tresses did the same,
  Her cheeks were tinged with bile, her eyes with rheum:
There was a throbbing at her heart within,
For, O! there was a shooting in her chin.

And, lo! upon her sad desponding brow
  The cruel trenches of besieging age,
With seams, but most unseemly, 'gan to show
  Her place was booking for the seventh stage;
And where her raven tresses used to flow,
  Some locks that time had left her in his rage,
And some mock ringlets, made her forehead shady,
A compound (like our Psalms) of tête and braidy.

Then for her shape — alas! how Saturn wrecks,
  And bends, and corkscrews all the frame about,

Doubles the hams, and crooks the straightest necks,
Draws in the nape, and pushes forth the snout,
Makes backs and stomachs concave or convex :
Witness those pensioners called In and Out,
Who, all day watching first and second rater,
Quaintly unbend themselves — but grow no straighter

So time with fair Bianca dealt, and made
Her shape a bow, that once was like an arrow;
His iron hand upon her spine he laid,
And twisted all awry her "winsome marrow."
In truth it was a change! — she had obeyed
The holy Pope before her chest grew narrow,
But spectacles and palsy seemed to make her
Something between a Glassite and a Quaker.

Her grief and gall meanwhile were quite extreme,
And she had ample reason for her trouble;
For what sad maiden can endure to seem
Set in for singleness, though growing double?
The fancy maddened her; but now the dream,
Grown thin by getting bigger, like a bubble,
Burst, — but still left some fragments of its size,
That, like the soap-suds, smarted, in her eyes.

And here — just here — as she began to heed
The real world, her clock chimed out its score;
A clock it was of the Venetian breed,
That cried the hour from one to twenty-four.
The works moreover standing in some need
Of workmanship, it struck some dozens more;
A warning voice that clenched Bianca's fears,
Such strokes referring doubtless to her years.

At fifteen chimes she was but half a nun,
By twenty she had quite renounced the veil;

She thought of Julio just at twenty-one,
And thirty made her very sad and pale,
To paint that ruin where her charms would run;
At forty all the maid began to fail,
And thought no higher, as the late dream crossed her,
Of single blessedness, than single Gloster.

And so Bianca changed; — the next sweet even,
With Julio in a black Venetian bark,
Rowed slow and stealthily — the hour, eleven,
Just sounding from the tower old St. Mark,
She sate with eyes turned quietly to heaven,
Perchance rejoicing in the grateful dark
That veiled her blushing cheek, — for Julio brought her
Of course — to break the ice upon the water.

But what a puzzle is one's serious mind
To open! — oysters, when the ice is thick,
Are not so difficult and disinclined;
And Julio felt the declaration stick
About his throat in a most awful kind;
However, he contrived by bits to pick
His trouble forth, — much like a rotten cork
Groped from a long-necked bottle with a fork.

But Love is still the quickest of all readers;
And Julio spent, besides those signs profuse
That English telegraphs and foreign pleaders,
In help of language, are so apt to use,
Arms, shoulders, fingers, all were interceders,
Nods, shrugs and bends, — Bianca could not choose
But soften to his suit with more facility,
He told his story with so much agility.

"Be thou my park, and I will be thy dear,
(So he began at last to speak or quote;)

Be thou my bark, and I thy gondolier,
  (For passion takes this figurative note;)
Be thou my light, and I thy chandelier;
  Be thou my dove, and I will be thy cote;
My lily be, and I will be thy river;
Be thou my life — and I will be thy liver."

This, with more tender logic of the kind,
  He poured into her small and shell-like ear,
That timidly against his lips inclined:
  Meanwhile her eyes glanced on the silver sphere
That even now began to steal behind
  A dewy vapor, which was lingering near,
Wherein the dull moon crept all dim and pale,
Just like a virgin putting on the veil: —

Bidding adieu to all her sparks — the stars,
  That erst had wooed and worshipped in her train
Saturn and Hesperus, and gallant Mars —
  Never to flirt with heavenly eyes again.
Meanwhile, remindful of the convent bars,
  Bianca did not watch these signs in vain,
But turned to Julio at the dark eclipse,
With words, like verbal kisses, on her lips.

He took the hint full speedily, and, backed
  By love, and night, and the occasion's meetness,
Bestowed a something on her cheek that smacked
  (Though quite in silence) of ambrosial sweetness;
That made her think all other kisses lacked
  Till then, but what she knew not, of completeness:
  Being used but sisterly salutes to feel,
  Insipid things — like sandwiches of veal.

  He took her hand, and soon she felt him wring
    The pretty fingers all, instead of one;

Anon his stealthy arm began to cling
 About her waist that had been clasped by none;
Their dear confessions I forbear to sing,
 Since cold description would but be outrun;
For bliss and Irish watches have the power
In twenty minutes to lose half an hour!

OVER THE WAY.

"I sat over against a window where there stood a pot with very pretty flowers; and had my eyes fixed on it, when on a sudden the window opened, and a young lady appeared whose beauty struck me." — ARABIAN NIGHTS.

ALAS! the flames of an unhappy lover
About my heart and on my vitals prey;
I've caught a fever that I can't get over,
 Over the way!

O! why are eyes of hazel? noses Grecian?
I've lost my rest by night, my peace by day,
For want of some brown Holland or Venetian,
 Over the way!

I've gazed too often, till my heart's as lost
As any needle in a stack of hay:
Crosses belong to love, and mine is crossed
 Over the way!

I cannot read or write, or thoughts relax —
Of what avail Lord Althorpe or Earl Grey?
They cannot ease me of *my* window-tax
 Over the way!

Even on Sunday my devotions vary,
And from St. Bennet Flint they go astray
To dear St. Mary Overy — the Mary
 Over the way!

O! if my godmother were but a fairy,
With magic wand, how I would beg and pray
That she would change me into that canary
Over the way!

I envy every thing that's near Miss Lindo,
A pug, a poll, a squirrel or a jay —
Blest blue-bottles! that buzz about the window
Over the way!

Even at even, for there be no shutters,
I see her reading on from grave to gay,
Some tale or poem, till the candle gutters,
Over the way!

And then — O! then — while the clear waxen taper
Emits, two stories high, a starlike ray,
I see twelve auburn curls put into paper
Over the way!

But how breathe unto her my deep regards,
Or ask her for a whispered ay or nay, —
Or offer her my hand, some thirty yards
Over the way!

Cold as the pole she is to my adoring;
Like Captain Lyon, at Repulse's Bay,
I meet an icy end to my exploring
Over the way!

Each dirty little Savoyard that dances
She looks on — Punch — or chimney-sweeps in May:
Zounds! wherefore cannot I attract her glances
Over the way!

Half out she leans to watch a tumbling brat,
Or yelping cur, run over by a dray;
But I'm in love — she never pities that!
Over the way!

I go to the same church — a love-lost labor;
Haunt all her walks, and dodge her at the play;
She does not seem to know she has a neighbor
Over the way!

At private theatres she never acts;
No Crown-and-Anchor balls her fancy sway;
She never visits gentlemen with tracts
Over the way!

To billets-doux by post she shows no favor —
In short there is no plot that I can lay
To break my window-pains to my enslaver
Over the way!

I play the flute — she heeds not my chromatics —
No friend an introduction can purvey;
I wish a fire would break out in the attics
Over the way!

My wasted form ought of itself to touch her:
My baker feels my appetite's decay;
And as for butcher's meat — O! she's my butcher
Over the way!

At beef I turn; at lamb or veal I pout;
I never ring now to bring up the tray;
My stomach grumbles at my dining out
Over the way!

I'm weary of my life; without regret
I could resign this miserable clay
To lie within that box of mignonette
Over the way!

I've fitted bullets to my pistol-bore;
I've vowed at times to rush where trumpets bray,
Quite sick of Number One — and Number Four
Over the way!

Sometimes my fancy builds up castles airy,
Sometimes it only paints a ferme ornée,
A horse — a cow — six fowls — a pig — and Mary,
Over the way!

Sometimes I dream of her in bridal white,
Standing before the altar, like a fay;
Sometimes of balls, and neighborly invite
Over the way!

I've cooed with her in dreams, like any turtle;
I've snatched her from the Clyde, the Tweed, and Tay:
Thrice I have made a grove of that one myrtle
Over the way!

Thrice I have rowed her in a fairy shallop,
Thrice raced to Gretna in a neat "po-shay,"
And showered crowns to make the horses gallop
Over the way!

And thrice I've started up from dreams appalling
Of killing rivals in a bloody fray —
There is a young man very fond of calling
Over the way!

O! happy man — above all kings in glory,
Whoever in her ear may say his say,
And add a tale of love to that one story
Over the way!

Nabob of Arcot — Despot of Japan —
Sultan of Persia — Emperor of Cathay —
Much rather would I be the happy man
    Over the way!

With such a lot my heart would be in clover —
But what — O, horror! — what do I survey!
Postilions and white favors! — all is over
    Over the way!

EPICUREAN REMINISCENCES OF A SENTIMENTALIST.

"My *Tables!* *Meat* it is, *I set it* down!" — HAMLET.

I THINK it was Spring — but not certain I am —
  When my passion began first to work;
But I know we were certainly looking for lamb,
  And the season was over for pork.

'Twas at Christmas, I think, when I met with Miss Chase,
  Yes, — for Morris had asked me to dine, —
And I thought I had never beheld such a face,
  Or so noble a turkey and chine.

Placed close by her side, it made others quite wild
  With sheer envy to witness my luck;
How she blushed as I gave her some turtle, and smiled
  As I afterwards offered some duck.

I looked and I languished, alas! to my cost,
  Through three courses of dishes and meats;
Getting deeper in love — but my heart was quite lost,
  When it came to the trifle and sweets!

With a rent-roll that told of my houses and land,
  To her parents I told my designs —

And then to herself I presented my hand,
  With a very fine pottle of pines!

I asked her to have me for weal or for woe,
  And she did not object in the least;—
I can't tell the date — but we married, I know,
  Just in time to have game at the feast.

We went to ———, it certainly was the sea-side;
  For the next, the most blessèd of morns,
I remember how fondly I gazed at my bride,
  Sitting down to a plateful of prawns.

O, never may memory lose sight of that year,
  But still hallow the time as it ought!
That season the "grass" was remarkably dear,
  And the peas at a guinea a quart.

So happy, like hours, all our days seemed to haste,
  A fond pair, such as poets have drawn,
So united in heart — so congenial in taste —
  We were both of us partial to brawn!

A long life I looked for of bliss with my bride,
  But then Death — I ne'er dreamt about that!
O, there's nothing is certain in life, as I cried
  When my turbot eloped with the cat!

My dearest took ill at the turn of the year,
  But the cause no physician could nab;
But something it seemed like consumption, I fear,—
  It was just after supping on crab.

In vain she was doctored, in vain she was dosed,
  Still her strength and her appetite pined;
She lost relish for what she had relished the most,
  Even salmon she deeply declined!

For months still I lingered in hope and in doubt,
  While her form it grew wasted and thin;
But the last dying spark of existence went out,
  As the oysters were just coming in!

She died, and she left me the saddest of men,
  To indulge in a widower's moan;
O, I felt all the power of solitude then,
  As I ate my first natives alone!

But when I beheld Virtue's friends in their cloaks,
  And with sorrowful crape on their hats,
O, my grief poured a flood! and the out-of-door folks
  Were all crying — I think it was sprats!

THE CARELESSE NURSE MAYD.

I SAWE a Mayd sitte on a Bank,
Beguiled by Wooer fayne and fond;
And whiles His flatterynge Vowes She drank,
Her Nurselynge slipt within a Pond!

All Even Tide they Talkde and Kist,
For She was fayre and He was Kinde;
The Sunne went down before She wist
Another Sonne had sett behinde!

With angrie Hands and frownynge Browe,
That deemd Her owne the Urchine's Sinne,
She pluckt Him out, but he was nowe
Past being Whipt for fallynge in.

She then beginnes to wayle the Ladde
With Shrikes that Echo answerede round —
O! foolishe Mayd to be soe sadde
The Momente that her Care was drownd!

ODE TO PERRY,

THE INVENTOR OF THE PATENT PERRYAN PEN.

"In this good work, Penn appears the greatest, usefullest of God's instruments. Firm and unbending when the exigency requires it — soft and yielding when rigid inflexibility is not a desideratum — fluent and flowing, at need, for eloquent rapidity — slow and retentive in cases of deliberation — never spluttering or by amplification going wide of the mark — never splitting, if it can be helped, with any one, but ready to wear itself out rather in their service — all things as it were with all men, — ready to embrace the hand of Jew, Christian, or Mahometan, — heavy with the German, light with the Italian, oblique with the English, upright with the Roman, backward in coming forward with the Hebrew, — in short, for flexibility, amiability, constitutional durability, general ability, and universal utility, it would be hard to find a parallel to the great Penn." — PERRY'S CHARACTERISTICS OF A SETTLER.

O! PATENT Pen-inventing Perrian Perry!
Friend of the goose and gander,
That now unplucked of their quill feathers wander,
Cackling, and gabbling, dabbling, making merry,
About the happy fen,
Untroubled for one penny-worth of pen,
For which they chant thy praise all Britain through,
From Goose-Green unto Gander-Cleugh! —

Friend to all Author-kind, —
Whether of Poet or of Proser, —
Thou art composer unto the composer
Of pens, — yea, patent vehicles for Mind
To carry it on jaunts, or more extensive
*Perry*grinations through the realms of thought;
Each plying from the Comic to the Pensive,
An Omnibus of intellectual sort!

Modern improvements in their course we feel;
And while to iron-railroads heavy wares,

Dry goods, and human bodies, pay their fares,
Mind flies on steel,
To Penrith, Penrhyn, even to Penzance;
Nay, penetrates, perchance,
To Pennsylvania, or, without rash vaunts,
To where the Penguin haunts!

In times bygone, when each man cut his quill,
With little Perryan skill,
What horrid, awkward, bungling tools of trade
Appeared the writing implements home-made!
What Pens were sliced, hewed, hacked, and haggled out,
Slit or unslit, with many a various snout,
Aquiline, Roman, crooked, square, and snubby,
Stumpy and stubby;
Some capable of ladye-billets neat,
Some only fit for ledger-keeping clerk,
And some to grub down Peter Stubbs his mark,
Or smudge through some illegible receipt;
Others in florid caligraphic plans,
Equal to ships, and wiggy heads, and swans!

To try in any common inkstands, then,
With all their miscellaneous stocks,
To find a decent pen,
Was like a dip into a lucky box:
You drew, — and got one very curly,
And split like endive in some hurly-burly;
The next unslit, and square at end, a spade;
The third, incipient pop-gun, not yet made;
The fourth a broom; the fifth of no avail,
Turned upwards, like a rabbit's tail;
And last, not least, by way of a relief,
A stump that Master Richard, James or John,

Had tried his candle-cookery upon,
Making "roast-beef!"

Not so thy Perryan Pens!
True to their M's and N's,
They do not with a whizzing zig-zag split,
Straddle, turn up their noses, sulk, and spit,
Or drop large dots,
Huge full-stop blots,
Where even semicolons were unfit.
They will not frizzle up, or, broom-like, drudge
In sable sludge —
Nay, bought at proper "Patent Perryan" shops,
They write good grammar, sense, and mind their stops:
Compose both prose and verse, the sad and merry —
For when the editor, whose pains compile
The grown-up Annual, or the Juvenile,
Vaunteth his articles, not women's, men's,
But lays "by the most celebrated Pens,"
What means he but thy Patent Pens, my Perry?

Pleasant they are to feel!
So firm! so flexible! composed of steel
So finely tempered — fit for tenderest Miss
To give her passion breath,
Or kings to sign the warrant stern of death —
But their supremest merit still is this,
Write with them all your days,
Tragedy, Comedy, all kinds of plays —
(No dramatist should ever be without 'em) —
And, just conceive the bliss, —
There is so little of the goose about 'em,
One's safe from any hiss!

Ah! who can paint that first great awful night,
  Big with a blessing or a blight,
When the poor dramatist, all fume and fret,
Fuss, fidget, fancy, fever, funking, fright,
Ferment, fault-fearing, faintness — more f's yet:
Flushed, frigid, flurried, flinching, fitful, flat,
Add famished, fuddled, and fatigued, to that;
Funeral, fate-foreboding — sits in doubt,
Or rather doubt with hope, a wretched marriage,
To see his play upon the stage come out;
No stage to him! it is Thalia's carriage,
And he is sitting on the spikes behind it,
Striving to look as if he didn't mind it!

  Witness how Beazley vents upon his hat
  His nervousness, meanwhile his fate is dealt:
He kneads, moulds, pummels it, and sits it flat,
Squeezes and twists it up, until the felt,
That went a beaver in, comes out a rat!
Miss Mitford had mis-givings, and in fright,
    Upon Rienzi's night
Gnawed up one long kid glove, and all her bag,
    Quite to a rag.
Knowles has confessed he trembled as for life,
    Afraid of his own "Wife;"
Poole told me that he felt a monstrous pail
Of water backing him, all down his spine, —
"The ice-brook's temper" — pleasant to the chine!
For fear that Simpson and his Co. should fail.
Did Lord Glengall not frame a mental prayer,
Wishing devoutly he was Lord knows where?
Nay, did not Jerrold, in enormous drouth,
While doubtful of Nell Gwynne's eventful luck,
    Squeeze out and suck

More oranges with his one fevered mouth
Than Nelly had to hawk from north to south?
Yea, Buckstone, changing color like a mullet,
Refused, on an occasion, once, twice, thrice,
From his best friend, an ice,
Lest it should hiss in his own red-hot gullet.

Doth punning Peake not sit upon the points
Of his own jokes, and shake in all his joints,
During their trial?
'Tis past denial.
And does not Pocock, feeling, like a peacock,
All eyes upon him, turn to very meacock?
And does not Planché, tremulous and blank,
Meanwhile his personages tread the boards,
Seem goaded by sharp swords,
And called upon himself to "walk the plank"?
As for the Dances, Charles and George to boot,
What have they more
Of ease and rest, for sole of either foot,
Than bear that capers on a hotted floor!

Thus pending — does not Mathews, at sad shift
For voice, croak like a frog in waters fenny? —
Serle seem upon the surly seas adrift? —
And Kenny think he's going to Kilkenny? —
Haynes Bayly feel Old ditto, with the note
Of Cotton in his ear, a mortal grapple
About his arms, and Adam's apple
Big as a fine Dutch codling in his throat?
Did Rodwell, on his chimney-piece, desire
Or not to take a jump into the fire?
Did Wade feel as composed as music can?
And was not Bernard his own Nervous Man?
Lastly, don't Farley, a bewildered elf,

Quake at the Pantomime he loves to cater,
And ere its changes ring transform himself? —
A frightful mug of human delf!
A spirit-bottle — empty of "the cratur"?
A leaden-platter ready for the shelf?
A thunderstruck dumb-waiter?

To clench the fact,
Myself, once guilty of one small rash act,
Committed at the Surrey,
Quite in a hurry,
Felt all this flurry,
Corporal worry,
And spiritual scurry,
Dram-devil — attic curry!
All going well,
From prompter's bell,
Until befell
A hissing at some dull imperfect dance —
There's no denying
I felt in all four elements at once!
My head was swimming, while my arms were flying!
My legs for running — all the rest was frying!

Thrice welcome, then, for this peculiar use,
Thy pens so innocent of goose!
For this shall dramatists, when they make merry,
Discarding port and sherry,
Drink — "Perry!"
Perry, whose fame, pennated, is let loose
To distant lands,
Perry, admitted on all hands,
Text, running, German, Roman,
For Patent Perryans approached by no man!
And when, ah me! far distant be the hour!

Pluto shall call thee to his gloomy bower,
Many shall be thy pensive mourners, many!
And Penury itself shall club its penny
To raise thy monument in lofty place,
Higher than York's or any son of War;
Whilst time all meaner effigies shall bury,
On due pentagonal base
Shall stand the Parian, Perryan, periwigged Perry,
Perched on the proudest peak of Penman Mawr!

NUMBER ONE.

VERSIFIED FROM THE PROSE OF A YOUNG LADY.

It's very hard! — and so it is, to live in such a row, —
And witness this that every miss but me has got a beau.
For Love goes calling up and down, but here he seems to shun;
I'm sure he has been asked enough to call at Number One!

I'm sick of all the double knocks that come to Number Four! —
That Number Three I often see a lover at the door; —
And one in blue, at Number Two, calls daily like a dun, —
It's very hard they come so near, and not to Number One!

Miss Bell, I hear, has got a dear exactly to her mind, —
By sitting at the window-pane without a bit of blind; —
But I go in the balcony, which she has never done,
Yet arts that thrive at Number Five don't take at Number One!

'Tis hard, with plenty in the street, and plenty passing
by, —
There's nice young men at Number Ten, but only rather
shy; —
And Mrs. Smith across the way has got a grown-up son,
But, la! he hardly seems to know there is a Number
One!

There's Mr. Wick at Number Nine, but he's intent on
pelf,
And though he's pious will not love his neighbor as him-
self. —
At Number Seven there was a sale — the goods had
quite a run!
And here I've got my single lot on hand at Number One!

My mother often sits at work and talks of props and
stays,
And what a comfort I shall be in her declining days: —
The very maids about the house have set me down a nun,
The sweethearts all belong to them that call at Number
One!

Once only when the flue took fire, one Friday afternoon,
Young Mr. Long came kindly in and told me not to
swoon:
Why can't he come again without the Phœnix and the
Sun?
We cannot always have a flue on fire at Number One!

I am not old, I am not plain, nor awkward in my gait —
I am not crooked, like the bride that went from Number
Eight: —
I'm sure white satin made her look as brown as any bun —
But even beauty has no chance, I think, at Number One!

At Number Six they say Miss Rose has slain a score of hearts,
And Cupid, for her sake, has been quite prodigal of darts.
The imp they show with bended bow, I wish he had a gun!
But if he had, he'd never deign to shoot with Number One.

It's very hard, and so it is, to live in such a row!
And here's a ballad-singer come to aggravate my woe; —
O, take away your foolish song and tones enough to stun —
There is "Nae luck about the house," I know, at Number One!

LINES ON THE CELEBRATION OF PEACE.

BY DORCAS DOVE.

AND is it thus ye welcome Peace,
From mouths of forty-pounding Bores?
O, cease, exploding Cannons, cease!
Lest Peace, affrighted, shun our shores!

Not so the quiet Queen should come;
But like a Nurse to still our Fears,
With shoes of List, demurely dumb,
And Wool or Cotton in her Ears!

She asks for no triumphal Arch;
No Steeples for their ropy Tongues;
Down, Drumsticks, down! She needs no March,
Or blasted Trumps from brazen Lungs.

She wants no Noise of mobbing Throats
To tell that She is drawing nigh:

Why this Parade of scarlet Coats,
  When War has closed his bloodshot Eye?

Returning to Domestic Loves,
  When War has ceased with all its Ills,
Captains should come like sucking Doves,
  With Olive Branches in their Bills.

No need there is of vulgar Shout,
  Bells, Cannons, Trumpets, Fife and Drum,
And Soldiers marching all about,
  To let Us know that Peace is come.

O, mild should be the Signs, and meek,
  Sweet Peace's Advent to proclaim!
Silence her noiseless Foot should speak,
  And Echo should repeat the same.

Lo! where the Soldier walks, alas!
  With Scars received on foreign Grounds;
Shall we consume in colored Glass
  The Oil that should be poured in Wounds?

The bleeding Gaps of War to close,
  Will whizzing Rocket-Flight avail?
Will Squibs enliven Orphans' Woes?
  Or Crackers cheer the Widow's Tale?

THE DEMON-SHIP.

'Twas off the Wash — the sun went down — the sea looked black and grim,
For stormy clouds with murky fleece were mustering at the brim;
Titanic shades! enormous gloom! — as if the solid night
Of Erebus rose suddenly to seize upon the light!

It was a time for mariners to bear a wary eye,
With such a dark conspiracy between the sea and sky!

Down went my helm — close reefed — the tack held freely in my hand —
With ballast snug — I put about, and scudded for the land.
Loud hissed the sea beneath her lee; my little boat flew fast,
But faster still the rushing storm came borne upon the blast.
Lord! what a roaring hurricane beset the straining sail!
What furious sleet, with level drift, and fierce assaults of hail!
What darksome caverns yawned before! what jagged steeps behind!
Like battle-steeds, with foamy manes, wild tossing in the wind.
Each after each sank down astern, exhausted in the chase,
But where it sank another rose and galloped in its place;
As black as night — they turned to white, and cast against the cloud
A snowy sheet, as if each surge upturned a sailor's shroud:
Still flew my boat; alas! alas! her course was nearly run!
Behold yon fatal billow rise — ten billows heaped in one!
With fearful speed the dreary mass came rolling, rolling fast,
As if the scooping sea contained only one wave, at last!
Still on it came, with horrid roar, a swift-pursuing grave!
It seemed as though some cloud had turned its hugeness to a wave!
Its briny sleet began to beat beforehand in my face —
I felt the rearward keel begin to climb its swelling base!

I saw its Alpine hoary head impending over mine!
Another pulse, and down it rushed, an avalanche of brine!
Brief pause had I, on God to cry, or think of wife and home;
The waters closed — and when I shrieked, I shrieked below the foam!
Beyond that rush I have no hint of any after deed —
For I was tossing on the waste, as senseless as a weed.

* * * * * *

"Where am I? in the breathing world, or in the world of death?"
With sharp and sudden pang I drew another birth of breath;
My eyes drank in a doubtful light, my ears a doubtful sound,
And was that ship a *real* ship whose tackle seemed around?

A moon, as if the earthly moon, was shining up aloft;
But were those beams the very beams that I had seen so oft?
A face that mocked the human face before me watched alone;
But were those eyes the eyes of man that looked against my own?

O! never may the moon again disclose me such a sight
As met my gaze, when first I looked on that accursed night!
I've seen a thousand horrid shapes begot of fierce extremes
Of fever; and most frightful things have haunted in my dreams —

Hyenas, cats, blood-loving bats, and apes with hateful stare,
Pernicious snakes, and shaggy bulls, the lion and she-bear,
Strong enemies, with Judas looks, of treachery and spite —
Detested features, hardly dimmed and banished by the light!

Pale-sheeted ghosts, with gory locks, upstarting from their tombs —
All fantasies and images that flit in midnight glooms —
Hags, goblins, demons, lemures, have made me all aghast, —
But nothing like that Grimly One who stood beside the mast!

His cheek was black — his brow was black — his eyes and hair as dark:
His hand was black, and where it touched it left a sable mark;
His throat was black, his vest the same; and when I looked beneath,
His breast was black — all, all was black, except his grinning teeth.
His sooty crew were like in hue, as black as Afric slaves!
O, horror! e'en the ship was black that ploughed the inky waves!

"Alas!" I cried, "for love of truth and blessed mercy's sake,
Where am I? in what dreadful ship? upon what dreadful lake?
What shape is that, so very grim, and black as any coal?
It is Mahound, the Evil One, and he has gained my soul!

O, mother dear! my tender nurse! dear meadows that
beguiled
My happy days, when I was yet a little sinless child, —
My mother dear—my native fields, I never more shall see:
I'm sailing in the Devil's Ship, upon the Devil's Sea!"

Loud laughed that SABLE MARINER, and loudly in return
His sooty crew sent forth a laugh that rang from stem
to stern —
A dozen pair of grimly cheeks were crumpled on the
nonce —
As many sets of grinning teeth came shining out at once;
A dozen gloomy shapes at once enjoyed the merry fit,
With shriek and yell, and oaths as well, like demons of
the Pit.
They crowed their fill, and then the Chief made answer
for the whole; —
"Our skins," said he, "are black, ye see, because we
carry coal;
You'll find your mother sure enough, and see your native
fields —
For this here ship has picked you up, the Mary Ann of
Shields!"

SPRING.

A NEW VERSION.

"*Ham.* The air bites shrewdly — it is very cold.
Hor. It is a nipping and an eager air." — HAMLET.

"COME, *gentle* Spring! ethereal *mildness*, come!"
O! Thomson, void of rhyme as well as reason,
How couldst thou thus poor human nature hum?
There's no such season.

The Spring! I shrink and shudder at her name!
  For why, I find her breath a bitter blighter!
And suffer from her *blows* as if they came
  From Spring the Fighter.

Her praises, then, let hardy poets sing,
  And be her tuneful laureates and upholders,
Who do not feel as if they had a *Spring*
  Poured down their shoulders.

Let others eulogize her floral shows;
  From me they cannot win a single stanza.
I know her blooms are in full blow — and so's
  The Influenza.

Her cowslips, stocks, and lilies of the vale,
  Her honey-blossoms that you hear the bees at,
Her pansies, daffodils, and primrose pale,
  Are things I sneeze at!

Fair is the vernal quarter of the year!
  And fair its early buddings and its blowings —
But just suppose Consumption's seeds appear
  With other sowings!

For me, I find, when eastern winds are high,
  A frigid, not a genial inspiration;
Nor can, like Iron-Chested Chubb, defy
  An inflammation.

Smitten by breezes from the land of plague,
  To me all vernal luxuries are fables;
O! where's the *Spring* in a rheumatic leg,
  Stiff as a table's?

I limp in agony, — I wheeze and cough,
  And quake with Ague, that great Agitator;
Nor dream, before July, of leaving off
  My Respirator.

What wonder if in May itself I lack
  A peg for laudatory verse to hang on ? —
Spring mild and gentle ! — yes, a Spring-heeled Jack
  To those he sprang on.

In short, whatever panegyrics lie
  In fulsome odes too many to be cited,
The tenderness of Spring is all my eye,
  And that is blighted !

FAITHLESS NELLY GRAY.

A PATHETIC BALLAD.

BEN BATTLE was a soldier bold,
  And used to war's alarms ;
But a cannon-ball took off his legs,
  So he laid down his arms !

Now, as they bore him off the field,
  Said he, " Let others shoot,
For here I leave my second leg,
  And the Forty-second Foot ! "

The army-surgeons made him limbs :
  Said he, " They're only pegs :
But there's as wooden members quite
  As represent my legs ! "

Now, Ben he loved a pretty maid,
Her name was Nelly Gray;
So he went to pay her his devours,
When he devoured his pay!

But when he called on Nelly Gray,
She made him quite a scoff;
And when she saw his wooden legs,
Began to take them off!

"O, Nelly Gray! O, Nelly Gray!
Is this your love so warm?
The love that loves a scarlet coat
Should be more uniform!"

Said she, "I loved a soldier once,
For he was blithe and brave;
But I will never have a man
With both legs in the grave!

"Before you had those timber toes,
Your love I did allow,
But then, you know, you stand upon
Another footing now!"

"O, Nelly Gray! O, Nelly Gray!
For all your jeering speeches,
At duty's call I left my legs
In Badajos's *breaches!*"

"Why then," said she, "you've lost the feet
Of legs in war's alarms,
And now you cannot wear your shoes
Upon your feats of arms!"

"O, false and fickle Nelly Gray!
  I know why you refuse: —
Though I've no feet — some other man
  Is standing in my shoes!

"I wish I ne'er had seen your face;
  But, now, a long farewell!
For you will be my death; — alas,
  You will not be my *Nell!*"

Now, when he went from Nelly Gray,
  His heart so heavy got,
And life was such a burthen grown,
  It made him take a knot!

So round his melancholy neck
  A rope he did entwine,
And, for his second time in life,
  Enlisted in the Line!

One end he tied around a beam,
  And then removed his pegs,
And, as his legs were off — of course
  He soon was off his legs!

And there he hung, till he was dead
  As any nail in town, —
For, though distress had cut him up,
  It could not cut him down!

A dozen men sat on his corpse,
  To find out why he died —
And they buried Ben in four cross-roads,
  With a *stake* in his inside!

THE FLOWER.

ALONE, across a foreign plain,
  The exile slowly wanders,
And on his isle beyond the main
  With saddened spirit ponders;

This lovely isle beyond the sea,
  With all its household treasures;
Its cottage homes, its merry birds,
  And all its rural pleasures;

Its leafy woods, its shady vales,
  Its moors, and purple heather;
Its verdant fields bedecked with stars
  His childhood loved to gather;

When, lo! he starts with glad surprise,
  Home-joys come rushing o'er him,
For "modest, wee, and crimson-tipped,"
  He spies the flower before him!

With eager haste he stoops him down,
  His eyes with moisture hazy,
And as he plucks the simple bloom,
  He murmurs, "Lawk-a-daisy!"

THE SEA-SPELL.

"*Cauld, cauld*, he lies beneath the deep." — *Old Scotch Ballad.*

IT was a jolly mariner!
The tallest man of three, —
He loosed his sail against the wind,
And turned his boat to sea:

The ink-black sky told every eye
A storm was soon to be!

But still that jolly mariner
Took in no reef at all,
For, in his pouch, confidingly,
He wore a baby's caul;
A thing, as gossip-nurses know,
That always brings a squall!

His hat was new, or, newly glazed,
Shone brightly in the sun;
His jacket, like a mariner's,
True blue as e'er was spun;
His ample trousers, like St. Paul,
Bore forty stripes save one.

And now the fretting, foaming tide
He steered away to cross;
The bounding pinnace played a game
Of dreary pitch and toss;
A game that, on the good dry land,
Is apt to bring a loss!

Good Heaven befriend that little boat,
And guide her on her way!
A boat, they say, has canvas wings,
But cannot fly away!
Though, like a merry singing-bird,
She sits upon the spray!

Still south by east the little boat,
With tawny sail, kept beating:
Now out of sight, between two waves,
Now o'er the horizon fleeting;

Like greedy swine that feed on mast, —
The waves her mast seemed eating!

The sullen sky grew black above,
The wave as black beneath;
Each roaring billow showed full soon
A white and foamy wreath;
Like angry dogs that snarl at first,
And then display their teeth.

The boatman looked against the wind,
The mast began to creak,
The wave, per saltum, came and dried,
In salt, upon his cheek!
The pointed wave against him reared,
As if it owned a pique!

Nor rushing wind nor gushing wave
The boatman could alarm,
But still he stood away to sea,
And trusted in his charm;
He thought by purchase he was safe,
And armed against all harm!

Now thick and fast and far aslant
The stormy rain came pouring,
He heard, upon the sandy bank,
The distant breakers roaring, —
A groaning intermitting sound,
Like Gog and Magog snoring!

The sea-fowl shrieked around the mast,
Ahead the grampus tumbled,
And far off, from a copper cloud,
The hollow thunder rumbled;
It would have quailed another heart,
But his was never humbled.

For why? he had that infant's caul;
And wherefore should he dread?
Alas! alas! he little thought,
Before the ebb-tide sped, —
That, like that infant, he should die,
And with a watery head!

The rushing brine flowed in apace;
His boat had ne'er a deck:
Fate seemed to call him on, and he
Attended to her beck;
And so he went, still trusting on,
Though reckless — to his wreck!

For as he left his helm, to heave
The ballast-bags a-weather,
Three monstrous seas came roaring on,
Like lions leagued together.
The two first waves the little boat
Swam over like a feather, —

The two first waves were past and gone,
And sinking in her wake;
The hugest still came leaping on,
And hissing like a snake.
Now helm a-lee! for through the midst
The monster he must take!

Ah, me! it was a dreary mount!
Its base as black as night,
Its top of pale and livid green,
Its crest of awful white,
Like Neptune with a leprosy, —
And so it reared upright!

With quaking sails the little boat
Climbed up the foaming heap,
With quaking sails it paused a while,
At balance on the steep;
Then, rushing down the nether slope,
Plunged with a dizzy sweep!

Look, how a horse, made mad with fear,
Disdains his careful guide;
So now the headlong, headstrong boat,
Unmanaged, turns aside,
And straight presents her reeling flank
Against the swelling tide!

The gusty wind assaults the sail;
Her ballast lies a-lee!
The sheet's to windward taut and stiff,
O! the Lively — where is she?
Her capsized keel is in the foam,
Her pennon's in the sea!

The wild gull, sailing overhead,
Three times beheld emerge
The head of that bold mariner,
And then she screamed his dirge!
For he had sunk within his grave,
Lapped in a shroud of surge!

The ensuing wave, with horrid foam,
Rushed o'er and covered all;
The jolly boatman's drowning scream
Was smothered by the squall,
Heaven never heard his cry, nor did
The ocean heed his *caul*.

A SAILOR'S APOLOGY FOR BOW-LEGS.

THERE's some is born with their straight legs by natur,
And some is born with bow-legs from the first —
And some that should have growed a good deal
straighter,
But they were badly nursed,
And set, you see, like Bacchus, with their pegs
Astride of casks and kegs:
I've got myself a sort of bow to larboard,
And starboard,
And this is what it was that warped my legs. —

'Twas all along of Poll, as I may say,
That fouled my cable when I ought to slip;
But on the tenth of May,
When I gets under weigh,
Down there in Hartfordshire, to join my ship,
I sees the mail
Get under sail,
The only one there was to make the trip.
Well — I gives chase,
But as she run
Two knots to one,
There warn't no use in keeping on the race!

Well — casting round about, what next to try on,
And how to spin,
I spies an ensign with a Bloody Lion,
And bears away to leeward for the inn,
Beats round the gable,
And fetches up before the coach-horse stable:
Well — there they stand, four kickers in a row,
And so
I just makes free to cut a brown 'un's cable.
But riding isn't in a seaman's natur —

So I whips out a toughish end of yarn,
And gets a kind of sort of a land-waiter
To splice me, heel to heel,
Under the she-mare's keel,
And off I goes, and leaves the inn a-starn!

My eyes! how she did pitch!
And wouldn't keep her own to go in no line,
Though I kept bowsing, bowsing at her bowline,
But always making lee-way to the ditch,
And yawed her head about all sorts of ways.
The devil sink the craft!
And wasn't she trimendous slack in stays!
We couldn't, nohow, keep the inn abaft!
Well — I suppose
We hadn't run a knot — or much beyond —
(What will you have on it?) — but off she goes,
Up to her bends in a fresh-water pond!
There I am! all a-back!
So I looks forward for her bridle-gears,
To heave her head round on the t'other tack;
But when I starts,
The leather parts,
And goes away right over by the ears!

What could a fellow do,
Whose legs, like mine, you know, were in the bilboes,
But trim myself upright for bringing-to,
And square his yard-arms, and brace up his elbows,
In rig all snug and clever,
Just while his craft was taking in her water?
I didn't like my berth, though, howsomdever,
Because the yarn, you see, kept getting tauter, —
Says I — I wish this job was rather shorter!

The chase had gained a mile
Ahead, and still the she-mare stood a-drinking:

Now, all the while
Her body didn't take of course to shrinking.
Says I, she's letting out her reefs, I'm thinking —
And so she swelled, and swelled,
And yet the tackle held,
Till both my legs began to bend like winkin.

My eyes! but she took in enough to founder!
And there's my timbers straining every bit,
Ready to split,
And her tarnation hull a-growing rounder!

Well, there — off Hartford Ness,
We lay both lashed and water-logged together,
And can't contrive a signal of distress;
Thinks I, we must ride out this here foul weather,
Though sick of riding out — and nothing less;
When, looking round, I sees a man a-starn: —
Hollo! says I, come underneath her quarter! —
And hands him out my knife to cut the yarn.
So I gets off, and lands upon the road,
And leaves the she-mare to her own consarn,
A-standing by the water.
If I get on another, I'll be blowed! —
And that's the way, you see, my legs got bowed!

THE BACHELOR'S DREAM.

My pipe is lit, my grog is mixed,
My curtains drawn and all is snug;
Old Puss is in her elbow-chair,
And Tray is sitting on the rug.
Last night I had a curious dream,
Miss Susan Bates was Mistress Mogg —

What d'ye think of that, my cat?
What d'ye think of that, my dog?

She looked so fair, she sang so well,
I could but woo and she was won;
Myself in blue, the bride in white,
The ring was placed, the deed was done!
Away we went in chaise-and-four,
As fast as grinning boys could flog —
What d'ye think of that, my cat?
What d'ye think of that, my dog?

What loving tête-à-têtes to come!
But tête-à-têtes must still defer!
When Susan came to live with me,
Her mother came to live with her!
With sister Belle she couldn't part,
But all *my* ties had leave to jog —
What d'ye think of that, my cat?
What d'ye think of that, my dog?

The mother brought a pretty Poll —
A monkey too, what work he made!
The sister introduced a beau —
My Susan brought a favorite maid.
She had a tabby of her own, —
A snappish mongrel christened Gog, —
What d'ye think of that, my cat?
What d'ye think of that, my dog?

The monkey bit — the parrot screamed,
All day the sister strummed and sung;
The petted maid was such a scold!
My Susan learned to use her tongue;
Her mother had such wretched health,

She sate and croaked like any frog —
What d'ye think of that, my cat?
What d'ye think of that, my dog?

No longer Deary, Duck, and Love,
I soon came down to simple "M!"
The very servants crossed my wish,
My Susan let me down to them.
The poker hardly seemed my own,
I might as well have been a log —
What d'ye think of that, my cat?
What d'ye think of that, my dog?

My clothes they were the queerest shape!
Such coats and hats she never met!
My ways they were the oddest ways!
My friends were such a vulgar set!
Poor Tomkinson was snubbed and huffed,
She could not bear that Mister Blogg —
What d'ye think of that, my cat?
What d'ye think of that, my dog?

At times we had a spar, and then
Mamma must mingle in the song —
The sister took a sister's part —
The maid declared her master wrong —
The parrot learned to call me "Fool!"
My life was like a London fog —
What d'ye think of that, my cat?
What d'ye think of that, my dog?

My Susan's taste was superfine,
As proved by bills that had no end;
I never had a decent coat —
I never had a coin to spend!
She forced me to resign my club,

Lay down my pipe, retrench my grog —
What d'ye think of that, my cat?
What d'ye think of that, my dog?

Each Sunday night we gave a rout
To fops and flirts, a pretty list;
And when I tried to steal away,
I found my study full of whist!
Then, first to come, and last to go,
There always was a Captain Hogg —
What d'ye think of that, my cat?
What d'ye think of that, my dog?

Now was not that an awful dream
For one who single is and snug —
With Pussy in the elbow-chair,
And Tray reposing on the rug? —
If I must totter down the hill,
'Tis safest done without a clog —
What d'ye think of that, my cat?
What d'ye think of that, my dog?

THE WEE MAN.

A ROMANCE.

It was a merry company,
  And they were just afloat,
When, lo! a man, of dwarfish span,
  Came up and hailed the boat.

"Good-morrow to ye, gentle folks,
  And will you let me in? —
A slender space will serve my case,
  For I am small and thin."

They saw he was a dwarfish man,
And very small and thin;
Not seven such would matter much,
And so they took him in.

They laughed to see his little hat,
With such a narrow brim;
They laughed to note his dapper coat,
With skirts so scant and trim.

But barely had they gone a mile,
When, gravely, one and all
At once began to think the man
Was not so very small.

His coat had got a broader skirt,
His hat a broader brim,
His leg grew stout, and soon plumped out
A very proper limb.

Still on they went, and as they went,
More rough the billows grew,—
And rose and fell, a greater swell,
And he was swelling too!

And, lo! where room had been for seven,
For six there scarce was space!
For five!—for four!—for three!—not more
Than two could find a place!

There was not even room for one!
They crowded by degrees—
Ay—closer yet, till elbows met,
And knees were jogging knees.

"Good sir, you must not sit astern,
The wave will else come in!"
Without a word he gravely stirred,
Another seat to win.

"Good sir, the boat has lost her trim,
You must not sit a-lee!"
With smiling face and courteous grace,
The middle seat took he.

But still, by constant quiet growth,
His back became so wide,
Each neighbor wight, to left and right,
Was thrust against the side.

Lord! how they chided with themselves,
That they had let him in!
To see him grow so monstrous now,
That came so small and thin.

On every brow a dew-drop stood,
They grew so scared and hot,—
"I' the name of all that's great and tall,
Who are ye, sir, and what?"

Loud laughed the Gogmagog, a laugh
As loud as giant's roar—
"When first I came, my proper name
Was Little—now I'm *Moore!*"

DEATH'S RAMBLE.

ONE day the dreary old King of Death
Inclined for some sport with the carnal,
So he tied a pack of darts on his back,
And quietly stole from his charnel.

His head was bald of flesh and of hair,
  His body was lean and lank;
His joints at each stir made a crack, and the cur
  Took a gnaw, by the way, at his shank.

And what did he do with his deadly darts,
  This goblin of grisly bone?
He dabbled and spilled man's blood, and he killed
  Like a butcher that kills his own.

The first he slaughtered it made him laugh,
  (For the man was a coffin-maker,)
To think how the mutes, and men in black suits,
  Would mourn for an undertaker.

Death saw two Quakers sitting at church;
  Quoth he, "We shall not differ."
And he let them alone, like figures of stone,
  For he could not make them stiffer.

He saw two duellists going to fight,
  In fear they could not smother;
And he shot one through at once — for he knew
  They never would shoot each other.

He saw a watchman fast in his box,
  And he gave a snore infernal;
Said Death, "He may keep his breath, for his sleep
  Can never be more eternal."

He met a coachman driving a coach
  So slow that his fare grew sick;
But he let him stray on his tedious way,
  For Death only wars on the *quick*.

Death saw a tollman taking a toll,
  In the spirit of his fraternity;

But he knew that sort of man would extort,
  Though summoned to all eternity.

He found an author writing his life,
  But he let him write no further;
For Death, who strikes whenever he likes,
  Is jealous of all self-murther!

Death saw a patient that pulled out his purse,
  And a doctor that took the sum;
But he let them be — for he knew that the "fee"
  Was a prelude to "faw" and "fum."

He met a dustman ringing a bell,
  And he gave him a mortal thrust;
For himself, by law, since Adam's flaw,
  Is contractor for all our dust.

He saw a sailor mixing his grog,
  And he marked him out for slaughter;
For on water he scarcely had cared for death,
  And never on rum-and-water.

Death saw two players playing at cards,
  But the game wasn't worth a dump,
For he quickly laid them flat with a spade,
  To wait for the final trump!

THE PROGRESS OF ART.

O HAPPY time! — Art's early days!
When o'er each deed, with sweet self-praise,
    Narcissus-like I hung!
When great Rembrandt but little seemed,
And such Old Masters all were deemed
    As nothing to the young!

Some scratchy strokes — abrupt and few,
So easily and swift I drew,
  Sufficed for my design;
My sketchy, superficial hand,
Drew solids at a dash — and spanned
  A surface with a line.

Not long my eye was thus content,
But grew more critical — my bent
  Essayed a higher walk;
I copied leaden eyes in lead —
Rheumatic hands in white and red,
  And gouty feet — in chalk.

Anon my studious art for days
Kept making faces — happy phrase,
  For faces such as mine!
Accomplished in the details then,
I left the minor parts of men,
  And drew the form divine.

Old gods and heroes — Trojan — Greek,
Figures — long after the antique,
  Great Ajax justly feared;
Hectors, of whom at night I dreamt,
And Nestor, fringed enough to tempt
  Bird-nesters to his beard.

A Bacchus, leering on a bowl,
A Pallas, that out-stared her owl,
  A Vulcan — very lame;
A Dian stuck about with stars,
With my right hand I murdered Mars —
  (One Williams did the same.)

But tired of this dry work at last,
Crayon and chalk aside I cast,

And gave my brush a drink;
Dipping — "as when a painter dips
In gloom of earthquake and eclipse," —
That is — in Indian ink.

O then, what black Mont Blancs arose,
Crested with soot, and not with snows!
What clouds of dingy hue!
In spite of what the bard has penned,
I fear the distance did not "lend
Enchantment to the view."

Not Radclyffe's brush did e'er design
Black forests half so black as mine,
Or lakes so like a pall;
The Chinese cake dispersed a ray
Of darkness, like the light of Day
And Martin, over all.

Yet urchin pride sustained me still;
I gazed on all with right good will,
And spread the dingy tint;
"No holy Luke helped me to paint;
The Devil, surely not a Saint,
Had any finger in't!"

But colors came! — like morning light,
With gorgeous hues displacing night,
Or Spring's enlivened scene:
At once the sable shades withdrew;
My skies got very, very blue;
My trees, extremely green.

And, washed by my cosmetic brush,
How Beauty's cheek began to blush!
With lock of auburn stain —

(Not Goldsmith's Auburn) — nut-brown hair
That made her loveliest of the fair;
    Not "loveliest of the plain!"

Her lips were of vermilion hue;
Love in her eyes, and Prussian blue,
    Set all my heart in flame!
A young Pygmalion, I adored
The maids I made — but time was stored
    With evil — and it came!

Perspective dawned — and soon I saw
My houses stand against its law;
    And "keeping" all unkept!
My beauties were no longer things
For love and fond imaginings;
    But horrors to be wept!

Ah! why did knowledge ope my eyes?
Why did I get more artist-wise?
    It only serves to hint
What grave defects and wants are mine;
That I'm no Hilton in design —
    In nature no Dewint!

Thrice happy time! — Art's early days!
When o'er each deed, with sweet self-praise,
    Narcissus-like I hung!
When great Rembrandt but little seemed,
And such Old Masters all were deemed
    As nothing to the young!

A FAIRY TALE.

On Hounslow heath — and close beside the road,
As western travellers may oft have seen, —
A little house some years ago there stood,
A minikin abode;
And built like Mr. Birkbeck's, all of wood;
The walls of white, the window-shutters green; —
Four wheels it had at North, South, East, and West
(Though now at rest,)
On which it used to wander to and fro,
Because its master ne'er maintained a rider,
Like those who trade in Paternoster Row;
But made his business travel for itself,
Till he had made his pelf,
And then retired — if one may call it so,
Of a roadsider.
Perchance, the very race and constant riot
Of stages, long and short, which thereby ran,
Made him more relish the repose and quiet
Of his now sedentary caravan;
Perchance, he loved the ground because 'twas common,
And so he might impale a strip of soil,
That furnished, by his toil,
Some dusty greens, for him and his old woman; —
And five tall hollyhocks, in dingy flower.
Howbeit, the thoroughfare did no ways spoil
His peace, — unless, in some unlucky hour,
A stray horse came and gobbled up his bower!

But, tired of always looking at the coaches,
The same to come, — when they had seen them one day!
And, used to brisker life, both man and wife

Began to suffer N U E's approaches,
And feel retirement like a long wet Sunday,—
So, having had some quarters of school-breeding,
They turned themselves, like other folks, to reading;
But setting out where others nigh have done,
    And being ripened in the seventh stage,
        The childhood of old age,
Began, as other children have begun,—
Not with the pastorals of Mr. Pope,
        Or Bard of Hope,
Or Paley ethical, or learned Porson,—
But spelt, on Sabbaths, in St. Mark, or John,
And then relaxed themselves with Whittington,
        Or Valentine and Orson—
But chiefly fairy tales they loved to con,
And being easily melted in their dotage,
        Slobbered,—and kept
        Reading,—and wept
Over the White Cat, in their wooden cottage.

Thus reading on—the longer
They read, of course, their childish faith grew stronger
In Gnomes, and Hags, and Elves, and Giants grim,—
If talking trees and birds revealed to him,
She saw the flight of Fairyland's fly-wagons,
        And magic fishes swim
In puddle ponds, and took old crows for dragons,—
Both were quite drunk from the enchanted flagons;
When, as it fell upon a summer's day,
    As the old man sat a feeding
        On the old babe-reading,
Beside his open street-and-parlor door,
        A hideous roar
Proclaimed a drove of beasts was coming by the way.

Long-horned, and short, of many a different breed,
Tall, tawny brutes, from famous Lincoln-levels,
Or Durham feed,
With some of those unquiet black dwarf devils,
From nether side of Tweed,
Or Firth of Forth;
Looking half wild with joy to leave the North,—
With dusty hides, all mobbing on together,—
When,—whether from a fly's malicious comment
Upon his tender flank, from which he shrank;
Or whether
Only in some enthusiastic moment,—
However, one brown monster, in a frisk,
Giving his tail a perpendicular whisk,
Kicked out a passage through the beastly rabble;
And after a pas seul,—or, if you will, a
Hornpipe before the basket-maker's villa,
Leapt o'er the tiny pale,—
Backed his beef-steaks against the wooden gable
And thrust his brawny bell-rope of a tail
Right o'er the page
Wherein the sage
Just then was spelling some romantic fable.

The old man, half a scholar, half a dunce,
Could not peruse—who could?—two tales at once;
And being huffed
At what he knew was none of Riquet's Tuft,
Banged-to the door,
But most unluckly enclosed a morsel
Of the intruding tail, and all the tassel:—
The monster gave a roar,
And bolting off with speed, increased by pain,

The little house became a coach once more,
And, like Macheath, "took to the road" again!

Just then, by fortune's whimsical decree,
The ancient woman stooping with her crupper
Towards sweet home, or where sweet home should be,
Was getting up some household herbs for supper:
Thoughtful of Cinderella, in the tale,
And quaintly wondering if magic shifts
Could o'er a common pumpkin so prevail,
To turn it to a coach, — what pretty gifts
Might come of cabbages, and curly kale:
Meanwhile she never heard her old man's wail,
Nor turned, till home had turned a corner, quite
Gone out of sight!

At last, conceive her, rising from the ground,
Weary of sitting on her russet clothing;
And looking round
Where rest was to be found,
There was no house — no villa there — no nothing!
No house!
The change was quite amazing;
It made her senses stagger for a minute,
The riddle's explication seemed to harden;
But soon her superannuated *nous*
Explained the horrid mystery; — and raising
Her hand to heaven, with the cabbage in it,
On which she meant to sup, —
"Well! this *is* Fairy Work! I'll bet a farden,
Little Prince Silverwings has ketched me up,
And set me down in some one else's garden!"

THE TURTLES.

A FABLE.

"The rage of the vulture, the love of the turtle." — BYRON.

ONE day, it was before a civic dinner,
  Two London aldermen, no matter which,—
Cordwainer, Girdler, Pattern-maker, Skinner,—
  But both were florid, corpulent, and rich,
And both right fond of festive demolition,
Set forth upon a secret expedition.
Yet not, as might be fancied from the token,
  To Pudding Lane, Pie Corner, or the Street
  Of Bread, or Grub, or any thing to eat,
Or drink, as Milk, or Vintry, or Portsoken,
But eastward, to that more aquatic quarter,
    Where folks take water,
Or, bound on voyages, secure a berth
For Antwerp or Ostend, Dundee or Perth,
Calais, Boulogne, or any port on earth!

    Jostled and jostling, through the mud,
    Peculiar to the town of Lud,
Down narrow streets and crooked lanes they dived,
    Past many a gusty avenue, through which
    Came yellow fog, and smell of pitch,
From barge, and boat, and dusky wharf derived;
With darker fumes, brought eddying by the draught,
    From loco-smoko-motive craft;
Mingling with scents of butter, cheese, and gammons,
    Tea, coffee, sugar, pickles, rosin, wax,
    Hides, tallow, Russia matting, hemp and flax,
Salt cod, red herrings, sprats, and kippered salmons,
    Nuts, oranges, and lemons,

Each pungent spice, and aromatic gum,
Gas, pepper, soaplees, brandy, gin, and rum;
Alamode beef and greens — the London soil —
Glue, coal, tobacco, turpentine, and oil,
Bark, asafœtida, squills, vitriol, hops,
In short, all whiffs, and sniffs, and puffs, and snuffs,
From metals, minerals, and dyewood stuffs,
Fruits, victual, drink, solidities, or slops —
In flasks, casks, bales, trucks, wagons, taverns, shops,
Boats, lighters, cellars, wharfs, and warehouse-tops,
That, as we walk upon the river's ridge,
Assault the nose — below the bridge.

A walk, however, as tradition tells,
That once a poor blind Tobit used to choose,
Because, incapable of other views,
He met with "such a sight of smells."

But on, and on, and on,
In spite of all unsavory shocks,
Progress the stout Sir Peter and Sir John,
Steadily steering ship-like for the docks —
And now they reach a place the Muse, unwilling,
Recalls for female slang and vulgar doing,
The famous Gate of Billing
That does not lead to cooing —
And now they pass that house that is so ugly
A customer to people looking smuggl'y —
And now along that fatal hill they pass
Where centuries ago an Oxford bled,
And proved — too late to save his life, alas! —
That *he* was "off his head."

At last before a lofty brick-built pile
Sir Peter stopped, and with mysterious smile

Tinkled a bell that served to bring
The wire-drawn genius of the ring,
A species of commercial Samuel Weller —
To whom Sir Peter, tipping him a wink,
  And something else to drink,
  "Show us the cellar."

Obsequious bowed the man, and led the way
Down sundry flights of stairs, where windows small,
Dappled with mud, let in a dingy ray —
A dirty tax, if they were taxed at all.
At length they came into a cellar damp,
With venerable cobwebs fringed around,
  A cellar of that stamp
Which often harbors vintages renowned,
The feudal Hock, or Burgundy the courtly,
  With sherry, brown or golden,
  Or port, so olden,
Bereft of body 'tis no longer portly
But old or otherwise — to be veracious —
That cobwebbed cellar, damp, and dim, and spacious,
Held nothing crusty — but crustaceous.

  Prone on the chilly floor,
Five splendid turtles — such a five!
Natives of some West Indian shore,
  Were flapping all alive,
Late landed from the Jolly Planter's yawl —
 A sight whereon the dignitaries fixed
 Their eager eyes, with ecstasy unmixed,
Like fathers that behold their infants crawl,
Enjoying every little kick and sprawl.
Nay — far from fatherly the thoughts they bred,
Poor loggerheads from far Ascension ferried!
The Aldermen too plainly wished them dead
   And Aldermanbury'd!

"There!" cried Sir Peter, with an air
Triumphant as an ancient victor's,
And pointing to the creatures rich and rare,
"There's picters!

"Talk of Olympic Games! They're not worth mention;
The real prize for wrestling is when Jack,
In Providence or Ascension,
Can throw a lively turtle on its back!"

"Ay!" cried Sir John, and with a score of nods,
Thoughtful of classical symposium,
"There's food for gods!
There's nectar! there's ambrosium!
There's food for Roman emperors to eat —
O, there had been a treat
(Those ancient names will sometimes hobble us)
For Helio-gobble-us!

"There were a feast for Alexander's Feast!
The real sort — none of your mock or spurious!"
And then he mentioned Aldermen deceased,
And "Epicurius,"
And how Tertullian had enjoyed such foison;
And speculated on that *verdigrease*
That isn't poison.

"Talk of your Spring, and verdure, and all that!
Give *me* green fat!
As for your poets with their groves of myrtles
And billing turtles,
Give me, for poetry, them Turtles there,
A-billing in a bill of fare!

"Of all the things I ever swallow —
Good, well-dressed turtle beats them hollow;

It almost makes me wish, I vow,
To have *two* stomachs, like a cow!"
And, lo! as with the cud, an inward thrill
Upheaved his waistcoat and disturbed his frill,
His mouth was oozing and he worked his jaw —
"I almost think that I could eat one raw!"

And thus, as "inward love breeds outward talk,"
The portly pair continued to discourse;
And then — as Gray describes of life's divorce —
With "longing, lingering look" prepared to walk, —
Having through one delighted sense, at least,
Enjoyed a sort of Barmecidal feast,
And with prophetic gestures, strange to see,
Forestalled the civic banquet yet to be,
Its callipash and callipee!

A pleasant prospect — but, alack!
Scarcely each Alderman had turned his back,
When, seizing on the moment so propitious,
And having learned that they were so delicious
To bite and sup,
From praises so high flown and injudicious, —
And nothing could be more pernicious!
The Turtles fell to work, and ate each other up!

Moral.

Never, from folly or urbanity,
Praise people thus profusely to their faces,
Till, quite in love with their own graces,
They're eaten up by vanity!

LOVE LANE.

If I should love a maiden more,
And woo her every hope to crown,
I'd love her all the country o'er,
But not declare it out of town.

One even, by a mossy bank,
That held a hornet's nest within,
To Ellen on my knees I sank, —
How snakes will twine around the shin!

A bashful fear my soul unnerved,
And gave my heart a backward tug;
Nor was I cheered when she observed,
Whilst I was silent, "What a slug!"

At length my offer I preferred,
And Hope a kind reply forebode —
Alas! the only sound I heard
Was, "What a horrid ugly toad!"

I vowed to give her all my heart,
To love her till my life took leave,
And painted all a lover's smart —
Except a wasp gone up his sleeve!

But when I ventured to abide
Her father's and her mother's grants —
Sudden she started up and cried,
"O dear! I am all over ants!"

Nay, when beginning to beseech
The cause that led to my rebuff,

The answer was as strange a speech —
A "Daddy-Longlegs, sure enough!"

I spoke of fortune — house, — and lands,
And still renewed the warm attack, —
'Tis vain to offer ladies hands
That have a spider on the back!

'Tis vain to talk of hopes and fears,
And hope the least reply to win,
From any maid that stops her ears
In dread of earwigs creeping in!

'Tis vain to call the dearest names
Whilst stoats and weasels startle by —
As vain to talk of mutual flames
To one with glowworms in her eye!

What checked me in my fond address,
And knocked each pretty image down?
What stopped my Ellen's faltering yes?
A caterpillar on her gown!

To list to Philomel is sweet —
To see the moon rise silver-pale, —
But not to kneel at lady's feet
And crush a rival in a snail!

Sweet is the eventide, and kind
Its zephyr, balmy as the south;
But sweeter still to speak your mind
Without a chafer in your mouth!

At last, emboldened by my bliss,
Still fickle.Fortune played me foul,

For when I strove to snatch a kiss
She screamed — by proxy, through an owl!

Then, lovers, doomed to life or death,
Shun moonlight, twilight, lanes and bats,
Lest you should have in self-same breath
To bless your fate — and curse the gnats!

DOMESTIC POEMS.

'It's hame, hame, hame." — A. CUNNINGHAM.
"There's no place like home." — CLARI.

I.

HYMENEAL RETROSPECTIONS.

O KATE! my dear partner, through joy and through strife!
When I look back at Hymen's dear day,
Not a lovelier bride ever changed to a wife,
Though you're now so old, wizened, and gray!

Those eyes, then, were stars, shining rulers of fate!
But as liquid as stars in a pool;
Though now they're so dim, they appear, my dear Kate,
Just like gooseberries boiled for a fool!

That brow was like marble, so smooth and so fair;
Though it's wrinkled so crookedly now,
As if Time, when those furrows were made by the share,
Had been tipsy whilst driving his plough!

Your nose, it was such as the sculptors all chose,
When a Venus demanded their skill;
Though now it can hardly be reckoned a nose,
But a sort of Poll-Parroty bill!

Your mouth, it was then quite a bait for the bees,
Such a nectar there hung on each lip;
Though now it has taken that lemon-like squeeze,
Not a blue-bottle comes for a sip!

Your chin, it was one of Love favorite haunts,
From its dimple he could not get loose;
Though now the neat hand of a barber it wants,
Or a singe, like the breast of a goose!

How rich were those locks, so abundant and full,
With their ringlets of auburn so deep!
Though now they look only like frizzles of wool,
By a bramble torn off from a sheep!

That neck, not a swan could excel it in grace,
While in whiteness it vied with your arms:
Though now a grave 'kerchief you properly place,
To conceal that scrag-end of your charms!

Your figure was tall, then, and perfectly straight,
Though it now has two twists from upright —
But bless you! still bless you! my partner! my Kate!
Though you be such a perfect old fright!

II.

THE sun was slumbering in the west, my daily labors past;
On Anna's soft and gentle breast my head reclined at last!
The darkness closed around, so dear to fond congenial souls;
And thus she murmured at my ear, "My love, we're out of coals!

"That Mister Bond has called again, insisting on his rent;

And all the Todds are coming up to see us, out of Kent;
I quite forgot to tell you John has had a tipsy fall; —
I'm sure there's something going on with that vile Mary Hall!

"Miss Bell has bought the sweetest silk, and I have bought the rest —
Of course, if we go out of town, Southend will be the best.
I really think the Jones's house would be the thing for us;
I think I told you Mrs. Pope had parted with her *nus.*

"Cook, by the way, came up to-day, to bid me suit myself —
And what d'ye think? the rats have gnawed the victuals on the shelf.
And, Lord! there's such a letter come, inviting you to fight!
Of course you don't intend to go — God bless you, dear, good-night!"

III.

A PARENTAL ODE TO MY SON, AGED THREE YEARS AND FIVE MONTHS.

Thou happy, happy elf!
(But stop, — first let me kiss away that tear) —
Thou tiny image of myself!
(My love, he's poking peas into his ear!)
Thou merry, laughing sprite!
With spirits feather-light,
Untouched by sorrow, and unsoiled by sin —
(Good heavens! the child is swallowing a pin!)

Thou little tricksy Puck!
With antic toys so funnily bestuck,
Light as the singing bird that wings the air —
(The door! the poor! he'll tumble down the stair!)
Thou darling of thy sire!
(Why, Jane, he'll set his pinafore afire!)
Thou imp of mirth and joy!
In Love's dear chain so strong and bright a link,
Thou idol of thy parents — (Drat the boy!
There goes my ink!)

Thou cherub — but of earth;
Fit playfellow for Fays, by moonlight pale,
In harmless sport and mirth,
(That dog will bite him if he pulls its tail!)
Thou human humming-bee, extracting honey
From every blossom in the world that blows,
Singing in youth's elysium ever sunny,
(Another tumble! — that's his precious nose!)

Thy father's pride and hope!
(He'll break the mirror with that skipping-rope!)
With pure heart newly stamped from Nature's mint —
(Where *did* he learn that squint?)
Thou young domestic dove!
(He'll have that jug off, with another shove!)
Dear nursling of the Hymeneal nest!
(Are those torn clothes his best?)
Little epitome of man!
(He'll climb upon the table, that's his plan!)
Touchéd with the beauteous tints of dawning life —
(He's got a knife!)

Thou enviable being!
No storms, no clouds, in thy blue sky foreseeing,

Play on, play on,
My elfin John!
Toss the light ball — bestride the stick —
(I knew so many cakes would make him sick!)
With fancies, buoyant as the thistle-down,
Prompting the face grotesque, and antic brisk,
With many a lamb-like frisk,
(He's got the scissors, snipping at your gown!)

Thou pretty opening rose!
(Go to your mother, child, and wipe your nose!)
Balmy and breathing music like the South,
(He really brings my heart into my mouth!)
Fresh as the morn, and brilliant as its star, —
(I wish that window had an iron bar!)
Bold as the hawk, yet gentle as the dove, —
(I'll tell you what, my love,
I cannot write unless he's sent above!)

IV.

A SERENADE.

"LULLABY, O, lullaby!"
Thus I heard a father cry,
"Lullaby, O, lullaby!
The brat will never shut an eye;
Hither come, some power divine!
Close his lids, or open mine!"

"Lullaby, O, lullaby!
What the devil makes him cry?
Lullaby, O, lullaby!
Still he stares — I wonder why,
Why are not the sons of earth
Blind, like puppies, from the birth?"

"Lullaby, O, lullaby!"
Thus I heard the father cry;
"Lullaby, O, lullaby!
Mary, you must come and try!—
Hush, O, hush, for mercy's sake—
The more I sing, the more you wake!"

"Lullaby, O, lullaby!
Fie, you little creature, fie!
Lullaby, O, lullaby!
Is no poppy-syrup nigh?
Give him some, or give him all,
I am nodding to his fall!"

"Lullaby, O, lullaby!
Two such nights and I shall die!
Lullaby, O, lullaby!
He'll be bruised, and so shall I,—
How can I from bed-posts keep,
When I'm walking in my sleep!"

"Lullaby, O, lullaby!
Sleep his very looks deny—
Lullaby, O, lullaby!
Nature soon will stupefy—
My nerves relax,—my eyes grow dim—
Who's that fallen—me or him?"

A PLAIN DIRECTION.

"Do you never deviate?"—JOHN BULL.

IN London once I lost my way in faring to and fro,
And asked a ragged little boy the way that I should go;

He gave a nod, and then a wink, and told me to get there
"Straight down the Crooked Lane, and all round the
Square."

I boxed his little saucy ears, and then away I strode;
But since I've found that weary path is quite a common
road.
Utopia is a pleasant place, but how shall I get there?
"Straight down the Crooked Lane, and all round the
Square."

I've read about a famous town that drove a famous trade,
Where Whittington walked up and found a fortune ready
made.
The very streets are paved with gold; but how shall I
get there?
"Straight down the Crooked Lane, and all round the
Square."

I've read about a Fairy Land, in some romantic tale,
Where dwarfs if good are sure to thrive, and wicked
giants fail;
My wish is great, my shoes are strong, but how shall I
get there?
"Straight down the Crooked Lane, and all round the
Square."

I've heard about some happy isle, where every man is
free,
And none can lie in bonds for life for want of L. S. D.
O! that's the land of Liberty! but how shall I get there?
"Straight down the Crooked Lane, and all round the
Square."

I've dreamt about some blessed spot, beneath the blessed
sky,
Where bread and justice never rise too dear for folks to
buy.

It's cheaper than the Ward of Cheap, but how shall I
get there?
"Straight down the Crooked Lane, and all round the
Square."

They say there is an ancient house, as pure as it is old,
Where members always speak their minds, and votes are
never sold.
I'm fond of all antiquities, but how shall I get there?
"Straight down the Crooked Lane, and all round the
Square."

They say there is a royal court maintained in noble state,
Where every able man, and good, is certain to be great!
I'm very fond of seeing sights, but how shall I get there?
"Straight down the Crooked Lane, and all round the
Square."

They say there is a temple too, where Christians come to
pray;
But canting knaves and hypocrites and bigots keep away.
O! that's the parish church for me! but how shall I get
there?
"Straight down the Crooked Lane, and all round the
Square."

They say there is a garden fair, that's haunted by the
dove,
Where love of gold doth ne'er eclipse the golden light
of love;
The place must be a Paradise, but how shall I get there?
"Straight down the Crooked Lane, and all round the
Square."

I've heard there is a famous land for public spirit known —
Whose patriots love its interests much better than their
own.

The Land of Promise sure it is! but how shall I get
there?
"Straight down the Crooked Lane, and all round the
Square."

I've read about a fine estate, a mansion large and strong;
A view all over Kent and back, and going for a song.
George Robins knows the very spot, but how shall I get
there?
"Straight down the Crooked Lane, and all round the
Square."

I've heard there is a company all formal and enrolled,
Will take your smallest silver coin and give it back in
gold.
Of course the office-door is mobbed, but how shall I get
there?
"Straight down the Crooked Lane, and all round the
Square."

I've heard about a pleasant land, where omelettes grow
on trees,
And roasted pigs run crying out, "Come eat me, if you
please."
My appetite is rather keen, but how shall I get there?
"Straight down the Crooked Lane, and all round the
Square."

EQUESTRIAN COURTSHIP.

It was a young maiden went forth to ride,
And there was a wooer to pace by her side;
His horse was so little, and hers so high,
He thought his angel was up in the sky.

His love was great, though his wit was small;
He bade her ride easy — and that was all.
The very horses began to neigh, —
Because their betters had nought to say.

They rode by elm, and they rode by oak,
They rode by a church-yard, and then he spoke: —
"My pretty maiden, if you'll agree
You shall always ramble through life with me."

The damsel answered him never a word,
But kicked the gray mare, and away she spurred.
The wooer still followed behind the jade,
And enjoyed — like a wooer — the dust she made.

They rode through moss, and they rode through moor,
The gallant behind, and the lass before; —
At last they came to a miry place,
And there the sad wooer gave up the chase.

Quoth he, "If my nag were better to ride,
I'd follow her over the world so wide.
O, it is not my love that begins to fail,
But I've lost the last glimpse of the gray mare's tail!"

AN OPEN QUESTION.

"It is the king's highway that we are in, and in this way it is that thou hast placed the lions." — BUNYAN.

WHAT! shut the gardens! lock the latticed gate!
  Refuse the shilling and the fellow's ticket!
And hang a wooden notice up to state,
  "On Sundays no admittance at this wicket!"
The Birds, the Beasts, and all the Reptile race,

Denied to friends and visitors till Monday!
Now, really, this appears the common case
Of putting too much Sabbath into Sunday—
But what is your opinion, Mrs. Grundy?

The Gardens,—so unlike the ones we dub
Of Tea, wherein the artisan carouses,—
Mere shrubberies without one drop of shrub,
Wherefore should they be closed like public houses?
No ale is vended at the wild Deer's Head,—
No rum—nor gin—not even of a Monday—
The Lion is not carved—or gilt—or red,—
And does not send out porter of a Sunday—
But what is your opinion, Mrs. Grundy?

The Bear denied! the Leopard under locks!
As if his spots would give contagious fevers!
The Beaver close as hat within its box;
So different from other Sunday beavers!
The Birds invisible—the Gnaw-way Rats—
The Seal hermetically sealed till Monday—
The Monkey tribe—the Family of Cats,—
We visit other families on Sunday—
But what is your opinion, Mrs. Grundy?

What is the brute profanity that shocks
The super-sensitively serious feeling?
The Kangaroo—is he not orthodox
To bend his legs, the way he does, in kneeling?
Was strict Sir Andrew, in his Sabbath coat,
Struck all a-heap to see a *Coati mundi?*
Or did the Kentish Plumtree faint to note
The Pelicans presenting bills on Sunday?—
But what is your opinion, Mrs. Grundy?

What feature has repulsed the serious set?
  What error in the bestial birth or breeding,
To put their tender fancies on the fret?
  One thing is plain — it is not in the feeding!
Some stiffish people think that smoking joints
  Are carnal sins 'twixt Saturday and Monday —
But then the beasts are pious on these points,
  For they all eat cold dinners on a Sunday —
  But what is your opinion, Mrs. Grundy?

What change comes o'er the spirit of the place,
  As if transmuted by some spell organic?
Turns fell Hyena of the Ghoulish race?
  The Snake, *pro tempore*, the true Satanic?
Do Irish minds, — (whose theory allows
  That now and then Good Friday falls on Monday) —
Do Irish minds suppose that Indian Cows
  Are wicked Bulls of Bashan on a Sunday? —
  But what is your opinion, Mrs. Grundy?

There are some moody Fellows, not a few,
  Who, turned by Nature with a gloomy bias,
Renounce black devils to adopt the blue,
  And think when they are dismal they are pious:
Is't possible that Pug's untimely fun
  Has sent the brutes to Coventry till Monday —
Or perhaps some animal, no serious one,
  Was overheard in laughter on a Sunday —
  But what is your opinion, Mrs. Grundy?

What dire offence have serious Fellows found
  To raise their spleen against the Regent's spinney?
Were charitable boxes handed round,
  And would not Guinea Pigs subscribe their guinea?
Perchance, the Demoiselle refused to moult

The feathers in her head — at least till Monday;
Or did the Elephant, unseemly, bolt
A tract presented to be read on Sunday? —
But what is your opinion, Mrs. Grundy?

At whom did Leo struggle to get loose?
Who mourns through Monkey tricks his damaged clothing?
Who has been hissed by the Canadian Goose?
On whom did Llama spit in utter loathing?
Some Smithfield Saint did jealous feelings tell
To keep the Puma out of sight till Monday,
Because he preyed extempore as well
As certain wild Itinerants on Sunday —
But what is your opinion, Mrs. Grundy?

To me it seems that in the oddest way
(Begging the pardon of each rigid Socius)
Our would-be Keepers of the Sabbath-day
Are like the Keepers of the brutes ferocious —
As soon the Tiger might expect to stalk
About the grounds from Saturday till Monday,
As any harmless man to take a walk,
If Saints could clap him in a cage on Sunday —
But what is your opinion, Mrs. Grundy?

In spite of all hypocrisy can spin,
As surely as I am a Christian scion,
I cannot think it is a mortal sin —
(Unless he's loose) — to look upon a lion.
I really think that one may go, perchance,
To see a bear, as guiltless as on Monday —
(That is, provided that he did not dance) —
Bruin's no worse than bakin' on a Sunday) —
But what is your opinion, Mrs. Grundy?

In spite of all the fanatic compiles,
I cannot think the day a bit diviner,
Because no children, with forestalling smiles,
Throng, happy, to the gates of Eden Minor—
It is not plain, to my poor faith, at least,
That what we christen "Natural" on Monday,
The wondrous history of Bird and Beast,
Can be unnatural because it's Sunday—
But what is your opinion, Mrs. Grundy?

Whereon is sinful fantasy to work?
The Dove, the winged Columbus of man's haven?
The tender Love-Bird—or the filial Stork?
The punctual Crane—the providential Raven?
The Pelican whose bosom feeds her young?
Nay, must we cut from Saturday till Monday
That feathered marvel with a human tongue,
Because she does not preach upon a Sunday—
But what is your opinion, Mrs. Grundy?

The busy Beaver—that sagacious beast!
The Sheep that owned an Oriental Shepherd—
That Desert-ship, the Camel of the East,
The horned Rhinoceros—the spotted Leopard—
The Creatures of the Great Creator's hand
Are surely sights for better days than Monday—
The Elephant, although he wears no band,
Has he no sermon in his trunk for Sunday?—
But what is your opinion, Mrs. Grundy?

What harm if men who burn the midnight-oil,
Weary of frame, and worn and wan of feature,
Seek once a week their spirits to assoil,
And snatch a glimpse of "Animated Nature"?
Better it were if, in his best of suits,

The artisan, who goes to work on Monday,
Should spend a leisure-hour amongst the brutes,
Than make a beast of his own self on Sunday —
But what is your opinion, Mrs. Grundy?

Why, zounds! what raised so Protestant a fuss
(Omit the zounds! for which I make apology)
But that the Papists, like some Fellows, thus
Had somehow mixed up *Dens* with their Theology?
Is Brahma's Bull — a Hindoo god at home —
A Papal Bull to be tied up till Monday —
Or Leo, like his namesake, Pope of Rome,
That there is such a dread of them on Sunday —
But what is your opinion, Mrs. Grundy?

Spirit of Kant! have we not had enough
To make Religion sad, and sour, and snubbish,
But Saints Zoological must cant their stuff,
As vessels cant their ballast — rattling rubbish!
Once let the sect, triumphant to their text,
Shut Nero up from Saturday till Monday,
And sure as fate they will deny us next
To see the Dandelions on a Sunday —
But what is your opinion, Mrs. Grundy?

A BLACK JOB.

"No doubt the pleasure is as great
Of being cheated as to cheat." — HUDIBRAS.

THE history of human-kind to trace
Since Eve — the first of dupes — our doom unriddled,
A certain portion of the human race
Has certainly a taste for being diddled.

Witness the famous Mississippi dreams!
  A rage that time seems only to redouble —
The Banks, Joint-Stocks, and all the flimsy schemes,
    For rolling in Pactolian streams,
That cost our modern rogues so little trouble.
No matter what, — to pasture cows on stubble,
  To twist sea-sand into a solid rope,
To make French bricks and fancy bread of rubble,
Or light with gas the whole celestial cope —
    Only propose to blow a bubble,
And, Lord! what hundreds will suscribe for soap!

Soap! it reminds me of a little tale,
  Though not a pig's, the hawbuck's glory,
When rustic games and merriment prevail —
    But here's my story:
Once on a time — no matter when —
A knot of very charitable men
  Set up a Philanthropical Society,
   Professing on a certain plan
   To benefit the race of man,
  And in particular that dark variety,
Which some suppose inferior — as in vermin,
    The sable is to ermine,
As smut to flour, as coal to alabaster,
  As crows to swans, or soot to driven snow,
  As blacking, or as ink to "milk below,"
  Or yet, a better simile to show,
As ragman's dolls to images in plaster!

However, as is usual in our city,
They had a sort of managing Committee,
  A board of grave, responsible Directors —
A Secretary, good at pen and ink —
A Treasurer, of course, to keep the chink,

And quite an army of Collectors!
Not merely male, but female duns,
Young, old, and middle-aged — of all degrees —
With many of those persevering ones,
Who mite by mite would beg a cheese!
And what might be their aim?
To rescue Afric's sable sons from fetters —
To save their bodies from the burning shame
Of branding with hot letters —
Their shoulders from the cowhide's bloody strokes,
Their necks from iron yokes?
To end or mitigate the ills of slavery,
The Planter's avarice, the Driver's knavery?
To school the heathen negroes and enlighten 'em,
To polish up and brighten 'em,
And make them worthy of eternal bliss?
Why, no — the simple end and aim was this —
Reading a well-known proverb much amiss —
To wash and whiten 'em!

They looked so ugly in their sable hides;
So dark, so dingy, like a grubby lot
Of sooty sweeps, or colliers, and besides,
However the poor elves,
Might wash themselves,
Nobody knew if they were clean or not —
On Nature's fairness they were quite a blot!
Not to forget more serious complaints
That even while they joined in pious hymn,
So black they were and grim,
In face and limb,
They looked like Devils, though they sang like Saints:
The thing was undeniable!
They wanted washing! not that slight ablution

To which the skin of the white man is liable,
Merely removing transient pollution —
  But good, hard, honest, energetic rubbing
      And scrubbing,
Sousing each sooty frame from heels to head
  With stiff, strong saponaceous lather,
  And pails of water — hottish rather,
But not so boiling as to turn 'em red!

So spoke the philanthropic man
Who laid, and hatched, and nursed the plan —
  And, O! to view its glorious consummation!
      The brooms and mops,
      The tubs and slops,
  The baths and brushes in full operation!
To see each Crow, or Jim, or John,
Go in a raven and come out a swan!
  While fair as Cavendishes, Vanes, and Russels,
Black Venus rises from the soapy surge,
And all the little Niggerlings emerge
  As lily-white as mussels.

Sweet was the vision — but, alas!
  However in prospectus bright and sunny,
To bring such visionary scenes to pass
  One thing was requisite, and that was — money!
Money, that pays the laundress and her bills,
For socks, and collars, shirts, and frills,
Cravats, and kerchiefs — money, without which
The Negroes must remain as dark as pitch;
  A thing to make all Christians sad and shivery,
To think of millions of immortal souls
Dwelling in bodies black as coals,
  And living — so to speak — in Satan's livery!

Money — the root of evil — dross and stuff!
  But, O! how happy ought the rich to feel,
Whose means enabled them to give enough
  To blanch an African from head to heel!
How blessed — yea, thrice blessed — to subscribe
    Enough to scour a tribe!
While he whose fortune was at best a brittle one,
Although he gave but pence, how sweet to know
He helped to bleach a Hottentot's great toe,
    Or little one!

Moved by this logic, or appalled,
  To persons of a certain turn so proper,
The money came when called,
In silver, gold, and copper,
Presents from "friends to blacks," or foes to whites,
"Trifles," and "offerings," and "widow's mites,"
Plump legacies, and yearly benefactions,
    With other gifts
    And charitable lifts,
Printed in lists and quarterly transactions.
    As thus — Elisha Brettel,
      An iron kettle.
      The Dowager Lady Scannel,
      A piece of flannel.
      Rebecca Pope,
      A bar of soap.
      The Misses Howels,
      Half-a-dozen towels.
      The Master Rush's
      Two scrubbing-brushes.
      Mr. T. Groom,
      A stable-broom,
      And Mrs. Grubb,
        A tub.

Great were the sums collected!
And great results in consequence expected.
But somehow, in the teeth of all endeavor,
According to reports
At yearly courts,
The Blacks, confound them! were as black as ever!

Yes! spite of all the water soused aloft,
Soap, plain and mottled, hard and soft,
Soda and pearlash, huckaback and sand,
Brooms, brushes, palm of hand,
And scourers in the office strong and clever,
In spite of all the tubbing, rubbing, scrubbing,
The routing and the grubbing,
The Blacks, confound them! were as black as ever!

In fact, in his perennial speech,
The Chairman owned the Niggers did not bleach,
As he had hoped,
From being washed and soaped,
A circumstance he named with grief and pity;
But still he had the happiness to say,
For self and the Committee,
By persevering in the present way,
And scrubbing at the Blacks from day to day,
Although he could not promise perfect white,
From certain symptoms that had come to light,
He hoped in time to get them gray!

Lulled by this vague assurance,
The friends and patrons of the sable tribe
Continued to subscribe,
And waited, waited on with much endurance —
Many a frugal sister, thrifty daughter —
Many a stinted widow, pinching mother —

With income by the tax made somewhat shorter,
Still paid implicitly her crown per quarter,
Only to hear, as every year came round,
That Mr. Treasurer had spent her pound;
And as she loved her sable brother,
That Mr. Treasurer must have another!

But, spite of pounds or guineas,
Instead of giving any hint
Of turning to a neutral tint,
The plaguy Negroes and their piccaninnies
Were still the color of the bird that caws —
Only some very aged souls,
Showing a little gray upon their polls,
Like daws!

However, nothing dashed
By such repeated failures, or abashed,
The Court still met; — the Chairman and Directors,
The Secretary, good at pen and ink,
The worthy Treasurer, who kept the chink,
And all the cash Collectors;
With hundreds of that class, so kindly credulous,
Without whose help no charlatan alive
Or Bubble Company could hope to thrive,
Or busy Chevalier, however sedulous —
Those good and easy innocents, in fact,
Who, willingly receiving chaff for corn,
As pointed out by Butler's tact,
Still find a secret pleasure in the act
Of being plucked and shorn!

However, in long hundreds there they were,
Thronging the hot, and close, and dusty court,

To hear once more addresses from the Chair,
        And regular Report.
Alas! concluding in the usual strain,
    That what with everlasting wear and tear,
    The scrubbing-brushes hadn't got a hair —
The brooms — mere stumps — would never serve again —
The soap was gone, the flannels all in shreds,
        The towels worn to threads,
The tubs and pails too shattered to be mended —
    And what was added with a deal of pain,
    But as accounts correctly would explain,
Though thirty thousand pounds had been expended —
    The Blackamoors had still been washed in vain!

"In fact, the Negroes were as black as ink,
Yet, still as the Committee dared to think,
And hoped the proposition was not rash,
A rather free expenditure of cash — "
But ere the prospect could be made more sunny —
    Up jumped a little, lemon-colored man,
    And with an eager stammer, thus began,
In angry earnest, though it sounded funny:
"What! More subscriptions! No — no — no, — not I!
You have had time — time — time enough to try!
They WON'T come white! then why — why — why — why — why,
            More money?"

"Why!" said the Chairman, with an accent bland,
And gentle waving of his dexter hand,
"Why must we have more dross, and dirt, and dust,
    More filthy lucre, in a word more gold —
    The why, sir, very easily is told,
Because Humanity declares we must!

We've scrubbed the Negroes till we've nearly killed 'em,
  And, finding that we cannot wash them white,
  But still their nigritude offends the sight,
      We mean to gild 'em!"

ODE TO RAE WILSON, ESQUIRE.

"Close, close your eyes with holy dread,
  And weave a circle round him thrice;
  For he on honey-dew hath fed,
  And drunk the milk of Paradise!" — COLERIDGE

"It's very hard them kind of men
  Won't let a body be." — OLD BALLAD.

A WANDERER, Wilson, from my native land,
Remote, O Rae, from godliness and thee,
Where rolls between us the eternal sea,
Besides some furlongs of a foreign sand, —
Beyond the broadest Scotch of London Wall;
Beyond the loudest Saint that has a call;
Across the wavy waste between us stretched,
A friendly missive warns me of a stricture,
Wherein my likeness you have darkly etched,
And though I have not seen the shadow sketched,
Thus I remark prophetic on the picture.

I guess the features: — in a line to paint
Their moral ugliness, I'm not a saint.
Not one of those self-constituted saints,
Quacks — not physicians — in the cure of souls,
Censors who sniff out moral taints,
And call the devil over his own coals —
Those pseudo Privy Councillors of God,
Who write down judgments with a pen hard-nibbed;

Ushers of Beelzebub's Black Rod,
Commending sinners not to ice thick-ribbed,
But endless flames, to scorch them like flax,—
Yet sure of heaven themselves, as if they'd cribbed
The impression of St. Peter's keys in wax!

Of such a character no single trace
Exists, I know, in my fictitious face;
There wants a certain cast about the eye;
A certain lifting of the nose's tip;
A certain curling of the nether lip,
In scorn of all that is, beneath the sky;
In brief, it is an aspect deleterious,
A face decidedly not serious,
A face profane, that would not do at all
To make a face at Exeter Hall,—
That Hall where bigots rant, and cant, and pray,
And laud each other face to face,
Till every farthing-candle *ray*
Conceives itself a great gas-light of grace!

Well!—be the graceless lineaments confest!
I do enjoy this bounteous beauteous earth;
And dote upon a jest
"Within the limits of becoming mirth;"—
No solemn sanctimonious face I pull,
Nor think I'm pious when I'm only bilious—
Nor study in my sanctum supercilious
To frame a Sabbath Bill or forge a Bull.
I pray for grace—repent each sinful act—
Peruse, but underneath the rose, my Bible;
And love my neighbor, far too well, in fact,
To call and twit him with a godly tract
That's turned by application to a libel.
My heart ferments not with the bigot's leaven,

All creeds I view with toleration thorough,
And have a horror of regarding heaven
As any body's rotten borough.

What else? No part I take in party fray,
With tropes from Billingsgate's slang-whanging Tartars,
I fear no Pope — and let great Ernest play
At Fox and Goose with Fox's Martyrs!
I own I laugh at over-righteous men,
I own I shake my sides at ranters,
And treat sham Abr'am saints with wicked banters;
I even own, that there are times — but then
It's when I've got my wine — I say d—— canters!

I've no ambition to enact the spy
On fellow-souls, a spiritual Pry —
'Tis said that people ought to guard their noses
Who thrust them into matters none of theirs:
And, though no delicacy discomposes
Your saint, yet I consider faith and prayers
Amongst the privatest of men's affairs.

I do not hash the Gospel in my books,
And thus upon the public mind intrude it,
As if I thought, like Otaheitan cooks,
No food was fit to eat till I had chewed it.

On Bible stilts I don't affect to stalk;
Nor lard with Scripture my familiar talk, —
For man may pious texts repeat,
And yet religion have no inward seat;
'Tis not so plain as the old Hill of Howth,
A man has got his belly full of meat
Because he talks with victuals in his mouth!

Mere verbiage, — it is not worth a carrot!
Why, Socrates or Plato — where's the odds? —

Once taught a Jay to supplicate the gods,
And made a Polly-theist of a Parrot!

A mere professor, spite of all his cant, is
Not a whit better than a Mantis, —
An insect, of what clime I can't determine,
That lifts its paws most parson-like, and thence,
By simple savages — through sheer pretence —
Is reckoned quite a saint amongst the vermin.
But where's the reverence, or where the *nous*,
To ride on one's religion through the lobby,
Whether as stalking-horse or hobby,
To show its pious paces to "the house."

I honestly confess that I would hinder
The Scottish member's legislative rigs,
That spiritual Pindar,
Who looks on erring souls as straying pigs,
That must be lashed by law, wherever found,
And driven to church as to the parish pound.
I do confess, without reserve or wheedle,
I view that grovelling idea as one
Worthy some parish clerk's ambitious son,
A charity-boy who longs to be a beadle.
On such a vital topic sure 'tis odd
How much a man can differ from his neighbor;
One wishes worship freely given to God,
Another wants to make it statute-labor —
The broad distinction in a line to draw,
As means to lead us to the skies above,
You say — Sir Andrew and his love of law,
And I — the Saviour with his law of love.

Spontaneously to God should tend the soul,
Like the magnetic needle to the Pole;

But what were that intrinsic virtue worth,
Suppose some fellow, with more zeal than knowledge,
        Fresh from St. Andrew's college,
Should nail the conscious needle to the north?
I do confess that I abhor and shrink
From schemes, with a religious willy-nilly,
That frown upon St. Giles's sins, but blink
The peccadilloes of all Piccadilly —
My soul revolts at such bare hypocrisy,
And will not, dare not, fancy in accord
The Lord of Hosts with an exclusive lord
Of this world's aristocracy.
It will not own a notion so unholy,
As thinking that the rich by easy trips
May go to heaven, whereas the poor and lowly
Must work their passage, as they do in ships.

One place there is — beneath the burial-sod,
Where all mankind are equalized by death;
Another place there is — the Fane of God,
Where all are equal who draw living breath; —
Juggle who will *elsewhere* with his own soul,
Playing the Judas with a temporal dole —
He who can come beneath that awful cope,
In the dread presence of a Maker just,
Who metes to every pinch of human dust
One even measure of immortal hope —
He who can stand within that holy door,
With soul unbowed by that pure spirit-level,
And frame unequal laws for rich and poor, —
Might sit for Hell, and represent the Devil!

Such are the solemn sentiments, O Rae,
In your last journey-work, perchance, you ravage,
Seeming, but in more courtly terms, to say
I'm but a heedless, creedless, godless, savage;

A very Guy, deserving fire and fagots,—
        A scoffer, always on the grin,
And sadly given to the mortal sin
Of liking Mawworms less than merry maggots!

The humble records of my life to search,
I have not herded with mere pagan beasts;
But sometimes I have "sat at good men's feasts,"
And I have been "where bells have knolled to church."
Dear bells! how sweet the sound of village bells
When on the undulating air they swim!
Now loud as welcomes! faint, now, as farewells!
And trembling all about the breezy dells,
As fluttered by the wings of Cherubim.
Meanwhile the bees are chanting a low hymn;
And lost to sight the ecstatic lark above
Sings, like a soul beatified, of love,
With, now and then, the coo of the wild pigeon:—
O pagans, heathens, infidels, and doubters!
If such sweet sounds can't woo you to religion,
Will the harsh voices of church cads and touters?

A man may cry Church! Church! at every word,
With no more piety than other people—
A daw's not reckoned a religious bird
Because it keeps a-cawing from a steeple;
The Temple is a good, a holy place,
But quacking only gives it an ill savor;
While saintly mountebanks the porch disgrace,
And bring religion's self into disfavor!

Behold yon servitor of God and Mammon,
Who, binding up his Bible with his ledger,
Blends Gospel texts with trading gammon,
A black-leg saint, a spiritual hedger,

Who backs his rigid Sabbath, so to speak,
Against the wicked remnant of the week,
A saving bet against his sinful bias —
"Rogue that I am," he whispers to himself,
"I lie — I cheat — do any thing for pelf,
But who on earth can say I am not pious!"

In proof how over-righteousness reacts,
Accept an anecdote well based on facts;
On Sunday morning — (at the day don't fret) —
In riding with a friend to Ponder's End,
Outside the stage, we happened to commend
A certain mansion that we saw To Let.
"Ay," cried our coachman, with our talk to grapple,
"You're right! no house along the road comes nigh it!
'Twas built by the same man as built yon chapel,
    And master wanted once to buy it, —
But t'other driv the bargain much too hard, —
    He axed sure-*ly* a sum prodigious!
But being so particular religious,
Why, *that*, you see, put master on his guard!"
    Church is "a little heaven below,
    I have been there, and still would go," —
Yet I am none of those who think it odd
    A man can pray unbidden from the cassock,
    And, passing by the customary hassock,
Kneel down remote upon the simple sod,
And sue in formâ pauperis to God.

As for the rest, — intolerant to none,
Whatever shape the pious rite may bear,
Even the poor pagan's homage to the sun
I would not harshly scorn, lest even there
I spurned some elements of Christian prayer —
An aim, though erring, at a "world ayont" —

Acknowledgment of good — of man's futility,
A sense of need, and weakness, and indeed
That very thing so many Christians want —
Humility.

Such, unto Papists, Jews, or Turbaned Turks,
Such is my spirit — (I don't mean my wraith !)
Such, may it please you, is my humble faith ;
I know, full well, you do not like my *works!*

I have not sought, 'tis true, the Holy Land,
As full of texts as Cuddie Hedrigg's mother,
The Bible in one hand,
And my own commonplace-book in the other —
But you have been to Palestine — alas !
Some minds improve by travel — others, rather,
Resemble copper wire or brass,
Which gets the narrower by going further !

Worthless are all such pilgrimages — very !
If Palmers at the Holy Tomb contrive
The human heats and rancor to revive
That at the Sepulchre they ought to bury.
A sorry sight it is to rest the eye on,
To see a Christian creature graze at Sion,
Then homeward, of the saintly pasture full,
Rush bellowing, and breathing fire and smoke,
At crippled Papistry to butt and poke,
Exactly as a skittish Scottish bull
Haunts an old woman in a scarlet cloak.

Why leave a serious, moral, pious home,
Scotland, renowned for sanctity of old,
Far distant Catholics to rate and scold
For — doing as the Romans do at Rome ?

With such a bristling spirit wherefore quit
The Land of Cakes for any land of wafers,
About the graceless images to flit,
And buzz and chafe importunate as chafers,
Longing to carve the carvers to Scotch collops? —
People who hold such absolute opinions
Should stay at home in Protestant dominions,
Not travel like male Mrs. Trollopes.

Gifted with noble tendency to climb,
Yet weak at the same time,
Faith is a kind of parasitic plant,
That grasps the nearest stem with tendril rings;
And as the climate and the soil may grant,
So is the sort of tree to which it clings.
Consider, then, before, like Hurlothrumbo,
You aim your club at any creed on earth,
That, by the simple accident of birth,
You might have been High Priest to Mumbo Jumbo.

For me — through heathen ignorance perchance,
Not having knelt in Palestine, — I feel
None of that griffinish excess of zeal
Some travellers would blaze with here in France.
Dolls I can see in Virgin-like array,
Nor for a scuffle with the idols hanker
Like crazy Quixotte at the puppet's play,
If their "offence be rank," should mine be *rancor*?

Mild light, and by degrees, should be the plan
To cure the dark and erring mind;
But who would rush at a benighted man,
And give him two black eyes for being blind?

Suppose the tender but luxuriant hop
Around a cankered stem should twine,

What Kentish boor would tear away the prop
So roughly as to wound, nay, kill the bine?

The images, 'tis true, are strangely dressed,
With gauds and toys extremely out of season;
The carving nothing of the very best,
The whole repugnant to the eye of Reason,
Shocking to Taste, and to Fine Arts a treason —
Yet ne'er o'erlook in bigotry of sect
One truly *Catholic*, one common form,
    At which unchecked
All Christian hearts may kindle or keep warm.

Say, was it to my spirit's gain or loss,
One bright and balmy morning, as I went
From Liege's lovely environs to Ghent,
If hard by the wayside I found a cross,
That made me breathe a prayer upon the spot —
While Nature of herself, as if to trace
The emblem's use, had trailed around its base
The blue significant Forget-Me-Not?
Methought, the claims of Charity to urge
More forcibly along with Faith and Hope,
The pious choice had pitched upon the verge
    Of a delicious slope,
Giving the eye much variegated scope! —
"Look round," it whispered, "on that prospect rare,
Those vales so verdant, and those hills so blue;
Enjoy the sunny world, so fresh and fair,
But" — (how the simple legend pierced me through!)
    "PRIEZ POUR LES MALHEUREUX."

With sweet kind natures, as in honeyed cells,
Religion lives, and feels herself at home;
But only on a formal visit dwells
Where wasps instead of bees have formed the comb.

Shun pride, O Rae! — whatever sort beside
You take in lieu, shun spiritual pride!
A pride there is of rank — a pride of birth,
A pride of learning, and a pride of purse,
A London pride — in short, there be on earth
A host of prides, some better and some worse;
But of all prides, since Lucifer's attaint,
The proudest swells a self-elected Saint.

To picture that cold pride so harsh and hard,
Fancy a peacock in a poultry-yard.
Behold him in conceited circles sail,
Strutting and dancing, and now planted stiff,
In all his pomp of pageantry, as if
He felt "the eyes of Europe" on his tail!
As for the humble breed retained by man,
  He scorns the whole domestic clan —
    He bows, he bridles,
    He wheels, he sidles,
As last, with stately dodgings in a corner,
He pens a simple russet hen, to scorn her
Full in the blaze of his resplendent fan!

  "Look here," he cries, (to give him words,)
  "Thou feathered clay, — thou scum of birds!"
Flirting the rustling plumage in her eyes, —
  "Look here, thou vile predestined sinner,
  Doomed to be roasted for a dinner,
Behold these lovely variegated dyes!
These are the rainbow colors of the skies,
That heaven has shed upon me *con amore* —
A Bird of Paradise? — a pretty story!
I am that Saintly Fowl, thou paltry chick!
    Look at my crown of glory!
Thou dingy, dirty, dabbled, draggled jill!"

And off goes Partlett, wriggling from a kick,
With bleeding scalp laid open by his bill!

That little simile exactly paints
How sinners are despised by saints.
By saints! — the Hypocrites that ope heaven's door
Obsequious to the sinful man of riches —
But put the wicked, naked, bare-legged poor,
In parish stocks, instead of breeches.

The Saints? — the Bigots that in public spout,
Spread phosphorus of zeal on scraps of fustian,
And go like walking "Lucifers" about,
Mere living bundles of combustion.

The Saints! — the aping Fanatics that talk
All cant and rant and rhapsodies high flown —
That bid you balk
A Sunday walk,
And shun God's work as you should shun your own.

The Saints! — the Formalists, the extra pious,
Who think the mortal husk can save the soul,
By trundling, with a mere mechanic bias,
To church, just like a lignum-vitæ bowl!

The Saints! — the Pharisees, whose beadle stands
Beside a stern coercive kirk,
A piece of human mason-work,
Calling all sermons contrabands,
In that great Temple that's not made with hands!

Thrice blessed, rather, is the man with whom
The gracious prodigality of nature,
The balm, the bliss, the beauty, and the bloom,
The bounteous providence in every feature,
Recall the good Creator to his creature,
Making all earth a fane, all heaven its dome!

To *his* tuned spirit the wild heather-bells
Ring Sabbath knells;
The jubilate of the soaring lark
Is chant of clerk;
For Choir, the thrush and the gregarious linnet;
The sod's a cushion for his pious want;
And, consecrated by the heaven within it,
The sky-blue pool, a font.
Each cloud-capped mountain is a holy altar;
An organ breathes in every grove;
And the full heart's a Psalter,
Rich in deep hymns of gratitude and love!

Sufficiently by stern necessitarians
Poor Nature, with her face begrimed by dust,
Is stoked, coked, smoked, and almost choked; but must
Religion have its own Utilitarians,
Labelled with evangelical phylacteries,
To make the road to heaven a railway trust,
And churches — that's the naked fact — mere factories?

O! simply open wide the temple door,
And let the solemn, swelling organ greet,
With *Voluntaries* meet,
The *willing* advent of the rich and poor!
And while to God the loud Hosannas soar,
With rich vibrations from the vocal throng —
From quiet shades that to the woods belong,
And brooks with music of their own,
Voices may come to swell the choral song
With notes of praise they learned in musings lone.

How strange it is, while on all vital questions,
That occupy the House and public mind,
We always meet with some humane suggestions

Of gentle measures of a healing kind,
Instead of harsh severity and vigor,
The saint alone his preference retains
For bills of penalties and pains,
And marks his narrow code with legal rigor!
Why shun, as worthless of affiliation,
What men of all political persuasion
Extol,—and even use upon occasion—
That Christian principle, conciliation?
But possibly the men who make such fuss
With Sunday pippins and old Trots infirm,
Attach some other meaning to the term,
As thus:

One market morning, in my usual rambles,
Passing along Whitechapel's ancient shambles,
Where meat was hung in many a joint and quarter,
I had to halt a while, like other folks,
To let a killing butcher coax
A score of lambs and fatted sheep to slaughter.
A sturdy man he looked to fell an ox,
Bull-fronted, ruddy, with a formal streak
Of well-greased hair down either cheek,
As if he dee-dashed-dee'd some other flocks
Besides those woolly-headed stubborn blocks
That stood before him, in vexatious huddle—
Poor little lambs, with bleating wethers grouped,
While, now and then, a thirsty creature stooped
And meekly snuffed, but did not taste the puddle.

Fierce barked the dog, and many a blow was dealt,
That loin, and chump, and scrag, and saddle felt,
Yet still, that fatal step they all declined it,—
And shunned the tainted door as if they smelt
Onions, mint-sauce, and lemon-juice behind it.

At last there came a pause of brutal force;
    The cur was silent, for his jaws were full
    Of tangled locks of tarry wool;
The man had whooped and bellowed till dead hoarse,
The time was ripe for mild expostulation,
And thus it stammered from a stander-by —
" Zounds ! — my good fellow, — it quite makes me — why
It really — my dear fellow — do just try
                    Conciliation ! "

    Stringing his nerves like flint,
The sturdy butcher seized upon the hint, —
At least he seized upon the foremost wether, —
And hugged and lugged and tugged him neck and crop
Just *nolens volens* through the open shop —
If tails come off he didn't care a feather, —
Then walking to the door, and smiling grim,
He rubbed his forehead and his sleeve together —
    " There ! — I've *con*ciliated him ! "

Again — good-humoredly to end our quarrel —
    (Good humor should prevail !)
    I'll fit you with a tale
    Whereto is tied a moral.

Once on a time a certain English lass
Was seized with symptoms of such deep decline,
Cough, hectic flushes, every evil sign,
That, as their wont is at such desperate pass,
The doctors gave her over — to an ass.

Accordingly, the grisly Shade to bilk,
Each morn the patient quaffed a frothy bowl
    Of asinine new milk,
Robbing a shaggy suckling of a foal

Which got proportionably spare and skinny —
Meanwhile the neighbors cried "Poor Mary Ann!
She can't get over it! she never can!"
When, lo! to prove each prophet was a ninny,
The one that died was the poor wet-nurse Jenny.

To aggravate the case,
There were but two grown donkeys in the place;
And, most unluckily for Eve's sick daughter,
The other long-eared creature was a male,
Who never in his life had given a pail
Of milk, or even chalk and water.
No matter: at the usual hour of eight
Down trots a donkey to the wicket-gate,
With Mister Simon Gubbins on his back, —
"Your sarvant, Miss, — a werry spring-like day, —
Bad time for hasses, though! good lack! good lack!
Jenny be dead, Miss, — but I'ze brought ye Jack, —
He doesn't give no milk — but he can bray."
So runs the story,
And, in vain self-glory,
Some Saints would sneer at Gubbins for his blindness;
But what the better are their pious saws
To ailing souls, than dry hee-haws,
Without the milk of human kindness?

A TABLE OF ERRATA.

(*Hostess loquitur.*)

Well! thanks be to Heaven,
The summons is given;
It's only gone seven,
And should have been six;

There's fine overdoing
In roasting and stewing,
And victuals past chewing
To rags and to sticks!

How dreadfully chilly!
I shake, willy-nilly;
That John is so silly,
And never will learn
This plate is a cold one,
That cloth is an old one, —
I wish they had told one
The lamp wouldn't burn.

Now then for some blunder
For nerves to sink under:
I never shall wonder,
Whatever goes ill.
That fish is a riddle!
It's broke in the middle.
A Turbot! a fiddle!
It's only a Brill!

It's quite over-boiled too,
The butter is oiled too,
The soap is all spoiled too,
It's nothing but slop.
The smelts looking flabby,
The soles are as dabby,
It all is so shabby
That Cook shall not stop!

As sure as the morning,
She gets a month's warning,
My orders for scorning —
There's nothing to eat!

I hear such a rushing,
I feel such a flushing,
I know I am blushing
  As red as a beet!

Friends flatter and flatter,
I wish they would chatter;
What *can* be the matter
  That nothing comes next?
How very unpleasant!
Lord! there is the pheasant!
Not wanted at present,
  I'm born to be vext!

The pudding brought on too,
And aiming at ton too!
And where is that John too,
  The plague that he is?
He's off on some ramble:
And there is Miss Campbell,
Enjoying the scramble,
  Detestable Quiz!

The veal they all eye it,
But no one will try it,
An Ogre would shy it
  So rudely as that!
And as for the mutton,
The cold dish it's put on
Converts to a button
  Each drop of the fat.

The beef without mustard!
My fate's to be flustered,
And there comes the custard
  To eat with the hare!

Such flesh, fowl, and fishing,
Such waiting and dishing,
I cannot help wishing
  A woman might swear!

O dear! did I ever —
But no, I did never —
Well, come, that is clever,
  To send up the brawn!
That Cook, I could scold her,
Gets worse as she's older;
I wonder who told her
  That woodcocks are drawn!

It's really audacious!
I cannot look gracious!
Lord help the voracious
  That came for a cram!
There's Alderman Fuller
Gets duller and duller.
Those fowls, by the color,
  Were boiled with the ham!

Well, where is the curry?
I'm all in a flurry.
No, Cook's in no hurry —
  A stoppage again!
And John makes it wider,
A pretty provider!
By bringing up cider
  Instead of champagne!

My troubles come faster!
There's my lord and master
Detects each disaster,
  And hardly can sit:

He cannot help seeing,
All things disagreeing;
If *he* begins d—ing
  I'm off in a fit!

This cooking?—it's messing!
The spinach wants pressing,
And salads in dressing
  Are best with good eggs.
And John—yes, already—
Has had something heady,
That makes him unsteady
  In keeping his legs.

How *shall* I get through it?
I never can do it,
I'm quite looking to it,
  To sink by and by.
O! would I were dead now,
Or up in my bed now,
To cover my head now,
  And have a good cry!

A ROW AT THE OXFORD ARMS.

"Glorious Apollo from on high behold us."—OLD SONG.

As latterly I chanced to pass
A Public House, from which, alas!
The Arms of Oxford dangle!
My ear was startled by a din,
That made me tremble in my skin,
A dreadful hubbub from within,
Of voices in a wrangle—

Voices loud, and voices high,
With now and then a party-cry,
Such as used in times gone by
To scare the British border:
When foes from North and South of Tweed—
Neighbors — and of Christian creed —
Met in hate to fight and bleed,
Upsetting Social Order.
Surprised, I turned me to the crowd,
Attracted by that tumult loud,
And asked a gazer, beetle-browed,
The cause of such disquiet.
When, lo! the solemn-looking man
First shook his head on Burleigh's plan,
And then, with fluent tongue, began
His version of the riot:

A row! — why, yes, — a pretty row, you might hear from this to Garmany,
And what is worse, it's all got up among the Sons of Harmony,
The more's the shame for them as used to be in time and tune,
And all unite in chorus like the singing-birds in June!
Ah! many a pleasant chant I've heard in passing here along,
When Swiveller was President a-knocking down a song;
But Dick's resigned the post, you see, and all them shouts and hollers
Is 'cause two other candidates, some sort of larned scholars,
Are squabbling to be Chairman of the Glorious Apollers!

Lord knows their names, I'm sure I don't, no more than any yokel,

But I never heard of either as connected with the vocal;
Nay, some do say, although of course the public rumor varies,
They've no more warble in 'em than a pair of hen canaries;
Though that might pass if they were dabs at t'other sort of thing,
For a man may make a song, you know, although he cannot sing;
But, lork! it's many folks' belief they're only good at prosing,
For Catnach swears he never saw a verse of their composing;
And when a piece of poetry has stood its public trials,
If pop'lar, it gets printed off at once in Seven Dials,
And then about all sorts of streets, by every little monkey,
It's chanted like the "Dog's Meat Man," or "If I had a Donkey."
Whereas, as Mr. Catnach says, and not a bad judge neither,
No ballad worth a ha'penny has ever come from either,
And him as writ "Jim Crow," he says, and got such lots of dollars,
Would make a better Chairman for the Glorious Apollers.

Howsomever that's the meaning of the squabble that arouses
This neighborhood, and quite disturbs all decent Heads of Houses,
Who want to have their dinners and their parties, as is reason,
In Christian peace and charity according to the season.
But from Number Thirty-Nine, since this electioneering job,
Ay, as far as Number Ninety, there's an everlasting mob;

Till the thing is quite a nuisance, for no creature passes by,
But he gets a card, a pamphlet, or a summut in his eye;
And a pretty noise there is! — what with canvassers and spouters,
For in course each side is furnished with its backers and its touters;
And surely among the Clergy to such pitches it is carried,
You can hardly find a Parson to get buried or get married;
Or supposing any accident that suddenly alarms,
If you're dying for a surgeon, you must fetch him from the "Arms:"
While the Schoolmasters and Tooters are neglecting of their scholars,
To write about a Chairman for the Glorious Apollers.

Well, that, sir, is the racket; and the more the sin and shame
Of them that help to stir it up, and propagate the same;
Instead of vocal ditties, and the social flowing cup, —
But they'll be the House's ruin, or the shutting of it up, —
With their riots and their hubbubs, like a garden full of bears,
While they've damaged many articles, and broken lots of squares,
And kept their noble Club Room in a perfect dust and smother,
By throwing *Morning Heralds*, *Times*, and *Standards* at each other;
Not to name the ugly language Gemmen ought n't to repeat,
And the names they call each other — for I've heard 'em in the street —

Such as Traitors, Guys, and Judases, and Vipers, and what not,
For Pasley and his divers an't so blowing-up a lot.
And then such awful swearing! — for there's one of them that cusses
Enough to shock the cads that hang on opposition 'busses;
For he cusses every member that's agin him at the poll,
As I wouldn't cuss a donkey, though it hasn't got a soul;
And he cusses all their families, Jack, Harry, Bob, or Jim,
To the babby in the cradle, if they don't agree with him.
Whereby, although as yet they have not took to use their fives,
Or, according as the fashion is, to sticking with their knives,
I'm bound there'll be some milling yet, and shakings by the collars,
Afore they choose a Chairman for the Glorious Apollers!

To be sure, it is a pity to be blowing such a squall,
Instead of clouds, and every man his song, and then his call —
And as if there was n't Whigs enough and Tories to fall out,
Besides politics in plenty for our splits to be about —
Why, a corn-field is sufficient, sir, as anybody knows,
For to furnish them in plenty who are fond of picking crows —
Not to name the Maynooth Catholics, and other Irish stews,
To agitate society and loosen all its screws;
And which all may be agreeable and proper to their spheres, —
But it's not the thing for musicals to set us by the ears.

And as to College larning, my opinion for to broach,
And I've had it from my cousin, and he driv a college
coach,
And so knows the University, and all as there belongs,
And he says that Oxford's famouser for sausages than
songs,
And seldom turns a poet out like Hudson that can
chant,
As well as make such ditties as the Free and Easies
want,
Or other Tavern Melodists I can't just call to mind —
But it's not the classic system for to propagate the
kind.
Whereby it so may happen as that neither of them
Scholars
May be the proper Chairman for the Glorious Apollers.

For my part in the matter, if so be I had a voice,
It's the best among the vocalists I'd honor with the
choice;
Or a poet as could furnish a new Ballad to the Bunch;
Or, at any rate, the surest hand at mixing of the punch;
'Cause why, the members meet for that and other tune-
ful frolics —
And not to say, like Muffincaps, their Catichiz and
Collec's.
But you see them there Initerants that preach so long
and loud,
And always take advantage like the prigs of any crowd,
Have brought their jangling voices, and as far as they
can compass,
Have turned a tavern shindy to a seriouser rumpus,
And him as knows most hymns — although I can't see
how it follers —
They want to be the Chairman of the Glorious Apollers!

Well, that's the row — and who can guess the upshot
after all?
Whether Harmony will ever make the "Arms" her
House of call,
Or whether this here mobbing — as some longish heads
foretell it,
Will grow to such a riot that the Oxford Blues must
quell it,
Howsomever, for the present, there's no sign of any
peace,
For the hubbub keeps a growing, and defies the New
Police;
But if I was in the Vestry, and a leading sort of Man,
Or a Member of the Vocals, to get backers for my
plan,
Why, I'd settle all the squabble in the twinkle of a
needle,
For I'd have another candidate — and that's the Parish
Beadle,
Who makes such lots of Poetry, himself, or else by
proxy,
And no one never has no doubts about his ortho-
doxy;
Whereby — if folks was wise — instead of either of
them Scholars,
And straining their own lungs along of contradictious
hollers,
They'll lend their ears to reason, and take my advice as
follers,
Namely — Bumble for the Chairman of the Glorious
Apollers!

ETCHING MORALIZED.

TO A NOBLE LADY.

"To point a moral." — JOHNSON.

FAIREST Lady and Noble, for once on a time,
Condescend to accept, in the humblest of rhyme,
  And a style more of Gay than of Milton,
A few opportune verses designed to impart
Some didactical hints in a Needlework Art,
  Not described by the Countess of Wilton.

An Art not unknown to the delicate hand
Of the fairest and first in this insular land,
  But in Patronage Royal delighting;
And which now your own feminine fantasy wins,
Though it scarce seems a lady-like work that begins
  In a *scratching* and ends in a *biting!*

Yet, O! that the dames of the Scandalous School
Would but use the same acid, and sharp-pointed tool,
  That are plied in the said operations —
O! would that our Candors on copper would sketch!
For the first of all things in beginning to etch
  Are — good *grounds* for our representations.

Those protective and delicate coatings of wax,
Which are meant to resist the corrosive attacks
  That would ruin the copper completely;
Thin cerements which whoso remembers the Bee,
So applauded by Watts, the divine LL. D.,
  Will be careful to spread very neatly.

For why? like some intricate deed of the law,
Should the ground in the process be left with a flaw,

Aquafortis is far from a joker;
And attacking the part that no coating protects
Will turn out as distressing to all your *effects*
As a landlord who puts in a broker.

Then carefully spread the conservative stuff,
Until all the bright metal is covered enough
To repel a destructive so active
For in Etching, as well as in Morals, pray note
That a little raw spot, or a hole in a coat,
Your ascetics find vastly attractive.

Thus the ground being laid, very even and flat,
And then smoked with a taper, till black as a hat,
Still from future disasters to screen it,
Just allow me, by way of precaution, to state,
You must hinder the footman from changing your *plate*,
Nor yet suffer the butler to clean it.

Nay, the housemaid, perchance, in her passion to scrub,
May suppose the dull metal in want of a rub,
Like the Shield which Swift's readers remember—
Not to mention the chance of some other mishaps,
Such as having your copper made up into caps
To be worn on the First of September.

But aloof from all damage by Betty or John,
You secure the veiled surface, and trace thereupon
The design you conceive the most proper:
Yet gently, and not with a needle too keen,
Lest it pierce to the wax through the paper between,
And of course play Old Scratch with the copper.

So in worldly affairs, the sharp-practising man
Is not always the one who succeeds in his plan,
Witness Shylock's judicial exposure;

Who, as keen as his knife, yet with agony found,
That while urging his *point* he was losing his *ground*,
  And incurring a fatal disclosure.

But, perhaps, without tracing at all, you may choose
To indulge in some little extempore views,
  Like the older artistical people;
For example, a Corydon playing his pipe,
In a Low Country Marsh, with a Cow after Cuyp,
  And a Goat skipping over a steeple.

A wild Deer at a rivulet taking a sup,
With a couple of Pillars put in to fill up,
  Like the columns of certain diurnals;
Or a very brisk sea, in a very stiff gale,
And a very Dutch boat, with a very big sail —
  Or a bevy of Retzsch's Infernals.

Architectural study — or rich Arabesque —
Allegorical dream — or a view picturesque,
  Near to Naples, or Venice, or Florence;
Or "as harmless as lambs and as gentle as doves,"
A sweet family cluster of plump little Loves,
  Like the Children by Reynolds or Lawrence.

But whatever the subject, your exquisite taste
Will insure a design very charming and chaste,
  Like yourself, full of nature and beauty —
Yet besides the *good points* you already reveal,
You will need a few others — of well-tempered steel,
  And especially formed for the duty.

For suppose that the tool be imperfectly set,
Over many *weak lengths in your line* you will fret,
  Like a pupil of Walton and Cotton
Who remains by the brink of the water, agape,

While the jack, trout, or barbel, effects its escape
  Through the gut or silk line being rotten.

Therefore let the steel point be set truly and round,
That the finest of strokes may be even and sound,
  Flowing glibly where fancy would lead 'em.
But, alas for the needle that fetters the hand,
And forbids even sketches of Liberty's land
  To be drawn with the requisite freedom!

O! the botches I've seen by a tool of the sort,
Rather hitching, than etching, and making, in short,
  Such stiff, crabbed, and angular scratches,
That the figures seemed statues or mummies from tombs,
While the trees were as rigid as bundles of brooms,
  And the herbage like bunches of matches!

The stiff clouds as if carefully ironed and starched,
While a cast-iron bridge, meant for wooden, o'er-arched
  Something more like a road than a river.
Prithee, who in such characteristics could see
Any trace of the beautiful land of the free —
  The Free-Mason — Free-Trader — Free-Liver!

But prepared by a hand that is skilful and nice,
The fine point glides along like a skate on the ice,
  At the will of the Gentle Designer,
Who impelling the needle just presses so much,
That each line of her labor *the copper may touch*,
  As if done by a penny-a-liner.

And, behold! how the fast-growing images gleam!
Like the sparkles of gold in a sunshiny stream,
  Till, perplexed by the glittering issue,
You repine for a light of a tenderer kind —
And in choosing a substance for making a blind,
  Do not sneeze at the paper called *tissue*.

For, subdued by the sheet so transparent and white,
Your design will appear in a soberer light,
And reveal its defects on inspection,
Just as Glory achieved, or political scheme,
And some more of our dazzling performances, seem
Not so bright on a *cooler reflection.*

So the juvenile Poet with ecstasy views
His first verses, and dreams that the songs of his Muse
Are as brilliant as Moore's and as tender —
Till some critical sheet scans the faulty design,
And, alas! *takes the shine out of every line*
That had formed such a vision of splendor.

Certain objects, however, may come in your sketch,
Which, designed by a hand unaccustomed to etch,
With a luckless result may be branded;
Wherefore add this particular rule to your code,
Let all vehicles take the *wrong* side of the road,
And man, woman, and child, be *left-handed.*

Yet regard not the awkward appearance with doubt,
But remember how often mere blessings fall out,
That at first seemed no better than curses;
So, till *things take a turn,* live in hope, and depend,
That whatever is wrong will come right in the end,
And console you for all your *reverses.*

But of errors why speak, when for beauty and truth
Your free, spirited Etching is worthy, in sooth,
Of that Club (may all honor betide it!)
Which, though dealing in copper, by genius and taste
Has accomplished *a service of plate* not disgraced
By the work of a Goldsmith beside it! *

* The Deserted Village, illustrated by the Etching Club.

So your sketch superficially drawn on the plate
It becomes you to fix in a permanent state,
   Which involves a precise operation,
With a keen-biting fluid, which *eating its way* —
As in other professions is common, they say —
   Has attained an artistical station.

And it's O! that some splenetic folks I could name,
If they *must* deal in acids, would use but the same
   In such innocent graphical labors!
In the place of the virulent spirit wherewith —
Like the polecat, the weasel, and things of that kith —
   They keep biting the backs of their neighbors!

But beforehand, with wax or the shoemaker's pitch,
You must build a neat dyke round the margin, in which
   You may pour the dilute aquafortis.
For if raw, like a dram, it will shock you to trace
Your design with a horrible froth on its face,
   Like a wretch in articulo mortis.

Like a wretch in the pangs that too many endure,
From the use of *strong waters,* without any pure,
   A vile practice, most sad and improper!
For, from painful examples, this warning is found,
That the raw burning spirit will *take up the ground,*
   In the church-yard, as well as on copper!

But the Acid has duly been lowered, and bites
Only just where the visible metal invites,
   Like a nature inclined to meet troubles;
And, behold! as each slender and glittering line
Effervesces, you trace the completed design
   In an elegant bead-work of bubbles!

And yet, constantly, secretly, eating its way,
The shrewd acid is making the substance its prey,
  Like some sorrow beyond inquisition,
Which is gnawing the heart and the brain all the while
That the face is illumed by its cheerfullest smile,
  And the wit is in bright ebullition.

But still stealthily feeding, the treacherous stuff
Has corroded and deepened some portions enough —
  The pure sky, and the water so placid —
And, these tenderer tints to defend from attack,
With some turpentine, varnish, and sooty lampblack,
  You must *stop* out the ferreting acid.

But before with the varnishing brush you proceed,
Let the plate with cold water be thoroughly freed
  From the other less innocent liquor —
After which, on whatever you want to protect,
Put a *coat* that will act to that very effect,
  Like the black one that hangs on the Vicar.

Then the varnish well dried — urge the biting again,
But how long at its meal the *eau forte* may remain,
  Time and practice alone can determine:
But of course not so long that the Mountain, and Mill,
The rude Bridge, and the Figures, whatever you will,
  Are as black as the spots on your ermine.

It is true, none the less, that a dark-looking scrap,
With a sort of Blackheath, and Black Forest, mayhap,
  Is considered as rather Rembrandty;
And that very black cattle, and very black sheep,
A black dog, and a shepherd as black as a sweep,
  Are the pets of some great Dilettante.

So with certain designers, one needs not to name,
All this life is a dark scene of sorrow and shame,
From our birth to our final adjourning —
Yea, this excellent earth and its glories, alack!
What with ravens, palls, cottons, and devils, as black
As a Warehouse for Family Mourning!

But before your own picture arrives at that pitch,
While the lights are still light, and the shadows, though rich,
More transparent than ebony shutters,
Never minding what Black-Arted critics may say,
Stop the biting, and pour the green fluid away,
As you please, into bottles or gutters.

Then removing the ground and the wax *at a heat*,
Cleanse the surface with oil, spermaceti, or sweet —
For your hand a performance scarce proper —
So some careful professional person secure —
For the Laundress will not be a safe amateur —
To assist you in *cleaning the copper.*

And, in truth, 'tis a rather unpleasantish job,
To be done on a hot German stove, or a hob —
Though as sure of an instant forgetting:
When — as after the dark clearing off of a storm —
The fair landscape shines out in a lustre as warm
As the glow of the sun in its setting!

Thus your Etching complete, it remains but to hint,
That with certain assistance from paper and print,
Which the proper Mechanic will settle,
You may charm all your Friends — without any sad tale
Of such perils and ills as bèset Lady Sale —
With *a fine India Proof of your Metal.*

ODE

ON A DISTANT PROSPECT OF CLAPHAM ACADEMY.

AH me! those old familiar bounds!
That classic house, those classic grounds,
My pensive thought recalls!
What tender urchins now confine,
What little captives now repine,
Within yon irksome walls!

Ay, that's the very house! I know
Its ugly windows, ten a-row!
Its chimneys in the rear!
And there's the iron rod so high,
That drew the thunder from the sky,
And turned our table-beer!

There I was birched! there I was bred!
There like a little Adam fed
From Learning's woful tree!
The weary tasks I used to con! —
The hopeless leaves I wept upon! —
Most fruitless leaves to me! —

The summoned class! — the awful bow! —
I wonder who is master now,
And wholesome anguish sheds!
How many ushers now employs,
How many maids to see the boys
Have nothing in their heads!

And Mrs. S * * *? — Doth she abet
(Like Pallas in the parlor) yet
Some favored two or three, —

The little Crichtons of the hour,
Her muffin-medals that devour,
And swill her prize — bohea?

Ay, there's the playground! there's the lime,
Beneath whose shade in summer's prime
So wildly I have read! —
Who sits there *now*, and skims the cream
Of young Romance, and weaves a dream
Of Love and Cottage-bread?

Who struts the Randall of the walk?
Who models tiny heads in chalk?
Who scoops the light canoe?
What early genius buds apace?
Where's Poynter? Harris? Bowers? Chase?
Hal Baylis? blithe Carew?

Alack! they're gone — a thousand ways!
And some are serving in "the Greys,"
And some have perished young! —
Jack Harris weds his second wife;
Hal Baylis drives the *wayne* of life;
And blithe Carew — is hung!

Grave Bowers teaches A B C
To Savages at Owhyee;
Poor Chase is with the worms! —
All, all are gone — the olden breed! —
New crops of mushroom boys succeed,
"And push us from our *forms!*"

Lo! where they scramble forth, and shout,
And leap, and skip, and mob about,
At play where we have played!

Some hop, some run, (some fall,) some twine
Their crony arms; some in the shine,
And some are in the shade!

Lo there what mixed conditions run!
The orphan lad; the widow's son;
And Fortune's favored care —
The wealthy born, for whom she hath
Macadamized the future path —
The nabob's pampered heir!

Some brightly starred — some evil born, —
For honor some, and some for scorn, —
For fair or foul renown!
Good, bad, indifferent — none they lack!
Look, here's a white, and there's a black!
And there's a creole brown!

Some laugh and sing, some mope and weep,
And wish *their* frugal sires would keep
Their only sons at home; —
Some tease the future tense, and plan
The full-grown doings of the man,
And pant for years to come!

A foolish wish! There's one at hoop;
And four at *fives!* and five who stoop
The marble taw to speed!
And one that curvets in and out,
Reining his fellow-cob about,
Would I were in his *steed!*

Yet he would gladly halt and drop
That boyish harness off, to swop
With this world's heavy van —
To toil, to tug. O little fool!

While thou canst be a horse at school
  To wish to be a man!

Perchance thou deem'st it were a thing
To wear a crown,—to be a king!
  And sleep on regal down!
Alas! thou know'st not kingly cares;
Far happier is thy head that wears
  That hat without a crown!

And dost thou think that years acquire
New added joys? Dost think thy sire
  More happy than his son?
That manhood's mirth?—O, go thy ways
To Drury-lane when ——— *plays*,
  And see how *forced* our fun!

Thy taws are brave!—thy tops are rare!—
Our tops are spun with coils of care,
  Our *dumps* are no delight!—
The Elgin marbles are but tame,
And 'tis at best a sorry game
  To fly the Muse's kite!

Our hearts are dough, our heels are lead,
Our topmost joys fall dull and dead,
  Like balls with no rebound!
And often with a faded eye
We look behind, and send a sigh
  Towards that merry ground!

Then be contented. Thou hast got
The most of heaven in thy young lot;
  There's sky-blue in thy cup!
Thou'lt find thy manhood all too fast—
Soon come, soon gone! and age at last
  A sorry *breaking up!*

A RETROSPECTIVE REVIEW.

O, WHEN I was a tiny boy
My days and nights were full of joy,
  My mates were blithe and kind! —
No wonder that I sometimes sigh,
And dash the tear-drop from my eye,
  To cast a look behind!

A hoop was an eternal round
Of pleasure. In those days I found
  A top a joyous thing; —
But now those past delights I drop;
My head, alas! is all my top,
  And careful thoughts the string!

My marbles, — once my bag was stored, —
Now I must play with Elgin's lord,
  With Theseus for a taw!
My playful horse has slipt his string!
Forgotten all his capering,
  And harnessed to the law!

My kite — how fast and far it flew!
Whilst I, a sort of Franklin, drew
  My pleasure from the sky!
'Twas papered o'er with studious themes,
The tasks I wrote — my present dreams
  Will never soar so high!

My joys are wingless all and dead;
My dumps are made of more than lead;
  My flights soon find a fall;
My fears prevail, my fancies droop,
Joy never cometh with a hoop,
  And seldom with a call!

My football's laid upon the shelf;
I am a shuttlecock myself
The world knocks to and fro; —
My archery is all unlearned,
And grief against myself has turned
My arrows and my bow!

No more in noontide sun I bask:
My authorship's an endless task,
My head's ne'er out of school;
My heart is pained with scorn and slight,
I have too many foes to fight,
And friends grown strangely cool!

The very chum that shared my cake
Holds out so cold a hand to shake,
It makes me shrink and sigh: —
On this I will not dwell and hang,
The changeling would not feel a pang
Though these should meet his eye!

No skies so blue or so serene
As then; — no leaves look half so green
As clothed the play-ground tree!
All things I loved are altered so,
Nor does it ease my heart to know
That change resides in me!

O, for the garb that marked the boy,
The trousers made of corduroy,
Well inked with black and red!
The crownless hat, ne'er deemed an ill —
It only let the sunshine still
Repose upon my head!

O, for the riband round the neck!
The careless dog's-ears apt to deck

My book and collar both!
How can this formal man be styled
Merely an Alexandrine child,
A boy of larger growth?

O, for that small, small beer anew!
And (heaven's own type) that mild sky-blue
That washed my sweet meals down;
The master even! — and that small Turk
That fagged me — worse is now my work —
A fag for all the town!

O, for the lessons learned by heart!
Ay, though the very birch's smart
Should mark those hours again;
I'd "kiss the rod," and be resigned
Beneath the stroke, and even find
Some sugar in the cane!

The Arabian Nights rehearsed in bed!
The Fairy Tales in school-time read,
By stealth, 'twixt verb and noun!
The angel form that always walked
In all my dreams, and looked and talked
Exactly like Miss Brown!

The *omne bene* — Christmas come!
The prize of merit, won for home —
Merit had prizes then!
But now I write for days and days,
For fame — a deal of empty praise,
Without the silver pen!

Then home, sweet home! the crowded coach —
The joyous shout — the loud approach —

The winding horns like rams'!
The meeting sweet that made me thrill,
The sweet-meats almost sweeter still,
No "satis" to the "jams!"—

When that I was a tiny boy
My days and nights were full of joy,
My mates were blithe and kind!
No wonder that I sometimes sigh,
And dash the tear-drop from my eye,
To cast a look behind!

FUGITIVE LINES ON PAWNING MY WATCH.

"Aurum *pot-a-bile:*"—Gold biles the pot.—FREE TRANSLATION.

FAREWELL then, my golden repeater,
We're come to my Uncle's old shop;
And hunger won't be a dumb-waiter,
The Cerberus growls for a sop.

To quit thee, my comrade diurnal,
My feelings will certainly scotch;
But O! there's a riot internal,
And Famine calls out for the Watch!

O! hunger's a terrible trial,
I really must have a relief—
So here goes the plates of your dial
To fetch me some Williams's beef!

As famished as any lost seaman,
I've fasted for many a dawn,
And now must play chess with the Demon,
And give it a *check* with a *pawn.*

I've fasted, since dining at Buncle's,
  Two days with true Perceval zeal —
And now must make up at my Uncle's,
  By getting a *duplicate* meal.

No Peachum it is, or young Lockit,
  That rifles my fob with a snatch;
Alas! I must pick my own pocket,
  And make gravy-soup of my watch!

So long I have wandered a starver,
  I'm getting as keen as a hawk;
Time's long hand must take up a carver,
  His short hand lay hold of a fork.

Right heavy and sad the event is,
  But O! it is Poverty's crime;
I've been such a Brownrigg's Apprentice,
  I thus must be "out of my Time."

Folks talk about dressing for dinner,
  But I have for dinner undrest;
Since Christmas, as I am a sinner,
  I've eaten a suit of my best.

I haven't a rag or a mummock
  To fetch me a chop or a steak;
I wish that the coats of my stomach
  Were such as my Uncle would take!

When dishes were ready with garnish
  My watch used to warn with a chime —
But now my repeater must furnish
  The dinner in lieu of the time!

39

My craving will have no denials,
  I can't fob it off, if you stay,
So go — and the old Seven Dials
  Must tell me the time of the day.

Your chimes I shall never more hear 'em,
  To part is a Tic Douloureux!
But Tempus has his edax rerum,
  And I have my Feeding-Time too!

Farewell then, my golden repeater,
  We're come to my Uncle's old shop —
And Hunger won't be a dumb-waiter,
  The Cerberus growls for a sop!

Alas! when in Brook Street the upper
  In comfort I lived between walls,
I've gone to a dance for my supper; —
  But now I must go to Three Balls!

THE BROKEN DISH.

WHAT'S life but full of care and doubt,
  With all its fine humanities?
With parasols we walk about,
  Long pigtails and such vanities.

We plant pomegranate trees and things,
  And go in gardens sporting,
With toys and fans of peacock's wings,
  To painted ladies courting.

We gather flowers of every hue,
  And fish in boats for fishes,

Build summer-houses painted blue—
  But life's as frail as dishes.

Walking about their groves of trees,
  Blue bridges and blue rivers,
How little thought them two Chinese,
  They'd both be smashed to shivers.

ODE TO PEACE.

WRITTEN ON THE NIGHT OF MY MISTRESS'S GRAND ROUT.

O PEACE! O come with me and dwell—
  But stop, for there's the bell.
O Peace! for thee I go and sit in churches,
    On Wednesday, when there's very few
      In loft or pew—
Another ring, the tarts are come from Birch's.
O Peace! for thee I have avoided marriage—
      Hush! there's a carriage.
O Peace! thou art the best of earthly goods—
      The five Miss Woods.
O Peace! thou art the Goddess I adore—
      There come some more.
O Peace! thou child of solitude and quiet—
That's Lord Drum's footman, for he loves a riot.
        O Peace!
      Knocks will not cease.
O Peace! thou wert for human comfort planned—
      That's Weippert's band.
O Peace! how glad I welcome thy approaches—
      I hear the sound of coaches.
O Peace! O Peace!—another carriage stops—
      It's early for the Blenkinsops.

O Peace! with thee I love to wander,
But wait till I have showed up Lady Squander,
And now I've seen her up the stair,
O Peace! — but here comes Captain Hare.
O Peace! thou art the slumber of the mind,
Untroubled, calm and quiet, and unbroken —
If that is Alderman Guzzle from Portsoken,
Alderman Gobble won't be far behind;
O Peace! serene in worldly shyness —
Make way there for his Serene Highness!

O Peace! if you do not disdain
To dwell amongst the menial train,
I have a silent place, and lone,
That you and I may call our own;
Where tumult never makes an entry —
Susan, what business have you in my pantry?
O Peace! but there is Major Monk,
At variance with his wife — O Peace!
And that great German, Vander Trunk,
And that great talker, Miss Apreece;
O Peace! so dear to poets' quills —
They're just beginning their quadrilles —
O Peace! our greatest renovator;
I wonder where I put my waiter —
O Peace! — but here my Ode I'll cease;
I have no peace to write of Peace.

POMPEY'S GHOST.

A PATHETIC BALLAD.

"Skins may differ, but affection
Dwells in white and black the same."
COWPER.

'TWAS twelve o'clock, not twelve at night,
But twelve o'clock at noon;
Because the sun was shining bright
And not the silver moon.
A proper time for friends to call,
Or Pots, or Penny Post;
When, lo! as Phœbe sat at work,
She saw her Pompey's Ghost!

Now when a female has a call
From people that are dead,
Like Paris ladies she receives
Her visitors in bed.
But Pompey's spirit would not come
Like spirits that are white,
Because he was a Blackamoor,
And wouldn't show at night!

But of all unexpected things
That happen to us here,
The most unpleasant is a rise
In what is very dear.
So Phœbe screamed an awful scream
To prove the seaman's text,
That after black appearances,
White squalls will follow next.

"O, Phœbe dear! O, Phœbe dear!
Don't go to scream or faint;

You think because I'm black I am
  The Devil, but I ain't!
Behind the heels of Lady Lambe
  I walked while I had breath;
But that is past, and I am now
  A-walking after Death!

"No murder, though, I come to tell
  By base and bloody crime;
So, Phœbe dear, put off your fits
  To some more fitting time.
No Coroner, like a boatswain's mate,
  My body need attack,
With his round dozen to find out
  Why I have died so black.

"One Sunday, shortly after tea,
  My skin began to burn
As if I had in my inside
  A heater, like the urn.
Delirious in the night I grew,
  And as I lay in bed,
They say I gathered all the wool
  You see upon my head.

"His Lordship for his Doctor sent,
  My treatment to begin;—
I wish that he had called him out,
  Before he called him in!
For though to physic he was bred,
  And passed at Surgeon's Hall,
To make his post a sinecure
  He never cured at all!

"The Doctor looked about my breast,
  And then about my back,

And then he shook his head and said,
  'Your case looks very black.'
And first he sent me hot cayenne
  And then gamboge to swallow,
But still my fever would not turn
  To Scarlet or to Yellow!

"With madder and with turmeric,
  He made his next attack;
But neither he nor all his drugs
  Could stop my dying black.
At last I got so sick of life,
  And sick of being dosed,
One Monday morning I gave up
  My physic and the ghost!

"O, Phœbe, dear, what pain it was
  To sever every tie!
You know black beetles feel as much
  As giants when they die.
And if there is a bridal bed,
  Or bride of little worth,
It's lying in a bed of mould,
  Along with Mother Earth.

"Alas! some happy, happy day,
  In church I hoped to stand,
And like a muff of sable skin
  Receive your lily hand.
But sternly with that piebald match
  My fate untimely clashes,
For now, like Pompe-double-i,
  I'm sleeping in my ashes!

"And now farewell! a last farewell!
  I'm wanted down below,

And have but time enough to add
  One word before I go —
In mourning crape and bombazine
  Ne'er spend your precious pelf.
Don't go in black for me — for I
  Can do it for myself.

"Henceforth within my grave I rest,
  But Death, who there inherits,
Allowed my spirit leave to come,
  You seemed so out of spirits;
But do not sigh, and do not cry,
  By grief too much engrossed,
Nor for a ghost of color, turn
  The color of a ghost!

"Again, farewell, my Phœbe dear!
  Once more a last adieu!
For I must make myself as scarce
  As swans of sable hue."
From black to gray, from gray to nought
  The shape began to fade —
And, like an egg, though not so white,
  The Ghost was newly laid!

TO DR. HAHNEMANN, THE HOMŒOPATHIST.

WELL, Doctor,
Great concoctor
Of medicines to help in man's distress;
Diluting down the strong to meek,
And making ev'n the weak more weak,

"Fine by degrees, and beautifully less"—
    Founder of a new system economic,
    To druggists any thing but comic;
Framed the whole race of Ollapods to fret
At profits, like thy doses, very small;
To put all Doctors' Boys in evil case,
Thrown out of bread, of physic, and of place—
And show us old Apothecaries' Hall
    "To Let."

How fare thy Patients? are they dead or living,
    Or well as can expected be, with such
    A style of practice, liberally giving
"A sum of more to that which had too much?"
Dost thou preserve the human frame, or turf it?
Do thorough draughts cure thorough colds or not?
    Do fevers yield to any thing that's hot?
Or hearty dinners neutralize a surfeit?
Is't good advice for gastronomic ills,
When Indigestion's face with pain is crumpling,
To cry, "Discard those Peristaltic Pills,
        Take a hard dumpling?"

    Tell me, thou German Cousin,
And tell me honestly, without a diddle,
Does an attenuated dose of rosin
Act as a *tonic* on the old *Scotch fiddle?*
Tell me, when Anhalt-Coethen babies wriggle,
    Like eels just caught by sniggle,
Martyrs to some acidity internal,
    That gives them pangs infernal,
Meanwhile the lip grows black, the eye enlarges;
Say, comes there all at once a cherub-calm,
Thanks to that soothing homœopathic balm,
The half of half of half a drop of "*varges?*"

Suppose, for instance, upon Leipzig's plain,
A soldier pillowed on a heap of slain,
In urgent want both of a priest and proctor;
When lo! there comes a man in green and red,
A featherless cocked hat adorns his head,
In short, a Saxon military doctor —
Would he, indeed, on the right treatment fix,
    To cure a horrid gaping wound,
    Made by a ball that weighed a pound,
If he well peppered it with number six?

Suppose a felon doomed to swing
    Within a *rope*,
    Might friends not hope
To cure him with a *string?*
Suppose his breath arrived at a full stop,
The shades of death in a black cloud before him,
Would a quintillionth dose of the New Drop
        Restore him?

Fancy a man gone rabid from a bite,
    Snapping to left and right,
And giving tongue like one of Sebright's hounds,
    Terrific sounds,
The pallid neighborhood with horror cowing,
To hit the proper homœopathic mark;
Now, might not "the last taste in life" of *bark*
    Stop his *bow-wow-ing?*
Nay, with a well-known remedy to fit him,
Would he not mend, if, with all proper care,
    He took "*a hair*
Of the dog that bit him?"

Picture a man — we'll say a Dutch Meinheer —
    In evident emotion,

Bent o'er the bulwark of the Batavier,
Owning those symptoms queer
Some feel in a *Sick Transit* o'er the ocean,
Can any thing in life be more pathetic
Than when he turns to us his wretched face ?—
But would it mend his case
To be decillionth-dosèd
With something like the ghost
Of an emetic ?

Lo! now a darkened room!
Look through the dreary gloom,
And see that coverlet of wildest form,
Tost like the billows in a storm,
Where ever and anon, with groans, emerges
A ghastly head!—
While two impatient arms still beat the bed,
Like a strong swimmer's struggling with the surges:
There Life and Death are on their battle-plain,
With many a mortal ecstasy of pain—
What shall support the body in its trial,
Cool the hot blood, wild dream, and parching skin,
And tame the raging Malady within—
A sniff of Next-to-Nothing in a phial ?

O! Doctor Hahnemann, if here I laugh
And cry together, half and half,
Excuse me, 'tis a mood the subject brings,
To think, whilst I have crowed like chanticleer,
Perchance, from some dull eye the hopeless tear
Hath gushed with my light levity at schism,
To mourn some Martyr of Empiricism:
Perchance, upon thy system, I have given
A pang, superfluous, to the pains of Sorrow,
Who weeps with Memory from morn till even;

Where comfort there is none to lend or borrow,
Sighing to one sad strain,
" She will not come again,
To-morrow, nor to-morrow, nor to-morrow!"

Doctor, forgive me, if I dare prescribe
A rule for thee thyself, and all thy tribe,
Inserting a few serious words by stealth;
Above all price of wealth
The Body's jewel — not for minds profane,
Or hands, to tamper with in practice vain —
Like to a Woman's Virtue is Man's Health.
A heavenly gift within a holy shrine!
To be approached and touched with serious fear,
By hands made pure, and hearts of faith severe,
Ev'n as the Priesthood of the ONE divine!

But, zounds! each fellow with a suit of black,
And, strange to fame,
With a diploma'd name,
That carries two more letters pick-a-back,
With cane, and snuffbox, powdered wig, and block,
Invents *his* dose, as if it were a chrism,
And dares to treat our wondrous mechanism
Familiar as the works of old Dutch clock;
Yet, how would common sense esteem the man,
O how, my unrelated German cousin,
Who having some such time-keeper on trial,
And finding it too fast, enforced the dial,
To strike upon the Homœopathic plan
Of fourteen to the dozen?

Take my advice, 'tis given without a fee,
Drown, drown your book ten thousand fathoms deep,

Like Prospero's, beneath the briny sea,
For spells of magic have all gone to sleep!
Leave no decillionth fragment of your works
To help the interest of quacking Burkes;
Aid not in murdering even widows' mites —
And now forgive me for my candid zeal,
I had not said so much, but that I feel
Should you *take ill* what here my Muse indites,
An Ode-ling more will set you all to rights.

ODE FOR ST. CECILIA'S EVE.

"Look out for squalls." — THE PILOT.

O COME, dear Barney Isaacs, come,
Punch for one night can spare his drum
As well as pipes of Pan!
Forget not, Popkins, your bassoon,
Nor, Mister Bray, your horn, as soon
As you can leave the Van;
Blind Billy, bring your violin;
Miss Crow, you're great in Cherry Ripe!
And Chubb, your viol must drop in
Its bass to Soger Tommy's pipe.
Ye butchers, bring your bones:
An organ would not be amiss;
If grinding Jim has spouted his,
Lend yours, good Mister Jones.
Do, hurdy-gurdy Jenny — do
Keep sober for an hour or two,
Music's charms to help to paint;
And, Sandy Gray, if you should not
Your bagpipes bring — O tuneful Scot!
Conceive the feelings of the Saint!

Miss Strummel issues an invite,
For music, and turn-out to-night
In honor of Cecilia's session;
But ere you go, one moment stop,
And with all kindness let me drop
A hint to you and your profession.
Imprimis then: Pray keep within
The bounds to which your skill was born;
Let the one-handed let alone Trombone,
Don't — Rheumatiz! seize the violin,
Or Ashmy snatch the horn!
Don't ever to such rows give birth,
As if you had no end on earth
Except to "wake the lyre;"
Don't "strike the harp," pray never do,
Till others long to strike it too,
Perpetual harping's apt to tire;
O I have heard such flat-and sharpers,
I've blest the head
Of good King Ned,
For scragging all those old Welsh Harpers!

Pray, never, ere each tuneful doing,
Take a prodigious deal of wooing;
And then sit down to thrum the strain
As if you'd never rise again —
The least Cecilia-like of things;
Remember that the Saint has wings.
I've known Miss Strummel pause an hour,
Ere she could "Pluck the Fairest Flower,"
Yet without hesitation, she
Plunged next into the "Deep, Deep Sea,"
And when on the keys she *does* begin,
Such awful torments soon you share,

She really seems like Milton's "Sin,"
  Holding the keys of — you know where!

Never tweak people's ears so toughly,
That urchin-like they can't help saying —
"O dear! O dear — you call this playing,
But O, it's playing very roughly!"
Oft, in the ecstasy of pain,
I've cursed all instrumental workmen,
Wished Broadwood Thurtelled in a lane,
And Kirke White's fate to every Kirkman —
I really once delighted spied
"Clementi Collard" in Cheapside.

Another word — don't be surprised,
Revered and ragged street Musicians,
You have been only half-baptized,
And each name proper, or improper,
Is not the value of a copper,
Till it has had the due additions,
    Husky, Rusky,
    Ninny, Tinny,
    Hummel, Bummel,
    Bowski, Wowski,
All these are very good selectables;
But none of your plain pudding-and-tames —
Folks that are called the hardest names
  Are music's most respectables.
   Ev'ry woman, ev'ry man,
   Look as foreign as you can,
   Don't cut your hair, or wash your skin,
   Make ugly faces and begin.

Each Dingy Orpheus gravely hears,
And now to show they understand it!

Miss Crow her scrannel throttle clears,
And all the rest prepare to band it.
Each scraper ripe for concertante,
Rozins the hair of Rozinante:
Then all sound A, if they know which,
That they may join like birds in June:
Jack Tar alone neglects to tune,
For he's all over concert-pitch.
A little prelude goes before,
Like a knock and ring at music's door,
Each instrument gives in its name;
            Then sitting in
            They all begin
To play a musical round game.
Scrapenberg, as the eldest hand,
Leads a first fiddle to the band,
      A second follows suit;
Anon the ace of Horns comes plump
On the two fiddles with a trump;
      Puffindorf plays a flute.
This sort of musical revoke,
The grave bassoon begins to smoke,
And in rather grumpy kind
Of tone begins to speak its mind;
The double drum is next to mix,
Playing the Devil on Two Sticks —
            Clamor, clamor,
            Hammer, hammer,
While now and then a pipe is heard,
Insisting to put in a word
   With all his shrilly best;
So to allow the little minion
Time to deliver his opinion,
   They take a few bars rest.

Well, little Pipe begins — with sole
And small voice going thro' the *hole,*
Beseeching,
Preaching,
Squealing,
Appealing,
Now as high as he can go,
Now in language rather low,
And having done — begins once more,
Verbatim what he said before.
This twiddling-twaddling sets on fire
All the old instrumental ire,
And fiddles, for explosion ripe,
Put out the little squeaker's pipe;
This wakes bass viol — and viol for that
Seizing on innocent little B flat,
Shakes it like terrier shaking a rat —
They all seem miching malico!
To judge from a rumble unawares,
The drum has had a pitch down stairs;
And the trumpet rash,
By a violent crash,
Seems splitting somebody's calico!
The viol too groans in deep distress,
As if he suddenly grew sick;
And one rapid fiddle sets off express —
Hurrying,
Scurrying,
Spattering,
Clattering,
To fetch him a Doctor of Music.
This tumult sets the Haut-boy crying
Beyond the Piano's pacifying,

The cymbal
Gets nimble,
Triangle
Must wrangle,
The band is becoming most martial of bands,
When just in the middle,
A quakerly fiddle,
Proposes a general shaking of hands!
Quaking,
Shaking,
Quivering,
Shivering,
Long bow — short bow — each bow drawing:
Some like filing — some like sawing;
At last these agitations cease,
And they all get
The flageolet,
To breathe "a piping time of peace."

Ah, too deceitful charm,
Like lightning before death,
For Scrapenberg to rest his arm,
And Puffindorf get breath!
Again without remorse or pity,
They play "The Storming of a City."
Miss S. herself composed and planned it —
When lo! at this renewed attack,
Up jumps a little man in black —
"The very Devil cannot stand it!"
And with that,
Snatching hat,
(Not his own,)
Off is flown,
Thro' the door,

In his black,
To come back,
Never, never, never, more!
O Music! praises thou hast had,
From Dryden and from Pope,
For thy good notes, yet none I hope,
But I, e'er praised the bad.
Yet are not saint and sinner even?
Miss Strummel on Cecilia's level?
One drew an angel down from heaven!
The other scared away the Devil!

THE LOST HEIR.

"O where, and O where
Is my bonnie laddie gone?" — OLD SONG.

ONE day, as I was going by
That part of Holborn christened High,
I heard a loud and sudden cry
That chilled my very blood;
And lo! from out a dirty alley,
Where pigs and Irish wont to rally,
I saw a crazy woman sally,
Bedaubed with grease and mud.
She turned her East, she turned her West,
Staring like Pythoness possest,
With streaming hair and heaving breast,
As one stark mad with grief.
This way and that she wildly ran,
Jostling with woman and with man —
Her right hand held a frying-pan,
The left a lump of beef.

At last her frenzy seemed to reach
A point just capable of speech,
And with a tone, almost a screech,
As wild as ocean birds,
Or female Ranter moved to preach,
She gave her "sorrow words."

"O Lord! O dear, my heart will break, I shall go stick stark staring wild!
Has ever a one seen any thing about the streets like a crying lost-looking child?
Lawk help me, I don't know where to look, or to run, if I only knew which way —
A Child as is lost about London streets, and especially Seven Dials, is a needle in a bottle of hay.
I am all in a quiver — get out of my sight, do, you wretch, you little Kitty M'Nab!
You promised to have half an eye to him, you know you did, you dirty deceitful young drab.
The last time as ever I see him, poor thing, was with my own blessed Motherly eyes,
Sitting as good as gold in the gutter, a playing at making little dirt pies.
I wonder he left the court, where he was better off than all the other young boys,
With two bricks, an old shoe, nine oyster-shells, and a dead kitten by way of toys.
When his Father comes home, and he always comes home as sure as ever the clock strikes one,
He'll be rampant, he will, at his child being lost; and the beef and the inguns not done!
La bless you, good folks, mind your own concarns, and don't be making a mob in the street;
O Serjeant M'Farlane! you have not come across my poor little boy, have you, in your beat?

Do, good people, move on! don't stand staring at me
  like a parcel of stupid stuck pigs;
Saints forbid! but he's p'r'aps been inviggled away up a
  court for the sake of his clothes by the priggs;
He'd a very good jacket, for certain, for I bought it my-
  self for a shilling one day in Rag Fair;
And his trousers considering not very much patched, and
  red plush, they was once his Father's best pair.
His shirt, it's very lucky I'd got washing in the tub, or
  that might have gone with the rest;
But he'd got on a very good pinafore with only two slits
  and a burn on the breast.
He'd a goodish sort of hat, if the crown was sewed in,
  and not quite so much jagged at the brim.
With one shoe on, and the other shoe is a boot, and not
  a fit, and you'll know by that if it's him.
Except being so well dressed, my mind would misgive,
  some old beggar woman in want of an orphan
Had borrowed the child to go a begging with; but I'd
  rather see him laid out in his coffin!
Do, good people, move on; such a rabble of boys! I'll
  break every bone of 'em I come near;
Go home — you're spilling the porter — go home —
  Tommy Jones, go along with your beer.
This day is the sorrowfullest day of my life, ever since
  my name was Betty Morgan.
Them vile Savoyards! they lost him once before all
  along of following a Monkey and an Organ:
O my Billy — my head will turn right round — if he's
  got kiddynapped with them Italians
They'll make him a plaster parish image boy, they will,
  the outlandish tatterdemalions.
Billy — where are you, Billy? — I'm as hoarse as a crow,
  with screaming for ye, you young sorrow!

And shan't have half a voice, no more I shan't, for crying
fresh herrings to-morrow.
O Billy, you're bursting my heart in two, and my life
won't be of no more vally,
If I'm to see other folks' darlins, and none of mine, play-
ing like angels in our alley.
And what shall I do but cry out my eyes, when I looks
at the old three-legged chair
As Billy used to make coach and horses of, and there
a'nt no Billy there!
I would run all the wide world over to find him, if I only
knowed where to run;
Little Murphy, now I remember, was once lost for a
month through stealing a penny-bun —
The Lord forbid of any child of mine! I think it would
kill me raily
To find my Bill holdin' up his little innocent hand at the
Old Bailey.
For though I say it as oughtn't, yet I will say, you may
search for miles and mileses
And not find one better brought up, and more pretty
behaved, from one end to t'other of St. Giles's.
And if I called him a beauty, it's no lie, but only as a
Mother ought to speak;
You never set eyes on a more handsomer face, only it
hasn't been washed for a week;
As for hair, though it's red, it's the most nicest hair when
I've time to just show it the comb;
I'll owe 'em five pounds, and a blessing besides, as will
only bring him safe and sound home.
He's blue eyes, and not to be called a squint, though a
little cast he's certainly got;
And his nose is still a good un, though the bridge is
broke, by his falling on a pewter pint pot;

He's got the most elegant wide mouth in the world, and very large teeth for his age;
And quite as fit as Mrs. Murdockson's child to play Cupid on the Drury Lane Stage.
And then he has got such dear winning ways — but O I never never shall see him no more!
O dear! to think of losing him just after nussing him back from death's door!
Only the very last month, when the windfalls, hang 'em, was at twenty a penny!
And the threepence he'd got by grottoing was spent in plums, and sixty for a child is too many.
And the Cholera man came and whitewashed us all, and, drat him, made a seize of our hog. —
It's no use to send the Cryer to cry him about, he's such a blunderin' drunken old dog;
The last time he was fetched to find a lost child, he was guzzling with his bell at the Crown,
And went and cried a boy instead of a girl, for a distracted Mother and Father about Town.
Billy — where are you, Billy, I say? come, Billy, come home, to your best of Mothers!
I'm scared when I think of them Cabroleys, they drive so, they'd run over their own Sisters and Brothers.
Or may be he's stole by some chimbly sweeping wretch, to stick fast in narrow flues and what not,
And be poked up behind with a picked pointed pole, when the soot has ketched, and the chimbly's red hot.
O I'd give the whole wide world, if the world was mine, to clap my two longin' eyes on his face.
For he's my darlin of darlins, and if he don't soon come back, you'll see me drop stone dead on the place.
I only wish I'd got him safe in these two Motherly arms, and wouldn't I hug him and kiss him!

Lauk! I never knew what a precious he was — but a child don't not feel like a child till you miss him.
Why, there he is! Punch and Judy hunting, the young wretch, it's that Billy as sartin as sin!
But let me get him home, with a good grip of his hair, and I'm blest if he shall have a whole bone in his skin!

THOSE EVENING BELLS.

"I'D BE A PARODY."

THOSE Evening Bells, those Evening Bells,
How many a tale their music tells,
Of Yorkshire cakes and crumpets prime,
And letters only just in time! —

The Muffin-boy has passed away,
The Postman gone — and I must pay,
For down below Deaf Mary dwells,
And does not hear those Evening Bells.

And so 'twill be when she is gone,
That tuneful peal will still ring on,
And other maids with timely yells
Forget to stay those Evening Bells.

www.ingramcontent.com/pod-product-compliance
Lightning Source LLC
LaVergne TN
LVHW020931110826
845150LV00004B/832

* 9 7 8 1 4 2 5 5 5 3 5 0 0 *